Trust Fall

Trust Fall

HOW WORKPLACE RELATIONSHIPS FAIL US

Sarah Mosseri

UNIVERSITY OF CALIFORNIA PRESS

University of California Press
Oakland, California

Cataloging-in-Publication data is on file at the Library of Congress.

ISBN 978-0-520-38736-2 (cloth)
ISBN 978-0-520-38737-9 (pbk.)
ISBN 978-0-520-38738-6 (ebook)

GPSR Authorized Representative: Easy Access System Europe,
Mustamäe tee 50, 10621 Tallinn, Estonia, gpsr.requests@easproject.com

35 34 33 32 31 30 29 28 27 26
10 9 8 7 6 5 4 3 2 1

Contents

Illustrations

TABLES

FIGURES

Note on Sensitivity

This book discusses sensitive topics related to workplace dynamics, including emotional and sexual harassment and abuse, racism, sexism, exploitation, and interpersonal conflict. Sensitive readers are encouraged to approach the material with care.

Introduction

Lanie wanted to trust the senior leaders at the marketing agency where she worked.[1] She wrestled out loud with the idea for several minutes as we sat in a dimly lit coffee shop on Manhattan's west side. Eventually she blurted out her central ambivalence, posing it as a hypothetical question to them: "Do you really care about my best interest, or am I just a machine to spin your wheels?"

DTC (Direct-to-Consumer) Communications was Lanie's first job out of college. Like many in her industry, she worked long hours—an expectation that didn't come with the lucrative salary or high prestige associated with overwork cultures in other professions like finance, law, and technology.[2] While Lanie would've welcomed a bigger paycheck, especially living in New York City, money wasn't her primary motivator. She joined DTC because she liked the creativity of the work, the culture of the company, and most of all, the people.

Over three years, her coworkers became close friends. They walked to nearby lunch spots, grabbed coffee, and went out drinking with one another, often debriefing the day's ups and downs as they did so. Occasionally they got together on weekends, too. Some of her colleagues were artists, others were business savvy, and Lanie learned a lot about work—and life—from them. She also had a fantastic manager, Constance, who treated her like a daughter. Constance pushed her to think differently and reach higher. "[She] makes you want to be the best version of yourself," Lanie explained.

I observed Lanie's dedicated passion in the office, watching her gesture excitedly one day as she tried to convince the team to incorporate the notion of "collective effervescence" into a music-focused marketing campaign. Yet there were challenges. Softening her voice to a whisper, Lanie described the humiliation she had felt a year prior when someone started a rumor she'd slept with a senior manager. She recounted a separate harrowing incident of sexual harassment from a supervisor. Company-wide gender inequities in pay and status constantly weighed on her, as did the ever-looming threat of layoffs. The latest degradation was learning she had been passed over for the company's training program for rising stars. "I want this agency to thrive," Lanie shared, "but I just don't think I'm valued enough here. I don't see the point in putting so much work into something that doesn't feel that way about me."

Nevertheless, despite interviewing with another company and receiving a competitive offer, Lanie decided to stay at DTC. She wasn't convinced the other company would be better, and at DTC she had Constance to protect her. Plus, Lanie was guilt ridden about the prospect of abandoning her team; they were a close-knit group, and she didn't want to leave them high and dry. Sounding as intent on convincing herself as on persuading me, she claimed the company higher-ups weren't necessarily "bad people"; they just lacked creative vision and were profit obsessed. In fact some leaders, like Donnie, a senior executive who'd taken Lanie under his wing, were different. "He really, *truly*, in the goodness of his heart, believes in the message of humanity for DTC," she said, referencing the newly adopted buzzword of "human" within the agency's culture. To Lanie, that meant Donnie liked to develop and promote from within—maybe even her eventually. With a deep sigh and a shrug of resignation, she circled back to the initial question of trust, redirecting it inward: "Trust is a choice, you know?"

Like so many others in today's workforce, Lanie was participating in a real-world trust fall: the team-building activity in which someone willingly falls backward, relying on group members to catch them before they get hurt. Would her managers and coworkers prevent her from hitting the ground, or was she naïvely buying into a relational safety net that would not hold?

This book deconstructs what we might think of as the *trust fall* of modern work: an acceptance of vulnerability in our work lives in the hope that the relationships we forge there will help us avoid (or at least endure) the all-too-common perils of contemporary labor. Like all workers, Lanie's adeptness at maneuvering within this trust fall was influenced by her class, race, and gender. Her risks were partially offset by her college degree and the option to move back into her parents' home during periods of unemployment—safeguards not widely available across the workforce. Her whiteness also acted as a safety harness within a setting tacitly designed to accommodate her, even as her femininity added a layer of complexity to trusting the arms extended to catch her.[3] Situating Lanie's experiences in existing employment conditions and comparing them to those of other workers, *Trust Fall* unpacks the relational mechanics of the modern workplace, revealing its uneven stakes and hidden costs.

From 2016 through 2018, I embedded myself in four different occupational settings, connecting with individuals like Lanie and observing the interpersonal dynamics within their workplaces. At Lanie's agency, I joined meetings spanning creative design to budgeting and watched as team camaraderie grew during late-night work sessions. I waited tables at a New York City (NYC) chain restaurant, balancing trays and schedules with my coworkers, while noting how team members helped each other build resilience in the face of never-ending chaos. I sat in a sun-soaked startup office in lower Manhattan where I "slacked" with techies sharing coding tips and industry memes.[4] I also camped out at the city's airport parking lots, where I listened to ride-hail drivers commiserate with one another over deteriorating conditions on platforms like Uber and Lyft as they waited in a digital queue for potentially profitable fares heading to the city.

Through my conversations and observations in these four distinct work settings, I witnessed how relations of interpersonal trust fill a critical void left by an insufficient and crumbling formal infrastructure of work. Federal work regulations, collective bargaining agreements, and internal promotion structures no longer hold significant sway over how work is organized.[5] Instead, I found that information, resources, protections, and opportunities flow primarily through networks of trust that have gendered, raced, and classed dimensions.[6] Trust may be a choice, as Lanie says, but it is a structured one—sometimes strategic, often coerced—within the context of dominant work cultures and labor relations in the United States (US).

Trust, however, serves as more than just a conduit of access and power. People are both pulled and pushed to *trust*: to let down their guard around, bracket doubt about, depend upon, and be vulnerable with those they work for and alongside.[7] Through these connections, they negotiate their sense of belonging at work, the value of their efforts, and their perceptions of what is acceptable and fair. These relationships help make work meaningful, but they are also vulnerable to abuse, especially when appropriated and controlled by those with privilege and power. Unfortunately, interpersonal relationships of trust rarely prove to be adequate insurance against the harshest realities of modern work, leaving people dangerously exposed to disrespect, exploitation, and precarity.

Trust Fall thus offers a deep immersion into the seduction and costs of everyday relational intimacy at work. Namely, it reveals how dominant processes of trust cultivate intimate social bonds that help people cope with the harsh realities of modern employment but ultimately undermine worker solidarity and power, and as a result, limit labor reform. More tangibly, it provides readers with a language and a framework to identify, talk about, and hopefully better navigate the promises and pitfalls of trust at work.

THE CURIOUS CASE OF WORKPLACE TRUST

Trust is both glue and lubricant, bonding people together in shared assumptions and agreements while simultaneously allowing them to keep moving in the face of uncertainty.[8] We trust the democratic system when casting our vote in an election, our doctor when undergoing an operation, our fellow citizens when gathering in public spaces, and our friends when we tell them personal information. Each example represents different forms of trust—institutional, expert, generalized, and interpersonal, respectively—but all comprise important threads of our social fabric.[9]

However, lately it seems trust is in short supply. The Pew Research Center in 2022 reported that only two in ten Americans trusted the federal government to do what's right, compared with about four in ten at the end of 2000 and more than seven in ten in 1964.[10] Multiple polls reveal declining public trust in other key institutions, such as the news media, banks, churches, and the criminal justice system.[11] Americans are becoming less likely to trust experts as well, with public health officials, college professors, and technologists (among others) experiencing greater scrutiny.[12] In marginalized and disadvantaged communities, institutional and expert distrust is even more pronounced, reflecting the nation's failure to actualize its stated ideals of liberty, equality, and justice.[13]

Surprisingly, the workplace appears to offer solid ground in the midst of the shifting sands of trust. Consistently since 2010, over 80 percent of General Social Survey (GSS) respondents say they trust their managers, and about 90 percent say they can rely on coworkers.[14] These expressions of trust at work are not only corroborated by other large-scale surveys, but they are also relatively consistent across income, race, and gender differences.[15] Americans may be "bowling alone," but they are still signing up for the company softball team.[16]

At first glance, one might attribute the contrast between trust within and outside of work to differences in form or type. Institutional trust, for example, rests on distant, often opaque systems, whereas social trust relies on human relationships.[17] Yet even when focusing solely on Americans' trust in one another, surveys show declines outside of work that contrast with the relatively stable—and much higher—levels within. Consider the question regularly posed in the GSS: "Generally speaking, would you say that most people can be trusted or that you can't be too careful in dealing with people?" In 2022, only a quarter of respondents said most people could be trusted, down from almost half in 1972 when the question was first posed.[18] This deficit of trust is shaped and deepened by long-standing societal disparities; trust, for instance, is far more common among the wealthy than the poor, and cross-racial relationships are less likely to be marked by trust than same-race ones.[19]

Yet such ruptures aren't confined to distant strangers. They increasingly appear even within our closest relationships. About one in four US adults reports being estranged from a family member, and people claim to rely less often on friends for personal support than in the past.[20] Stories of strained holiday get-togethers and contentious school board meetings are becoming more common.[21] Political division and associated mis- and disinformation campaigns drive much of this distrust, with Democrats and Republicans professing an inability to agree even on "basic facts."[22] This broader social fracturing makes the resilience of workplace trust all the more striking.

So why is it that these same divisions do not disrupt workplaces, especially as it becomes ever more difficult to find apolitical ground? One possibility is that work is a task-oriented space, requiring people to put aside differences in the name of coordination. But we also come together with family, friends, and neighbors to accomplish tasks, whether cooking dinner, arranging childcare, or working out a school budget. Still, workplace relationships appear uniquely resistant to the polarization affecting other spheres. To understand why, we need to consider what trust actually means—and does—within workplace settings.

It could be that the stakes of trust are simply lower at work, with people limiting its meaning to something more cursory or one dimensional. In *The Tumbleweed Society,* sociologist Allison Pugh argues that people take a rather pragmatic approach to employment. They view job insecurity as inevitable—an inherent and unavoidable part of contemporary work—and expect to be let down within formal employment relationships.[23] This may suggest a shallow form of trust bounded by narrow expectations: not trust in mutual loyalty or care, but in employers to act in the best interest of the business. As we will see, however, precarity and pragmatism don't eliminate trust; they reshape it. Trust becomes more selective, more concentrated. Insecurity fuels a desire to count on someone—anyone—within a system that offers few guarantees. And when trust does surface, it takes on heightened emotional weight, setting the stage for interpersonal work relationships to become emotionally overburdened.

To understand why trust carries so much weight in today's workplace, it's necessary to first examine the structural conditions that surround it. Today, the US labor system gives workers very little on which to rely. A legal framework of "at-will" employment in the private sector permits the firing of workers with little notice and for almost any reason.[24] This system enables employers to shed labor costs without much legal liability—and they routinely do so, implementing strategies like downsizing, outsourcing, and automation to attract and satisfy investors and shareholders.[25] While job holders technically have a corresponding freedom to leave at any time, doing so jeopardizes the references they typically need to get hired elsewhere.

This imbalance of power is exacerbated by lengthy hiring processes and vague job descriptions that make employment transitions tedious and risky. Additional factors like market concentration, restrictive occupational licensing, and noncompete agreements further inhibit job seekers' negotiating position.[26] Such asymmetries in employment relationships were once countered by unions. But decades of conservative governance and corporate activism have left these defenders defanged—guard dogs barking without bite.[27]

In this context, roles characterized by fair pay, long-term security, and avenues for advancement—what we might call "good" jobs—are scarce.[28] While business narratives celebrate spartan conditions as a catalyst for innovation and profit generation, workers scramble in a game of musical chairs, chasing ever-vanishing seats.[29] Indeed, most workers now spend less than five years in any given job, and almost all workers experience at least one period of unemployment—six on average—by the age of fifty-two.[30] Even those fortunate enough to land relatively good jobs rarely feel nurtured or secure, depleted by a blend of survivor's guilt, ongoing job loss anxiety, and the strain of shouldering more responsibilities with fewer resources.[31]

Rampant employment churn is especially tumultuous for Black and Brown workers and for women of all races, who are disproportionately pushed out during times of market turbulence and face systemic barriers to reemployment.[32] These same workers are often corralled into "bad" jobs, where they are undervalued and overmanaged.[33] Yet they are not alone. Many working-class white men also find themselves trapped in unstable, low-quality work, sometimes juggling multiple bad jobs just to scrape by.[34]

Despite this precarious employment structure, America's threadbare public safety net continues to rely on employers for basic social protections, tethering people to insecure work.[35] Workers move from one subpar job to the next, stitching together family care solutions and navigating fragmented assistance programs.[36] A discourse of entrepreneurialism—stressing passion over job tenure, risk-taking over prudence, and social networking over institutional loyalty—wraps these efforts in gauzy individualized narratives, papering over the structural barriers and policy failures that fuel inequality and insecurity.[37] Stuck in an insomniac's daze as they chase the American Dream, many workers are white-knuckling it until a daybreak that never comes.

One might think this confluence of income insecurity, job inequality, and self-reliance would make contemporary workplaces either cold, rational spaces or hotbeds of interpersonal competition and conflict—certainly not bastions of trust.[38] Yet this context of insecurity and turmoil is precisely what makes trust meaningful and raises its stakes.[39] In fact, trust creates a bubble of "normalcy" and a sense of ease amid uncertainty and risk, enabling people to continue on "as if" threats were contained or a particular future was certain.[40] It is the contrast between this fabricated cocoon and the risks outside of it that gives interpersonal trust at work its significance and weight.

To that point, trust is not the expectation of security.[41] Instead, trust entails an acute awareness of one's fragility and the active creation of pockets of hope and exceptionalism. Lanie constructed such pockets via her relationships with supervisor Constance and executive Donnie; these vectors of vertical trust offered her comfort and guidance in a turbulent environment. Horizontal trust across her team further helped to keep her workplace apprehensions at bay, with bonds of mutual reliance making Lanie feel less alone and affirming her sense of worth. Lanie reluctantly acknowledged journalist Sarah Jaffe's warning that "work won't love you back" and no longer assumed her efforts would pay off within the company, but she held out her individual relationships with colleagues as different due to the trust that defined them.[42]

Lanie's story is not an isolated one. I watched people working in both good and bad jobs rely on trust as they navigated the vicissitudes of work. They turned to mentors, peers, and junior colleagues for advice, favors, or a sympathetic ear. Without structural protections, these interpersonal connections often eased the impact of seemingly inevitable tumbles and falls. Yet these lifelines did not come free of charge. Workers sacrificed their time to help close team members; they opened themselves up to microaggressions; they gave trusted leaders latitude and grace in the face of questionable decision-making; and they lingered in roles that no longer served their needs, feeling as though they would let others down if they left.

Across the four sites I observed, trust fluctuated across relationships and over time, influenced by the dynamics of gender, race, and hierarchical authority within the workplace. Yet even in its most fragile form, trust functioned as an essential scaffolding—propping up an employment system that was otherwise rickety and uneven.

MANUFACTURING TRUST

An unsettled environment may accentuate trust's salience, but it doesn't in and of itself produce trust. If it did, we'd likely see trust flourishing in other destabilized realms of society. Crucially, managerial discourse actively encourages folks to develop trust at work. Open any popular business magazine and you will be greeted by articles like, "How Leaders Can Build a Culture of Trust—And Why They Should" and "Want Your Employees to Trust You? Show You Trust Them."[43] Big-name companies such as Amazon, Walgreens, Procter & Gamble, and Salesforce all proudly proclaim trust as a core organizational value.[44]

This emphasis on trust at work isn't new. Employers have invested in the social and emotional lives of workplace actors since at least the 1920s, when the famous Hawthorne experiments highlighted the importance of group dynamics and social sentiment in worker motivation.[45] Not much has changed a century later: interpersonal skills such as communication, empathy, and conflict resolution are regularly prioritized within job descriptions and built into leadership training programs. As the cultural theorist Eva Illouz astutely points out, the ultimate aim in today's workplace is "to increase others' trust in oneself [and] also to make oneself trust others."[46]

For employers, the goal of trust cultivation is to transition their operations from rigid bureaucratic structures to flexible, team-based designs said to be more adaptable to market changes.[47] As a bonus, team-based setups telegraph a democratic culture that bolsters company reputations and entices workers.[48] However, the inequities and ambiguities involved in trust—what sociologist Adia Harvey Wingfield calls the "gray area"—are masked by this broad embrace.[49] Consider the case of minoritized individuals who often work harder to find pathways of trust that don't simply rely on social similarity or taken-for-granted status. Their surplus labor is obscured by narratives celebrating team cohesion.[50] Regardless of its equivocations and contradictions, however, trust persists as a popular buzzword, resonating from the boardroom to the point-of-sale front lines.

The cultivation of a cultural lexicon of trust at work matters. It contributes to the available vocabulary people have for thinking through, making sense of, and talking about their workplace relationships.[51] Consider, for instance, Lanie's declaration about trust. "At the end of the day, it's number one! I can't imagine *not* feeling [like] I can trust my coworkers," she gasped. "I couldn't work there!" As Lanie's words demonstrate, the language of trust is difficult to escape in modern work settings, and this language shapes what aspects of our workplace relationships are most legible and the kinds of connections we seek to forge.[52]

Trust is also more than just a standard of everyday work talk; it's a symbol of success. Empirically linked with positive outcomes such as leadership effectiveness, employee commitment, and organizational performance, trust has come to stand for these positive attributes.[53] Indeed, Great Place to Work, the consulting agency that produces the widely read "Best Companies to Work For" lists, bases its ratings on the degree of trust reported in a workplace.[54] A business goal in itself, trust is a fetishized commodity, endorsed at face value regardless of whether or not it truly reflects or contributes to positive work relationships in a given setting. High levels of purported trust signify happy employees and a productive workplace. Trust is so reflexively idealized in this context that when I've raised the idea of its potential downsides, people often respond with bafflement, asking, "But who wouldn't aspire to trust at work?"

But trust isn't just manufactured through company cultures; it finds traction in part because of the broader cultural and institutional meaning we attach to work itself. Our jobs are, as Tressie McMillan Cottom put it, "the basic units of U.S. citizenship."[55] They are not only how we earn our livelihoods but also the gateway to public goods like health care and social security benefits. Work is where many seek social connection, dignity, and moral worth: a space that offers fun and friendship for some and promises personal fulfillment and transcendence for others.[56] The pandemic laid bare this social dimension, as concerns about how remote work might deepen America's loneliness epidemic revealed just how central the workplace has become to people's emotional and relational lives.[57] Such anxieties hold traction only in a cultural environment where work is the de facto cornerstone of our lives—a notion reinforced by the structural double helix of employment-centric welfare policies and company perks that bind us to our jobs.[58]

While trust has long mattered at work, shifting labor conditions make it more consequential. The relentless campaign by elites to dismantle employment protections, unions, and stable work arrangements not only exacerbates job insecurity but also transfers risks and responsibilities away from institutions and onto individuals.[59] As a result, social networks—the people one knows—are ever more crucial.

White men have disproportionately benefited from networks when it comes to landing jobs, managing career obstacles, and achieving professional advancement.[60] Indeed, gender, race, and class shape network access and placement, frequently barring traditionally disadvantaged groups from high-resource contacts.[61] Notwithstanding such deficiencies, today's transient job market and portfolio-style career paths make building and maintaining strong social networks practically compulsory for all workers.[62] New technologies intensify network pressures, with employers increasingly scrutinizing the online presence of potential and existing workers with an eye toward using their connections to enhance company recruiting and branding operations.[63] Thus, disparities in accessing and mobilizing one's social network have become a decisive factor in workplace outcomes.

Importantly, trust is a critical determinant of whether one's networks pay off.[64] Work scholar Megan Tobias Neely demonstrates how in the hedge fund industry, relationships of trust, loyalty, and tradition—often rooted in familiarity—buttress a patronage system that disproportionately secures wealth and power for white men.[65] At the other end of the socioeconomic spectrum, sociologists Judith Levine and Sandra Smith show how a lack of trust among low-income individuals impedes their ability to discover and seize valuable opportunities.[66] For instance, low-income Black job seekers often hesitate to provide job references for peers, fearing damage to their own reputations in a challenging market;

assistance is typically extended only after careful evaluation of others' trustworthiness.[67]

Debates abound over whether strong ties (such as those with family and friends) or weak ties (with acquaintances) provide better access to resources.[68] Yet it is workplace ties—those with coworkers, supervisors, subordinates, and clients—that arguably wield the most influence in today's labor market, underscoring the imperative to forge and sustain trust in these relationships.[69]

In short, the modern system of US labor runs on trust. In today's workplace, the premium placed on teamwork and interpersonal negotiation drives operations and shapes company cultures. In the process, perceived trustworthiness is turned into a key competency and personal guardedness a professional failing.[70] Along work's periphery, the lack of meaningful guardrails (e.g., worker protections and public safety nets) unencumbers employers and keeps costs low. But as a result, workers are susceptible to every bump in the road, dependent on fellow travelers to warn them of upcoming potholes and to assist them when they break down.[71]

In other words, social policies, institutions, and practices foster an environment in which even the most cynical and reticent individuals are driven to forge trust. Engaging in the trust fall is universally encouraged, even as exposure to its risk varies greatly across participants. Questions of whether others are deserving of trust are rendered seemingly irrelevant, with the answer only revealed when one is or is not caught by the arms of colleagues. And while workers and managers scramble to fulfill their roles in this routine, employers mine the resulting intimacy for its useful parts.

REAL IN ITS CONSEQUENCE

Trust isn't just manufactured at work; it's put to work. Relations of trust help people adapt to insecurity, but they also distribute power, reinforcing hierarchies and deepening dependency. Trust can feel like connection or care, but in unequal relationships, it can also become obligation cloaked in choice. Business leaders exploit this dynamic, using a fractured labor system, the moral ideal of work, and a climate of social unease to turn workplace trust into a salve—and a lever.

Yet just because workplace trust is ripe for employer exploitation, its expression is not entirely under managerial control. While employers undeniably seek to impose trust at work through cultural expectations, professional standards, and organizational frameworks, these messages are often diluted or convoluted by the time they reach workers' ears, weakening their impact.[72] But even more to the point, as leadership expert Simon Sinek has dryly noted, trust can't simply be produced on command.[73] Human sentiment doesn't work like that.

Trust at work, therefore, is not solely an expression of emotional labor—a compelled and alienating performance for pay.[74] Indeed, rigid definitions of emotional labor have come under scrutiny for failing to account for how people shift and reshape who they are in response to different roles and relationships.[75]

Take the restaurant server, smiling and chatting as they move between tables, serving an endless stream of guests. To some, this might look like submission: a performance to satisfy customer expectations. And it often is, each grin a concession to role expectations. But that cheerful facade can also serve as a protective shield, deflecting on-the-job indignities.[76] Or, much like David Bowie stepping into Ziggy Stardust or Nicki Minaj channeling Roman Zolanski, the performance can feel like slipping into a liberating alter ego, unlocking parts of the server's personality that might otherwise be repressed. The point is, affects are dynamic and layered. While conditioned by workplace dynamics, they remain deeply personal and can be a medium for agency and resistance.

In the chapters that follow, I move beyond common depictions of trust that lean toward one-dimensional, insular, or overdetermined understandings.[77] Instead I approach trust as a dynamic social accomplishment, motivated by individual pursuits and shaped by the structures, practices, vocabularies, and values that define one's world.[78] As I argue, this process unfolds in negotiation and collaboration with others, as we distinguish between what is legitimate within our social environment and what requires greater vigilance and scrutiny.[79] By engaging in this process, we contribute to a shared construct: a collective belief in and a leap of faith toward a certain interpretation of reality.[80]

Of course, we do not all participate equally in this rendering. People with more power and resources often have an easier time being seen as trustworthy—and can afford to take more risks in trusting others.[81] If something goes wrong, they're more likely to recover thanks to financial cushions, social connections, or second chances.[82] But for workers from historically marginalized groups, trust can be harder to give and even harder to earn. They're often judged against biased standards and pushed to prove themselves in ways others are not, simply because they don't match the image of who typically gets trusted in an organization.[83]

How we individually and collectively accomplish trust at work matters because it shapes how we interpret and navigate our workplace realities: what we do, what we yearn for, what we think is fair, what we're willing to offer or endure, with whom we interact and how.[84] Regardless of whether they are contrived or genuine, expressions and enactments of trust at work are real in their consequences.[85]

People don't just interpret their sense of reality through trust. In many cases they actually transform their world in light of it.[86] Take Lanie: she trusted her manager, regularly confiding in Constance and going to her for guidance. In doing so, she increased her vulnerability and dependence within that relationship, giving Constance considerably more power than the baseline outlined within her managerial role. At the same time, in acting out her dependency, Lanie made a bid for Constance's attention and care. Constance's own power—and the responsibility that goes along with it—became more visible and harder to ignore when Lanie explicitly placed trust in her. Conversely when Constance gave Lanie more autonomy, she wasn't just empowering her. She was also relying on her, creating new obligations in the process. Trust, in other words, does not just describe our social relationships; it also defines (and redefines) them.

Nor is it simply about whether we trust or not; *how* we trust matters, a point that social scientist Nissim Mizrachi and his colleagues show in their study of an Israeli textile plant operating in Jordan. They observed how, at the plant's opening, Jordanian managers sought to develop "normative" trust with Israeli executives, emphasizing respect, honor, and hospitality to ingratiate themselves with these higher-ups. A few years later, however, when political unrest made the multinational business collaboration unpopular in Jordan, the plant managers switched to a more "calculative" form of trust, emphasizing professional competence and efficiency. In switching the meaning and form of trust, the Jordanian managers sought to transform the relationship with their Israeli colleagues to create a more perfunctory yet still highly functional bond. Doing so helped them negotiate emergent tensions between their national and professional identities.[87] As it turns out, there is not just one way to trust, and trust is not stable; rather, meanings and performances of trust shift across contexts and evolve over time, with significant consequences.[88]

However conceived, trust involves envisioning a desired or hoped-for version of reality, and it is understandable that we are reluctant to acknowledge—or even see—cracks in this vision once established. The unsettling possibility that those we trust might ignore our needs or exploit our earnestness can be paralyzing, slowing us down in an economy that constantly urges us to push forward. Thus, against our better judgment, we accept an uneven social contract that requires we give much more than we receive in our jobs. We overlook or disregard signs of danger, and we sidestep betrayal until the urgency of the situation makes it impossible to ignore, by which point we are likely already overwhelmed with pain. Worse, the emotional and relational labor required to sustain workplace trust depletes the resources we need to express our humanity in other spheres of life, particularly in personal relationships and civic engagement. This acceptance therefore not only harms individuals but also undermines the social fabric outside of work.

The vignettes and voices in this book lay bare both the fantasy and futility of workplace trust. They expose the cruel optimism driving each of us to hold up a system that doesn't really work instead of building one that does.[89]

GETTING PERSONAL

Trust is notoriously difficult to study, with debates over its conceptualization plaguing scholars for decades.[90] Is trust a thought, a feeling, or a behavior? What encapsulates trusting versus being trusted versus trustworthiness? Given its many shades, simply talking to people about trust at work, separate from their work contexts and relationships, jeopardizes analytic rigor. Without diving fully into the social milieu, it's easy to miss out on the full palette of trust in the workplace, particularly its more subtle and negotiated aspects—its collective rituals, ripple effects, and its tensions.

I therefore embedded myself in US workplaces to better understand what's happening with trust at work. We already know a little about how trust works in extremely polarized jobs, at elite levels and below the poverty line. In the former, the most privileged tend to ride the currents of trust to greater power and wealth, while in the latter, trust passes over the working poor, washing away access to opportunities and resources with it.[91] But we know less about how trust operates among people with incomes closer to the median and at workplaces that don't require Ivy League or advanced degrees.

Mainstream discussions of cubicles and nine-to-five schedules often assume a professional office environment, making this setting a cultural touchpoint for work and therefore appropriate for my purposes. Yet we encounter people at work in other arenas as well: retail spaces, salons, warehouses, factories, health-care facilities, homes, construction sites, planes, and vehicles. Such spaces are equally intrinsic to the reality of work, making them compelling comparative sites of study.

These physical distinctions often (though not always) map onto status hierarchies: office-based jobs tend to be seen as professional and high status, while nonoffice roles are more often interactive, public facing, and lower in organizational rank. Conventional wisdom suggests that trust thrives in professional settings—bolstered by espoused values like transparency and egalitarianism—and falters in frontline environments marked by surveillance and limited autonomy. While this framework has intuitive appeal, my own past experience working across both types of environments revealed a more complex reality, which prompted the closer empirical investigation that followed.

I moved, husband and dog in tow, to NYC. I'd spent time in the city earlier in my career and had stayed in touch with people working in the kinds of settings I now aimed to study. My old connections came through. A coworker turned friend from my restaurant days, who was active in the NYC hospitality space, referred me to a chef at the midtown location of The Jones, a busy regional restaurant chain where I was subsequently hired as a paid server. Months later, I reconnected with a former advertising colleague who brokered an introduction to the human resources team at DTC, and after several meetings, I was invited to join them as an unpaid consultant.

I spent about thirty hours "in the field" each week for nine months, slowly becoming rooted in both The Jones and DTC communities. Shortly after being hired at the former, management added me to the employee listserv and the corresponding digital scheduling app. My phone immediately lit up with messages from my new coworkers asking if I could cover shifts, but it took a while before I felt like more than just a new name on the roster. Hoping to build rapport, I arrived early before each shift, frequently taking advantage of the pre-shift "family" meal (concoctions of leftovers made specifically for staff).

As I became more of a known entity, my coworkers began directing jovial quips in my direction and inviting me to join them for after-shift drinks at a nearby pub. I generally said "yes" whenever anyone invited me to do something outside of work, whether it was bar hopping, rock climbing at a nearby gym, or even watching my coworkers (many of whom were aspiring entertainers) perform in comedy shows and plays. These interactions weren't just social perks; they became an informal currency. I learned that trust—at least the kind that opened doors or softened the job's sharper edges—often emerged through these shared moments, quietly negotiated at the margins of the formal workday.

The social environment at DTC was equally challenging to enter. After obtaining an office ID, I set up at a rotating "hot desk" early each morning, engaging in friendly chitchat with arriving colleagues. Many people initially kept their distance, with one skeptical manager jokingly referring to me as a "narc." Despite a bumpy first few weeks, I remained persistent, asking people if I could tag along for meetings or coffee runs and even joining the company softball team. Gradually, I became a regular at project meetings, training sessions, happy hours, client meetings, and off-site promotional events. It wasn't always seamless, but in time I found my footing.[92]

From that vantage point, I gleaned a lot about trust at work. I noticed how people helped one another out; who enjoyed greater flexibility and autonomy; when, where, and with whom people vented; and what caught people off guard. Once immersed in each setting, I was also able to talk one-on-one with my coworkers, which helped me delve deeper into how individuals experienced, interpreted, and expressed various work situations and relationships.[93]

At both The Jones and DTC, I conducted private interviews with staff members, managers, and senior leaders, including the CEO of each organization. The most prominent organizational boundary at The Jones was between "front-of-house" positions, which are customer-facing positions on the restaurant floor, and "back-of-house" positions, which are in the kitchen or out of customers' sight. At DTC, more than a third of staff members were contract workers, many of them working outside the office to facilitate client relationships and promotional events. Within the office, the core teams were defined by functional area (e.g., client services, project management, production, creative, finance, human resources).[94] Some teams, especially those directed toward day-to-day client services, tended to focus on only one client, while others worked across clients and projects. To get a more representative picture of what was happening in each setting, I invited people from across these various divides to participate in the interviews, although my data is skewed toward The Jones's front-of-house and DTC's in-office landscapes.[95]

Despite our NYC location, I was initially struck by the overwhelming whiteness of both work settings. Employees, especially white senior leaders, often described their companies as "diverse," yet racial diversity was relegated to small corners and crevices within their organizational structures.[96] For example, DTC's creative studio—the only function led by a person of color—was much more racially diverse than the rest of the agency. Unlike the tokenized representation often seen elsewhere, the studio team reflected the rich diversity within Black, Asian, and Latinx communities. This team, however, was the exception rather than the rule across the agency.

On the whole, The Jones's workforce was more racially diverse than at DTC, but Black and Brown workers were overrepresented in back-of-house positions and underrepresented in front-of-house and leadership roles.[97] Similarly, senior leaders at both organizations were primarily men, while women made up the bulk of the junior-level workforce. Seven of the ten most senior figures at The Jones (and seven of the nine most senior figures at DTC) were white cis men, reflecting inequities that also exist in the broader workforce and which are upheld by widespread policies and practices that systematically advantage this demographic at work.[98] In general, my interview sample reflects this gendered and racialized institutional structure, and throughout the book, I pay close attention to how social hierarchies map onto organizational hierarchies in ways that shape the tenor, tone, and rhythm of trust relationships.

Interviews were formal in that they were planned, recorded, and followed a list of prepared topics and questions. However, I approached each conversation with a casual demeanor.[99] Conversations usually began with a brief review of the person's career journey leading up to their current role, memorable moments they'd experienced at work, and identification of key mentors and close colleagues. When we turned to trust, my goal was different than that of national surveys. I was less interested in counting up people's self-declarations of trust at work than in accessing how they thought about it: what trust meant to them, the tensions and contradictions they wrestled with as they forged and maintained trust, what it felt like to trust or be trusted, and what emotions felt acceptable when people betrayed their trust. I often pressed them for examples and stories.[100] Sometimes multiple people described a similar situation or described events I personally witnessed firsthand. This deepened my understanding of what was happening, not because it enabled "fact-checking" but because it gave me access to the plurality of experience and the ways in which trust—collectively developed—could shape what people saw and how it made them feel.[101]

As has become even more prominent postpandemic, two trends were emerging within the 2016 work landscape: digital communication and platform technologies were becoming more central, while workers were becoming more geographically dispersed. There were glimpses of these patterns at DTC and The Jones. At DTC, senior leaders frequently discussed the agency's ability to compete in the "digital economy," and while I was there, they created an "innovation and technology" executive role to manage technology investments. At The Jones, schedules were published and maintained on mobile apps; orders were input on point-of-sale terminals (Micros); and the team regularly interfaced with digital reservation, review, and delivery platforms like OpenTable, Yelp, and UberEats. Yet both marketing and in-house dining are fairly traditional industries

Table 1. Research Sites

	Traditional Setting *(more bureaucratic, greater physical proximity between workers, less tech centered)*	**Emergent Setting** *(less bureaucratic, less physical proximity between workers, more tech centered)*
Higher-paid, higher-status work	DTC Communications marketing firm	Disruption Technology start-up
Lower-paid, lower-status work	The Jones restaurant	ride-hail circuit

adapting to a changing work environment rather than being at the cutting edge of developments. I therefore expanded the study to include two additional settings in which such trends might be more pronounced in order to understand whether and how these trends impacted trust dynamics (see table 1).

I spent several months at Disruption, a technology consulting start-up. Disruption was unique in that I didn't access it through my social network. Rather, I cold emailed the head of human resources, who wrote back, intrigued about how their company (which consisted of fourteen people) could better build and maintain trust.[102] Most of Disruption's staff were either full time or contracted consultants experienced in coding, software development, and website and app design, and they typically worked on-site at client offices for extended periods. Meanwhile, the operations team (a euphemistic name for leadership in a company that rejected traditional hierarchies) and consultants not logging billable hours (dubbed "on the bench") worked out of a small, shared space in the financial district with other entrepreneurs, remote workers, and independent contractors. Everyone stayed in touch via the digital messaging platform Slack, which I had access to for five months. For two months, I joined them in their office for eight to ten hours each week, attending regular operations and company-wide, all-hands meetings. I interviewed all fourteen employees, participated in a team dinner and karaoke event, and joined the team at an industry-wide exhibition where they sought to lure new investors, clients, and employees and attract press coverage.

The second emergent work setting—my final research site—was the NYC ride-hail circuit. I observed and interviewed various actors involved in this ecosystem, including drivers, platform providers (e.g., Uber and Lyft representatives), riders, local regulators, labor advocates, the press, and the general public.[103] Like Disruption, technology was central to the ride-hail circuit, and workers were often spread across the city; like The Jones, the platform driver workforce is frequently characterized as lower-status, interactive service work. At the time of the study, the industry was under scrutiny from academics, journalists, regulators, and drivers themselves, creating challenges for my research because both drivers and platform representatives were wary of talking with outsiders.[104] Platform representatives in particular cited privacy policies and institutional partnerships with other academics as reasons not to speak with me.[105] As a result, interview data at this setting are more limited; nevertheless, I was still able to converse with two platform representatives, two labor advocates, and fourteen drivers.

To better understand worker interactions in the ride-hail sector, I visited driver "hubs" where drivers met face-to-face with platform representatives, reviewed public online driver forums, and spent time with drivers at NYC airports as they awaited fares. I also attended relevant NYC Taxi and Limousine Commission meetings, tracked pertinent news stories, engaged local industry experts in information-gathering conversations, and conducted audits of platform company websites, downloading their official reports and communiqués.

In total, over the course of a year and a half, I spent over twelve hundred hours in participant observation at these four different sites and interviewed a total of 122 managers and workers (see table 2 for interview sample characteristics).

I originally expected to map different patterns and configurations of trust across the sites, but striking convergences in the ways trust unfolded within DTC, The Jones, and Disruption were undeniable and brought some of the broader patterns of trust at work into sharp relief. Most of the book, therefore, paints across these three sites, using stories from each to highlight different aspects of trust at work that were consistent. While I point out differences across the sites as relevant, my emphasis on the common threads allows me to dig deeper into the very meaningful differences

Table 2. Interview Sample Characteristics

	The Jones		*DTC*		*Disruption*		*Ride-Hail*		*Total Sample*	
Social Status Category	*Sample Size (39 total)*	*% of Site n*	*Sample Size (51 total)*	*% of Site n*	*Sample Size (14 total)*	*% of Site n*	*Sample Size (18 total)*	*% of Site n*	*Sample Size (122 total)*	*% of Site n*
Organization position										
Manager	15	38	24	47	3	21	3	17	45	37
Worker	24	62	27	53	11	79	15	83	77	63
Gender identity										
Cis woman	24	62	29	57	2	14	5	28	60	49
Cis man	15	38	22	43	10	71	13	72	60	49
Trans fem.	0	0	0	0	2	14	0	0	2	2
Trans masc.	0	0	0	0	0	0	0	0	0	0
Nonbinary	0	0	0	0	0	0	0	0	0	0
Race/ethnic identity										
Asian	1	3	4	8	1	7	1	6	7	6
Black	4	10	4	8	1	7	5	28	14	11
Latinx	3	8	5	10	0	0	6	33	14	11
White	28	72	35	69	10	71	6	33	79	65
Multiracial	3	8	3	6	2	14	0	0	8	7

Social Status Category	The Jones		DTC		Disruption		Ride-Hail		Total Sample	
	Sample Size (39 total)	*% of Site n*	*Sample Size (51 total)*	*% of Site n*	*Sample Size (14 total)*	*% of Site n*	*Sample Size (18 total)*	*% of Site n*	*Sample Size (122 total)*	*% of Site n*
Annual net income*										
	(35 responses)		(48 responses)		(14 responses)		(15 responses)		(112 responses)	
Less than $20K	3	9	0	0	0	0	2	13	5	4
$21K–$35K	14	40	4	8	1	7	3	20	22	20
$36K–$50K	9	26	16	33	0	0	1	7	26	23
$51K–$75K	4	11	11	23	4	29	8	53	27	24
$76K–$100K	2	6	7	15	8	57	1	7	18	16
$100K+	3	9	10	21	1	7	0	0	14	13
Education										
HS or less	11	28	2	4	3	21	12	67	28	23
Bachelors	25	64	42	82	11	79	5	28	83	68
Grad degree	3	8	7	14	0	0	1	6	11	9
Age										
Twenties	21	54	18	35	6	43	6	33	51	42
Thirties	13	33	21	41	3	21	6	33	43	35
Forties	5	13	8	16	3	21	5	28	21	17
Fifties	0	0	3	6	1	7	1	6	5	4
Sixties	0	0	1	2	1	7	0	0	2	2

NOTE: Data are self-reported.

*According to Census Current Population Survey data, approximately 25% of US workers earned less than $20,000 and 60% less than $50,000 in 2016. At the other end of the income spectrum, about 20% earned more than $75,000 and 10% above $100,000. The median income level was approximately $37,000, and the poverty threshold was about $12,000.

that I observed *within* them, particularly the ways in which workplace authority intersected with race and gender categories to influence trust.[106] The ride-hail circuit was a unique case, with trust playing out differently. I outline the distinct patterns in this work setting within a single chapter, discussing how these differences illuminate taken-for-granted assumptions in the other sites and how the specific workplace solidarities observed might inform labor activism moving forward.

OVERVIEW OF THE BOOK

Chapter 1 offers an overarching framework and vocabulary as a foundation for making sense of trust in contemporary American work. Specifically, I outline three processes through which trust emerges from within adverse work conditions—processes that strengthen meaningful workplace connections, sustaining employee commitment and productivity in bad jobs.

Chapters 2 and 3 present prominent rituals of workplace trust. Chapter 2 dissects the trauma bonding that occurs in frenetic work environments, fostering a form of solidarity that prioritizes resilience over resistance. Chapter 3 delves into the in-between moments of work, where people drink, vent, and banter with one another in ways that forge connection but also amplify vulnerabilities.

In Chapter 4 managerial performances of trust are revealed to be highly gendered and raced, showcasing how trust serves as a mechanism of inequality in the workplace. Disheveled personas and rule-breaking bolster white men's authenticity, while women supervisors and managers of color are forced to balance personability with a meticulous professionalism to keep at bay underlying doubts about their capabilities.

Chapters 5 and 6 examine how employers encourage vulnerability and then prey on it. Chapter 5 demonstrates how workers often bear the burden of trust, managing obligation, reputation, and risk to facilitate employer agility, while their employers maintain institutional safeguards that undermine trust and protect their own interests. Chapter 6 juxtaposes the "warm fuzzies" of workplace cultures with the vilification of the "dirty" aspects of business, demonstrating how the former obscure the latter and shield employer structures and practices from accountability.

The case of ride-hail workers, presented on its own in chapter 7, demonstrates how the patterns of workplace trust observed in the other work sites are not inevitable and how new technologies and ways of organizing work may present an opportunity to reconfigure workplace relations in ways that better serve worker interests. In the conclusion, I outline how the book's arguments might inform new workplace conversations, and I provide recommendations for strengthening and rebuilding labor infrastructures, thereby reducing the relevance and impact of the trust fall.

CONCLUSION

The stories in this book reveal how trust greases the wheels of insecure work. Namely, trust sustains performance and commitment through interpersonal relationships, which in turn patch the gaps between cultural ideals of work as a source of identity and worth and material realities marred by insecurity and inequality. Team members and colleagues pick up the slack of underresourced work environments and ill-fitting workplace policies, shielding one another from daily indignities, advising one another through difficult decisions, and offering comfort when things do not work out as planned. In jobs that often consume an outsized proportion of people's time and energy, coworkers and colleagues offer each other a sense of belonging and validation, motivating one another's tenacity through challenging, disorganized, or undervalued work.

But the personal burdens are heavy, and the individual risks are great, and not everyone can afford or is willing to serve in this role. Gaps and imbalances exist across workplace trust networks; some employees lack necessary interpersonal support, while others bear excessive and disproportionate emotional and relational burdens. Certain individuals, better positioned due to financial stability or social advantages, can afford to take risks and are more likely to prosper when doing so.[107] Conversely, those living paycheck to paycheck or supporting extended kin may face dire circumstances or devastating setbacks when their networks fail them.[108] A reliance on workplace trust exposes all workers to substantial risk, but the effects of job loss, forfeited promotions, and missing workplace protections unequally affect people when labor markets are polarized by class, gender, and race.[109]

In the end, when workers like Lanie perceive trust to be a choice, they tend to look inward and question themselves when outcomes fall short of expectations.[110] Their introspection not only shields from accountability those who betray them, but more crucially, it lets a system that hinges on interpersonal trust off the hook for its failings.

1 Flash Intimacy

THE PROCESSES AND POLITICS OF TRUST AT WORK

As we sat at a bodega across the street from The Jones, Nelly admitted feeling worn down; she was dreading her upcoming serving shift. But there was a silver lining. "As soon as I get there, everyone's kind of on the same page," she said, a smile creeping onto her face. She chuckled, almost embarrassed at her own earnestness. "I just really like everyone we work with." One never knew what obstacles a restaurant shift might hold, from bustling crowds and order mishaps to poor tips, but Nelly rejoiced in the idea of being "in it together" with her coworkers. "Whenever I actually am *at* work," Nelly said, citing the conviviality of the group, "I'm like, 'This is nice!'"

The mutual recognition and care that inhabit intimate work relationships replenish the stamina a capitalist economy depletes and cushion the pain of job-based injustices and indignities, with such benefits affecting even senior leaders. Disruption's CEO Shane, for example, credited his start-up team's support to explain his perseverance over a prolonged period of intense work stress. Struggling to describe his colleagues' relational labor in detail, Shane contrasted it with more conventional professional traits and behaviors. "It wasn't so much the team with the credentials or the competence and the skillsets that we needed," he clarified.

"It's not a practical thing. It was an emotional thing, right? That I wasn't in it alone." Decoupling these relational dynamics from typical job operations and proficiencies, Shane framed the team's connection in transcendent terms, giving it an intangible quality others echoed.

Employers like Shane seek to harness this interpersonal "magic," and many books about workplace trust respond to that hunger, offering how-to guides for optimizing workplace relationships to improve business efficiency and productivity.[1] *Trust Fall* takes the opposite approach. I aim to demystify processes of workplace trust, bringing workers' relational skills, sacrifices, and creative interpretations to the fore so their efforts can be better accounted for within business processes.[2] In doing so, I demonstrate how workers' relational dynamics, which often imbue them with the fortitude to forge ahead in challenging times, are co-opted by employers in ways that ultimately deprive them of a more just system of work.

Chiefly, I reveal how expressions and rituals of trust at work facilitate and nurture what I call *flash intimacy*. Akin to a flash mob, flash intimacy reflects meaningful social connections that spark a sense of exuberance, in part because they are unexpected and largely out of sync with the broader social context. Beguiling in their improbability, moments of flash intimacy amid the hardships of modern work can feel thrilling and fun, like a radical act or form of resistance. They emerge amid the chaos and brutality of business to become a lifeline for workers.

However, while invigorating, flash intimacy tends to entrench workers in oppressive and unequal work environments, with bonds of localized support deflecting attention from broader workplace arrangements that don't serve them. Consider Constance and Lanie from the introduction. Motivated by the mutuality they enjoyed within their relationship, they doubled down in their efforts—the by-products of which benefited their employer greatly. Yet reward and recognition primarily came through the reciprocities of their bond. The women protected and advocated for one another within what they described as a "boys' club," but their marginal status in this relational web constrained their ability to secure substantial outcomes for one another.[3] In the end, Constance and Lanie's hard work and loyalty, while fulfilling within their relationship, profited DTC, the marketing firm they worked for, without compelling the company to equitably recognize and reward their contributions.

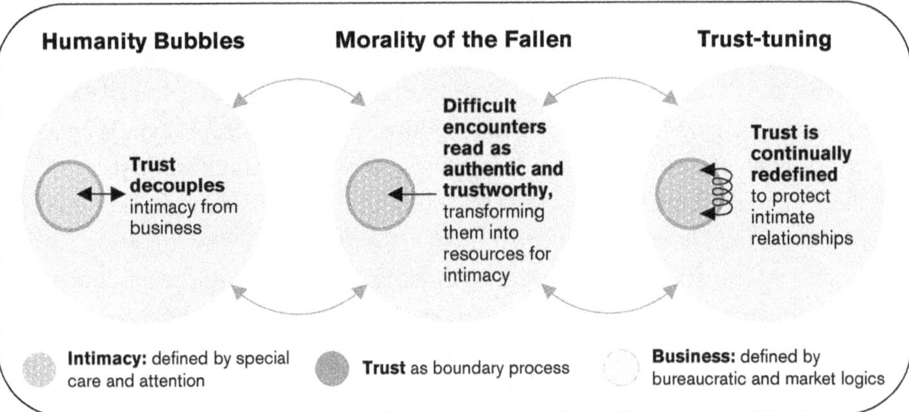

Figure 1. The processes of trust contributing to flash intimacy. Illustration by author.

This chapter details three dominant and overlapping processes of trust that foster flash intimacy (see figure 1). First, rituals of trust help to create and maintain *humanity bubbles*, serving as the means by which intimate relationships are distinguished from "normal" business operations. In other words, trust is both bridge and boundary, connecting these two workplace dimensions while preserving their autonomy. Second, socially constructed understandings of authenticity inform trust-building, contributing to a *morality of the fallen* that celebrates dysfunction and suffering. This ethos transforms challenging work conditions and professional flaws into resources for intimacy. Third and finally, intimate relationships—especially those defined by power differentials—are protected and sustained by practices of *trust-tuning*, through which people creatively adjust the meanings of trust rather than admit betrayal or abuse. By dissociating harsh working conditions from intimate workplace relationships, valorizing transgressive behavior and haphazard work processes as authentic, and reframing betrayal in empathetic terms, these trust processes help to facilitate social bonds that aren't grounded in longevity or even mutual obligation.

Although intimacy sometimes fortifies existing power structures, it doesn't inevitably serve the status quo. Indeed, we'll see glimpses of the potential intimacy harbors for defiance, resistance, and a reimagining of existing conditions across the chapters that follow, in workers' venting sessions or in their one-off protests on behalf of mistreated colleagues.[4] In chapter 7 we'll also explore a more persistent form of collective dissent among NYC ride-hail workers, tracing how they orchestrated bonds centered more on solidarity than trust. Nevertheless, the dominant story of flash intimacy depicted across DTC, The Jones, and Disruption is one of organizational homeostasis; trust moderates the relationship between intimacy and business, offsetting instrumental doubts enough to let people forge meaningful ties, but marking them as distinct in ways that keep personal entanglements from intruding on operations.

Understanding flash intimacy is critical because it encapsulates both the allure and the danger that animate the trust fall: the urgency and drama of interdependence in the midst of insecure and unequal work, highlighted by intense emotions felt at a visceral level. But the rapid pulse of flash intimacy also keeps workers in a heightened state that overwhelms their defenses, drawing them deeper into their jobs. By providing a framework and vocabulary for recognizing and pushing back on the workplace patterns that raid human connections for profit, this chapter seeks to name and identify the issues that have upset and unbalanced the rhythm of our work lives.

HUMANITY BUBBLES

"People who I trust at work are the people that are helpful," Nelly explained, while those she distrusted were more focused on "keeping score." While prior experiences of colleagues' helpfulness likely shaped Nelly's trust in them, what stood out was how she and others used trust as a gatekeeping device to regulate their expectations of workplace relationships.[5] Only within trusted relationships did they allow themselves to hope for special treatment and consideration, whether in the form of extra attention or care, greater autonomy and flexibility from standard practice, or access to privileged information and resources.

Like many others I met at The Jones, DTC, and Disruption, Nelly used trust to delineate intimate relationships within the workplace—relationships that economic sociologist Viviana Zelizer describes as offering people "knowledge and attention that are not widely available to third parties."[6] I refer to these spaces, guided by the logic of intimacy but cordoned off and insulated by trust, as humanity bubbles. Within these spaces, workplace relationships seemed less transactional, actions didn't always need to be accounted for, and people felt valued regardless of their utility. In a humanity bubble, one was more than a number on a spreadsheet or a cog in the machine. Rather than usurp the bureaucratic and market-based aspects of work, however, the language and rituals of trust compartmentalized workplace intimacy, recreating *within* the workplace a version of the "haven in a heartless world" trope that has long defined the relationship *between* domestic life and paid work.[7]

People felt protected and supported within humanity bubbles, even as they assumed most employers were driven primarily by impersonal bureaucratic and market-based logics. For instance, while people are acutely aware of the constant threat of layoffs, they believe a trusted mentor will advocate for them in critical decisions and that a close colleague, aware of impending changes, will discreetly warn them in advance. But the expectations and protections of intimacy didn't just come to the fore in dire situations like layoffs. At The Jones, server Shawn admitted he could sometimes behave unprofessionally on the job, taking shortcuts and making irreverent jokes. Although he expected most managers and coworkers to rebuke his behavior, Shawn believed the reaction would be different among those he trusted: "If I slack off or say something crazy, they won't say anything 'cause they're friends." According to Shawn, trusted colleagues gave him the benefit of the doubt and put his behaviors in context.

By separating out moments and relationships of intimacy from regular business, people reinforced the notion that these were two separate social spheres—"hostile worlds" that risked contamination or corruption should they come into contact. Of course, this separation is more illusion than reality, as business and intimacy are deeply intertwined in practice.[8] Financial provision and formal recognition are, for example, forms of care, with a pay raise or promotion providing people not just with material stability but also with a greater sense of belonging and moral worth in their jobs.[9] In this way, money underwrites intimacy. Conversely, intimate workplace ties promote business operations.[10] Indeed, referral-based hiring, managerial coaching, and team-based structures are designed to harness workplace intimacies and reorient their gains toward company profits.[11] Regardless of the intrinsic rewards these ties may bring, cultivating this intimacy requires labor—effort that is shaped by the bureaucratic and financial systems that commodify, regulate, and mediate these exchanges.[12]

Nevertheless, the language and practices of trust frame care as transcending power dynamics and market logics. At DTC, for instance, Account Director Russ emphasized the high degree of trust that defined his team: "There's a 'we have each others' back' mentality. Always. Even if it [is] something outside of what you do." Russ went on to clarify what this meant: "If I saw something needed to get done, I'm not going to sit around. I'm going to get in there and get my hands dirty and do it. And everybody on that team has that attitude." In his mind, trust freed the team from the constraints of formal job descriptions, liberating their ability to support each other.

Across DTC, The Jones, and Disruption, workers who were willing to step up and get things done (regardless of their actual duties) were heralded as trusted team players, while managers who abandoned the privileges of their authority and got "in the trenches" or "led from behind" were beloved and celebrated. In contrast, individuals who violated the symbolic separation between intimate relations and the material aspects of work by actively striving for recognition and reward for their team-focused efforts were viewed skeptically and labeled as "calculating," "ego-driven," and "power hungry."

The repudiation of appeals to workplace rewards and hierarchies within trusted relationships—undergirded by the myth of intimacy and business as mutually exclusive—shares some tendencies with broader cultural taboos around explicitly discussing one's salary, wealth, or financial situation. As sociologist Rachel Sherman argues in her book *Uneasy Street*, these norms not only protect the wealthiest among us from experiencing shame about having so much more than those in need, but also muddle the moral conversation around inequality, directing attention *away* from structural decisions about how resources should be distributed fairly and instead *toward* individual judgments about how people should politely occupy privilege (or the lack thereof).[13]

The same is true in the workplace. Downplaying the material aspects of work (e.g., job title, job security, salary or wages) does not eliminate their importance but rather decenters them in workplace discourse, often in ways that benefit the most privileged and powerful by continuing to normalize the status quo. Workplace actors accordingly focus their attention on individual actions, such as whether and how people enact "good" teamwork or leadership, marked by selflessness, humility, and hard work, as opposed to structural considerations, such as whether one is paid fairly, how promotion and compensation processes are implemented, or how strategic business decisions are made. These often unclear processes are put to the side and categorized under a different and distinct logic that is uncritically accepted and taken for granted as "just doing business."

Since traditional bureaucratic workplace structures and rewards are seen as incompatible with the warmth and attachment of interpersonal collegiality and care, workers and managers opt instead for the language of gifts and favors to describe the dynamics inside humanity bubbles.[14] Although these exchanges tend to be framed in neutral terms, in reality they remain underpinned by relations of power and inequality.[15] For example, Russ's willingness to jump in and get his hands dirty is more likely to benefit him both materially and symbolically than anyone else on his team. As team leader, he was ultimately seen as responsible for the team's output and was rewarded accordingly. Moreover, because his structural position allowed him greater agency, Russ's discretionary efforts were more likely to be perceived as a personal choice, creating the impression of generosity. For lower-ranking workers whose agency is more limited and their job descriptions broader in scope, such "gifts" hold less weight, as their contributions are often implicitly expected and not individually rewarded.[16] Their "favors"—whether assisting a teammate, staying late to finish a task, or working an undesirable shift or on an unappealing assignment—are likely to be coded as showing initiative and commitment, met with appreciation, yet ultimately framed as part and parcel of "doing a good job."

Ashley, whose middle management position at The Jones made her acutely aware of the crosscurrents within this "economy of gratitude," wrestled with conflicting interpretations of the relationship between business and intimacy.[17] Reflecting on her decision to show up for work all week despite being sick with the flu, she described how her precarious financial situation and the unrelenting demands of her role compelled her to push through. Even so, Ashley emphasized how "lucky" she felt to have supervisors who temporarily relaxed their expectations of her and even stepped in to help her manage the workload amid her illness. She saw their tolerance and support as a gift—a voluntary act of kindness and care in an otherwise rigid environment.

As she articulated her gratitude, however, Ashley started to second-guess this perspective, exposing an underlying ambivalence. "Yeah, like, 'Thank you so much,'" she said with a sarcastic edge creeping into her voice. "Thank you for actually doing what you should be doing because you're my superior and should be understanding that I can't get this done right now, physically. You know?" With this remark, Ashley rejected the idea that her managers' help was a personal favor and reframed it as a professional obligation. In this view, intimacy and kindness were not exceptions but embedded expectations within business. And her simmering irritation points to a deeper truth: because the meaning of gift giving and favor granting hinge on having power and privilege to begin with, it's hard for those at the bottom (or even the middle) of workplace hierarchies to leverage the norms of gratitude and reciprocity that govern intimate workplace exchange.

Yet somewhat ironically, Ashley reverted to the "hostile worlds" perspective when adopting the role of manager herself. From this position, she worried about how displays of care might be exploited by workers in ways that threatened her authority. Framing intimacy in opposition to business practice, she questioned workers' potential calculus: "Are you taking advantage of our mutual respect because you think that you can get away with something?" Ashley defended herself against this vulnerability by highlighting how she had no problem firing workers she liked. "I'll do it," she said resolutely. "I *like you*, but I'll do it. Because at the end of the day, I have to run a business." In her quick turn, Ashley revealed the fragile and conditional nature of trust and care within humanity bubbles, exposing how easily they yield to the imperatives of authority and control.

Despite a contemporary work landscape marred by insecurity, abuse, and inequality, the intimacy created within humanity bubbles—what I've referred to as flash intimacy—serves as a source of passion and devotion to the job for individuals and provides content for people-centric, family-like work cultures.[18] Because trust marks an exception to the presumed standard of cold rationality and profit maximization in business, what happens in humanity bubbles is scrutinized and assigned moral weight.

Yet the dominance of the surrounding business logic remains untouched. Workplace intimacies are thus perceived not only as separate from the normal workings of business but also as inherently provisional: able to pump life into a work environment but never stable or powerful enough to override business-as-usual operations. They offer succor in the moment but often can be leveraged to prop up the very system they were meant to circumvent in the first place.

MORALITY OF THE FALLEN

A second trust process contributing to the development and maintenance of flash intimacy foregrounds notions of suffering and authenticity within the workplace. In particular, folks relished finding and exploring the cracks in what Donnie, a senior leader at DTC, called others' professional "veneer." Donnie explained how breaking through that barrier could be a tender, even uncomfortable experience: "Some people feel very, I don't know if it's embarrassed or whatever, but once it's out, it's like 'Oh, shit. Now you know this about me, and now I feel very vulnerable, like super vulnerable.'" Nevertheless, after the professional shell was punctured and the person inside revealed in their messiness and imperfection, people were usually more relaxed. "In a way, it's like breathing," Donnie commented. "Like, can I actually breathe for a little bit?" By bringing the interaction down to this basic level, he mused, they set the conditions for "true connection."

Others agreed. Workers and managers alike chronicled how challenging work situations stripped people down to their core, revealing who could be trusted (and who could not). They also recounted building trust through unfiltered venting sessions that erupted when folks were pushed past their limits and during workplace hangouts where alcohol doubled as a "truth serum." Whether pushed or pulled into a vulnerable state of exposure, the resulting unscriptedness was mined for meaning—unvarnished authenticity treasured as the rare, natural resource at the heart of human relationships.

These common beliefs in the power of pain and the purity of impulsiveness constitute the morality of the fallen. The morality of the fallen vilifies professionalism, reframes difficult situations as a test of character, and celebrates the unrestrained and imperfect as authentic, all of which inform workplace trust. This ethos is integral to the production and maintenance of flash intimacy, as it helps people make sense of and even cherish social cohesion amid chaos, dysfunction, and distress.

The morality of the fallen was thus central to many collective rituals of workplace trust. At The Jones, for example, server Liz said she built trust with people by working alongside them on the hardest shifts at the restaurant. "When you work brunch with someone," she explained, "and you survive what we do at that fucking place, and what we go through [. . .] you see someone's true colors."[19] As hard as these moments were, Liz craved such occasions, perceiving them as an opportunity to really get to know her coworkers. "I base my respect levels of people and kind of categorize them and their identities based on their work ethic," Liz said. "I need to see someone in the utmost distressing moments of their career to see how they handle it—to see how they work." To emphasize the point, she added, "Like, if I'm going to marry someone, I need to see them at Sunday brunch level."

Workers like Liz frequently revisited such heightened moments when talking about developing workplace relationships. Not only did they revel in the voyeuristic thrill of peeking behind others' professional fronts, but they described a unity and collective identity forged through shared experiences of adversity. For instance, Lynn, another server at The Jones, referenced the fellowship restaurant workers develop through their common exposure to difficult guests. "Every single person has had that type of experience," she said, contrasting this insider viewpoint with how outsiders who hadn't worked in the service industry talked. "Other people are like, 'Oh, that's so *hard*. I couldn't imagine doing that all day!'" There was both a knowledge and a pride among those who'd endured such travails, and the shared brand of workplace hardship connected them, strengthening their collective will.

The idea of drawing strength from suffering is deeply embedded in US culture.[20] It's a dominant ethos serving as the backbone of a diverse array of social groups, from substance-abuse collectives to cancer patients and military units. It supplies a powerful and dramatic arc to the hero's journey that structures many movies and books. And it's foundational to the rags-to-riches stories that give moral fuel to the American Dream. At work, people draw upon this idea of productive suffering to create meaning from job challenges and crises, assuming "them's the breaks," and how people make do—individually and together—is what really matters. This framing is useful in driving worker resilience and cooperation, but because the focus is oriented toward enduring adverse conditions as opposed to confronting the nature of those circumstances, it does little to address or subvert the root causes of workers' suffering.[21]

Beyond glorifying difficult working conditions as a test of character and a basis for deep mutuality, people also interpreted others' behaviors through this moral lens. Read through the morality of the fallen, unprofessional acts were frequently branded as authentic and thereby deemed ethically unassailable. In a telling example, Donnie recalled a former colleague who drank heavily on the job, describing the man's transgressive behavior as endearingly earnest. "He felt that he could be his true self, no matter what," Donnie said. "He could be drinking, doing his work, and he was himself. And that kind of made him charming and disarming to people." Further romanticizing authenticity, Donnie posited that the man's innate capabilities excused and perhaps were even inextricably intertwined with his troubled behavior, admirably calling him a "profound talent [. . .] kind of a tormented soul, you know? Genius type." Eventually, when the man's liabilities began to outweigh his contributions to the company, he was let go. Nevertheless, Donnie's nostalgia reveals how a celebration of the raw and irreverent aspects of work life can lead people to conflate dysfunction with genuineness.

From Taylor Swift's confessional lyrics to Donald Trump's unfiltered rhetoric, Americans crave access to the gritty and unstable realities they believe lie just beneath the surface.[22] This yearning is intensified by the proliferation of social media filters, auto-tuning, and generative AI technologies that bend notions of reality.[23] Yet social scientists warn against placing too much inherent value in notions of authenticity.[24] Authenticity, they contend, is not a natural resource to be unearthed; rather, it is a culturally mediated invention, dependent upon both a successful performance and its validation from others. Rather than being discovered, authenticity is socially accomplished.[25]

Generally, successful performances of authenticity tend to be reactive, drawing on (sometimes stereotypical) cultural narratives to counter dominant norms.[26] Authentic performances at Disruption, The Jones, and DTC loosely followed this template, with people often signaling their "realness" by rejecting traditional markers of corporate conformity: dressing casually, flouting rules, broaching taboo topics, or demeaning formal credentials. These performances resonated in companies that took great pride in their self-made origins and where there was growing resentment of the formal processes, organizational charts, and strict budgets that accompanied their recent expansions. At Disruption, for instance, the edict to "be authentic" was built into the company manifesto, with Shane claiming to have founded the start-up to escape the typical trappings of corporate life. Seeking to galvanize the team following an era of disorienting growth, Shane returned to this mantra of authenticity during one "all-hands" meeting, saying, "It is who we are—we have a responsibility, both internally and externally, to be authentic."

Performances of authenticity that challenge established workplace norms can be empowering, especially for traditionally marginalized groups.[27] This was the case for Nylah, a Disruption consultant who identified as a transgender woman. Nylah spoke adamantly about bringing her "whole self" to the office, which she modeled for others by deviating from traditional business attire and speaking openly about sensitive topics (like politics) typically avoided in the workplace. While her approach invited accusations of unprofessionalism among some, Nylah justified her behavior through an appeal to authenticity. "You can't be at home and be like, 'I have these views, and I'm this type of person,' and in the office, I'm gonna be a totally different person," she said. Assimilating to dominant norms meant denying a piece of herself, which Nylah contended meant building workplace relationships on shaky ground: "Automatically, you're lying to your coworkers at that point." Noting how the tech industry was "a utopia for this one single demographic," Nylah sought to perform an authenticity that deconstructed professional norms in ways that created space not only for her but for other marginalized groups.

Yet people don't stand on equal footing when they push boundaries or defy convention at work; the acceptance of nonconformity is conditional on social status and mediated through implicitly gendered and racialized expectations.[28] Thus, the return on investment for such performances—particularly in gendered and racialized organizations like DTC, The Jones, and Disruption—tended to be greater for dominant groups. When white cis men acted unconventionally, their colleagues often praised them as visionary, candid, or down to earth. For example, Ronald, who led DTC's production team, described himself as "a very blunt, forthcoming person" and a "bulldog." He saw his job not necessarily as an exercise in collaboration—a key tenet of the company's culture—but as a constant fight against colleagues and clients whom he felt held unrealistic expectations of his team. Despite his adversarial approach, Ronald was frequently praised by others both within and outside of his team as "passionate" and a "good leader."

In an environment where their presence and power were taken for granted, white cis men's norm deviations rarely led to questions about their competence or legitimacy; rather, they denoted an authenticity that further legitimized their belonging.[29] Even when their authentic performances went so far as to violate basic norms of civility—entailing emotional outbursts, inappropriate comments, and bullying behavior—they rarely invited censure. In fact, when positioned against progressive norms of "cultural sensitivity," "political correctness," or "wokeness," they signaled a freedom from pretense that often reinforced the personas of those "transgressing" as honest and relatable.

In contrast, the behaviors of women, people of color, and LGBTQIA+ people were typically filtered through cultural stereotypes that trapped them between a person and an archetype.[30] For example, when Black men veered from traditional professional dress norms by wearing casual clothing (e.g., hoodies), they risked provoking prevailing images that depicted them as dangerous or threatening.[31] And when mothers deviated from professional norms of work devotion to attend to family matters, they risked being cast as distracted and uncommitted.[32] These examples highlight the biased valuation of rule-breaking.[33] Those at the top of social hierarchies are often free to express themselves in dynamic and multidimensional ways, while those at the margins struggle to be seen and heard on their own terms, continually confronting stereotypes that threaten to flatten them into caricatures.

Highly aware of their vulnerability to misrepresentation and stigmatization, members of nondominant groups had to balance their self-expression with self-preservation. Doing so made the effortlessness of authenticity harder to achieve, prompting demeaning labels like "poser" or "striver" that undermined their perceived trustworthiness.[34] Not wanting to be thought of as lazy or incompetent on the job, Liz at The Jones took a diligent approach to work, carefully learning restaurant policies and consistently modeling them. Doing so, however, attracted mixed reactions from her colleagues. While new trainees extolled Liz as a deep well of knowledge, and team members regularly depended on her proficiency during the height of the rush, others derided her meticulousness as neurotic. One manager even went so far as to casually remark to a group of servers, "She's not a sociopath, but she has some sociopathic tendencies."[35] Liz made the cardinal mistake of trying too hard, failing to achieve the sense of "ease" that typically fostered trust and comradery.[36]

The morality of the fallen offers people a lens through which they can understand discomfort as a conduit to meaningful relationships, enabling difficult workplace situations to serve as kindling that continually revives and fuels flash intimacy. Dysfunctional work operations are recast as tests of character and fortitude, "trauma bonding" as a noble mechanism for achieving team cohesion, and indecencies as authentic expressions beyond reproach—all in the pursuit of genuine connection.[37] But in reality, intensity functions as a questionable foundation for healthy intimacies, prioritizing urgent fervor over consistent care. The scars of work life brandished as marks of individual character and tight-knit work cultures are revealed to be the outcome of stubborn inequalities. Consequently, the "reality" brought to the fore through the morality of the fallen tends to reflect rather than confer power.

TRUST-TUNING

Consultant Lionel had observed disturbing patterns at Disruption over the previous year. People were let go without explanation, financial documents contained inaccuracies, and he was promised a raise that hadn't materialized. Yet when I asked if he trusted the three-person operations team leading the company, he replied affirmatively. "As much as there might be things that I have to gripe about," Lionel explained, "I definitely think that the three of them care about us as individuals." Delicately threading the needle between his grievances and his faith in leadership, he added, "Obviously, they have to look out for business interests and shit like that, but they're willing to go to bat to help people with particular situations of various types." Lionel's defense of the company's leaders reveals a robust sense of trust, which was expansive enough to withstand contradictory experiences of discomfort and care within these relationships.

In my conversations with people at Disruption, DTC, and The Jones, workers displayed a remarkable dexterity in avoiding outright admissions of feeling "betrayed" within their work relationships.[38] Indeed, one Jones's server condemned the term, calling it "so dramatic." This desire to evade betrayal makes sense within the cultural glorification of workplace trust discussed in the introduction, but it requires significant relational work that often goes unnoticed.

I call the dance of meaning making that people perform in this regard trust-tuning. Rather than approach workplace trust like a light switch to be either turned on or off, people act like sound mixers, experimentally "tuning" their understandings of trust to reflect complex and even contradictory workplace realities. When faced with opportunities to express betrayal, people instead adjusted the "volume" across various connotations of trust—authenticity, integrity, competence, loyalty, allyship, freedom, protection, and empathy—until they found a meaning that resonated. They mixed and matched understandings of trust to bring their experiences of neglect, disappointment, and even deceit into harmony with their belief that those they trusted cared for them, thereby sustaining flash intimacy.[39]

I observed trust-tuning in action while talking with Lark, a senior DTC executive. Early on in our conversation, Lark expressed an unwavering faith in Adam, the company's CEO. As she described it, this trust was grounded in Adam's candor: "He's very open. . . . [H]e and I have really deep talks about personal stuff and challenges and like honesty and all of that, vulnerability." When asked about some of the tougher aspects of working so closely with the CEO, Lark shifted uncomfortably in her seat. "It's almost, you want to, almost, keep your distance. When you're too much on the radar, almost, you can become a target. . . . [Y]ou're kind of in the lion's den. So, like, he could redirect anger at you." But she quickly excused Adam's occasional outbursts, rationalizing, "He doesn't really mean to; you're just there." Wrestling with her admission of tumult within the relationship, she searched for language to make sense of it. "He's extremely, um, uh, what's the word I'm looking for?" she wondered, mentally flipping through her linguistic Rolodex. "Passionate, I guess, is the word," she unconvincingly offered, trying to justify her continued willingness to trust this powerful man who periodically lashed out at her.

Suddenly, Lark's voice strengthened as she exclaimed, "But, most of the time, he's right!" Casting aside empathy and doubling down on competence as a basis for her sustained trust, she explained how Adam was always ten steps ahead of everyone else. Perhaps his means left something to be desired, but the ends were justified: "The way that he delivers it is like—[gasps]—Like, he's had to yell. He's yelled at me several times, and I'm like, 'You're totally right.'" Even during these confrontations, Adam's competence was strong enough to vindicate Lark's continued allegiance.

Typically, researchers try to impose analytic order on the multifaceted nature and fluidity of trust, breaking it down into typologies and dimensions and making bold declarations about its sources, boundaries, and impacts.[40] While this process may be useful for quantitative modeling and algorithmic coding, it does little to explain the complexity of trust in dynamic workplace relationships. Crucially, it erases the cultural and relational work of trust-tuning that helps people reconcile workplace intimacies with experiences of betrayal.

There is good reason to sustain these intimacies in the face of duplicity. Job references are born from close workplace ties, and advice and opportunities travel through them.[41] Moreover, intimacy is a marker of workplace belonging; employers make job offers—and applicants choose to accept them (or not)—based in large part on a sense of interpersonal "fit."[42] Workers also rely on colleagues and mentors to navigate workplace climates, especially the informal rules that can't be found in employee manuals.[43] Beyond these practical benefits of workplace intimacy, people bear witness to each other's lives while at work, confiding their anxieties and desires to colleagues and joking around with them to stave off boredom and relieve stress.[44] As jobs demand more through overwork and erratic schedules, draining not only the spaces but also the energy needed for other forms of social connection, workplace intimacies stand out as a steadfast oasis for friendship.[45]

Despite often idyllic depictions of intimacy—both at work and beyond—it's important to remember that close relationships have a dark side. Cases of domestic abuse perhaps most acutely highlight the potential perils of intimacy, but the exploitation of women's household labor is also indicative of the oppressive dynamics of close ties.[46] At work, people confront intimate dangers in incidents of sexual harassment and in practices of normative and relational control, in which employers seek to unduly capitalize on workers' intrinsic motivations and manipulate peer-to-peer relationships for surveillance.[47] Yet the hazards of workplace intimacy are often more quotidian and less institutionalized.

At Disruption, for example, consultants grew annoyed with colleagues who brought private conversations to the full group without their consent and with managers who overshared personal struggles, resulting in awkward emotional demands and unwanted stress. At The Jones, food runners, bussers, and bartenders were dismayed when servers they'd shared a drink with the night before snapped at them over a mistaken food placement, rushed their drink tickets at the service bar, or lowballed their shared portion of the tip pool. At DTC, junior workers were discouraged when mentors didn't defend their ideas in a meeting and when colleagues failed to publicly celebrate their accomplishments with others. Indeed, workplace friends and allies could often inflict the deepest pains.

Work intimacies, especially those defined by power imbalances, are thus characterized by a profound ambivalence: a sense of danger within familiarity, desire within dependence, and repulsion within compulsion.[48] We want intimate relationships at work—we often need them in order to succeed—yet they are fraught with unique dangers. Explaining this widespread human challenge of affirming trust in the face of intimate danger, the anthropologist Peter Geschiere calls on the wisdom of his Duala research participants in Cameroon, saying, "You have to learn to live with your witch."[49] In other words, trust is about finding ways to connect—and stay connected—despite the risk of getting hurt by those you let get close to you.

Through trust-tuning, people harness the *slipperiness* of language to make space for this ongoing ambivalence, their practice reminiscent of a passage from Lewis Carroll's novel *Through the Looking Glass*. "When I use a word," Humpty Dumpty tells Alice, "it means just what I choose it to mean—neither more nor less." When asked whether one can make words mean so many different things, Carroll's creation responds resolutely: "The question is [. . .] which is to be master—that's all."[50] Like Humpy Dumpty, workers often harness the power of language through processes of trust-tuning. They draw on trust's plurality to improvise within practical constraints and deficiencies, bending meanings to meet circumstances. Lark, for example, adroitly leveraged one meaning of trust—competence—to bring Adam's "openness" into alignment with normative workplace expectations, overcoming the personal trepidation she sometimes felt within the relationship.

In other cases, people tapped into the expansiveness of trust to identify points of commonality and connection amid conflicting agendas, embracing the term's indeterminacy to persist in relationships and on projects despite ongoing contingency and risk. At DTC, for example, Constance described an unguardedness in her relationship with Donnie: "I can be *very* candid with him—I don't hold back." When she confided her frustration to Donnie regarding her lack of promotion within the company, she felt recognized and heard: "He listens. I think he hears the frustration in my voice."

Given Donnie's stature and power within the company, I asked Constance why he hadn't successfully negotiated her promotion. "In terms of whether he'll have my back, I hope so," she replied, reflecting the leap of faith she was taking. She noted how Donnie told her changes were coming; however, she admitted, "He didn't tell me definitively where this whole thing is going," revealing a striking one-sidedness to their interpersonal candor. Nevertheless, trust kept their relationship afloat. Rationalizing the delay, Constance said, "Things are a little bit in disarray. . . . He's so busy right now, it's very hard for him to stay 'clued into' the NY office." A smile of reassurance spread across her face as she added, "He's going to jump back in—I think that's because he misses us." Constance's trust not only informed her patience, but it also helped her to creatively interpret Donnie's actions (or lack thereof) in ways that preserved their intimacy.

Trust-tuning therefore sustains flash intimacy by continually rerouting people through different frequencies of trust, forging a course that enables them to navigate (sometimes difficult) organizational realities while remaining attuned to the ideals of their workplace cultures. Notably, this does not render workplace trust vacuous. Quite the opposite: it allows people to hold contradictory ideas and inhabit the liminal spaces betwixt and between certainties and absolutes, reflecting a rich conception of the social landscape. In doing so, they define workplace relationships on their terms, even while constrained by the cultural dominance of workplace trust and the insufficient conditions of their jobs.[51] Yet our ability to navigate these complex dynamics through language remains inherently limited and imperfect. As author Rachel Aviv writes, "there are stories that save us, and stories that trap us," and it can be hard to know which is which.[52] Without public discourse that holds trust relationships accountable to certain standards—such as fairness and reciprocity—it is difficult to build solidarity around unmet expectations and broken promises within the workplace, leaving people grappling with disappointment and discontent on their own.

CONCLUSION

The production and maintenance of flash intimacy through these three processes of trust helps to explain a confounding characteristic of contemporary work: how it continues to serve as an important site of purpose, identity, and social connection even as jobs become more precarious and transient. Through the development of humanity bubbles, people create cherished spaces of intimacy that cut across but do not impede business operations. Workers draw on the morality of the fallen to invert norms of right and wrong, upholding sources of pain and suffering in the workplace as sacred and noble. And through trust-tuning, employees protect relationships beset by differing priorities and uneven power dynamics.

Said more succinctly, trust is the cost of participating in flash intimacy. However, because trust involves a deliberate submission to the potential for harm, it inadvertently shields the purveyors of pain. When trust is violated, the judgment of the one who trusted is brought into question, while the violation itself is reframed and minimized. With blame internalized, breaches of trust back into a corner those who trust: either reconcile their feelings, or adopt a posture of distrust that not only forces them to face the harsh realities of modern work alone but also stigmatizes them in a system that runs on trust.[53] As a result, people are motivated to sustain trust, even as doing so contributes to conditions at odds with their own flourishing.

The following chapters show these processes of trust in action, revealing how the trust fall may serve workplace teams, but does so at the expense of individual workers. Chapter 7, in contrast, presents an alternative framework for workplace relations. Through the case of the NYC ride-hail circuit, we'll see what happens when workers are willing to puncture humanity bubbles, focus on a morality of repair versus falling, and tune out trust.

2 Communions of Crisis

TRUST-BUILDING AT THE EXTREMES

The alarm pierced the 6:00 a.m. silence, driving me out of bed for my first scheduled Sunday brunch shift at The Jones restaurant. Liz, a server introduced in the last chapter, ominously described the shift as "the worst day of my life, once a week." She warned me: "By 3:30, you're considering suicide or becoming a trophy wife, all these things that are not in your character, just to never have to do that again."

The Sunday brunch shift wasn't just long—upward of ten hours versus the typical six- to eight-hour shifts—but also incredibly busy. My coworkers often said we were one of the three busiest restaurants in the city, and on Sundays we genuinely earned that label. The real kicker was that the shift wasn't a guaranteed moneymaker for front-of-house staff like me; free juice and cocktail specials added work but kept customer bills—and thus tips—relatively low.[1] I clocked in, bracing myself for a challenge.

David, the manager, told me I'd be in a back section of the restaurant floor, responsible for seven tables. As the doors swung open, the crowd outside was unleashed upon us, kicking the pace into high gear. The Jones's policy required us to greet each table within forty-five seconds, a standard that seemed superhuman to me as my section almost instantly filled with guests. I wondered how any server could possibly manage the restaurant's rigorous twenty-one-step protocol for each table on time without messing up.

Now working at warp speed, I replayed a running list of tasks in my head over and over: cappuccino for table 52, input 61's order, maple syrup for 53, coffee refills everywhere, greet 64, take the order at 71. Tom, a senior server, made eye contact and asked, "Are you okay?" I paused, thinking through my list, and he smiled knowingly. "If you've got a list in your head, you're not fully in the weeds yet," he said, grabbing a coffee pot and refilling my guests' cups. Another server, Brittany, came up with bar drinks in her hand. "Table 53?" she asked. I nodded appreciatively as she took them to one of my tables.

Four hours into my shift, I was shocked—and somewhat proud—that I hadn't made any big mistakes despite the dizzying pace, largely thanks to the support of my coworkers. But with each new turn of the tables, the restaurant became more of a blur. I wasn't sure how much longer I could keep it up. Finally, close to 5:00 p.m., the managers cut me, and I was done for the day. Tom, the server who'd checked in on me earlier, smirked as he asked, "Did you survive your first brunch?" "Is this normal?" I gasped. "Yes," he said flatly.

The Jones's brunch rush represents what might usefully be described as a "crisis": a period of extremity that disrupts the scripted functioning of a setting. The Jones wasn't unique in being a site of work crises; I observed similar "crises" erupt at DTC marketing and the start-up Disruption, although in those workplaces the impetus was often new business pitches and program implementations as opposed to acute demand surges. Crises are noteworthy in that they bring people to the edge of normal functioning, where they confront and negotiate the boundaries of order and disorder, making trust particularly salient.[2] In these moments, typical routines are often sidelined, and through relations of trust, improvised measures like triage, firefighting, and patchwork problem-solving take their place.[3]

Consequently, crises spawn both challenge and change to standard protocols and structures, subtly reshaping how work is conducted. Writing on national crises, author and activist Naomi Klein observes how leaders seize on the disorientation and volatility of such moments to advance contentious policies and practices, often invoking the logic that one should "never let a crisis go to waste."[4] Crises, she argues, disorient and destabilize, creating openings for maneuvering that might otherwise face resistance. While Klein focuses on political elites, the idea that crisis creates room for strategic action resonates in the workplace too, though at a different scale and with different stakes. At The Jones, DTC, and Disruption, both managers and workers saw utility in the crises they encountered at work. For them, crises were sacred and fertile ground for pressure-testing workplace relationships—the "trust fall on crack," as one DTCer put it.

I grasped this logic at a visceral level as I clocked out of my first Sunday brunch shift. The fast-paced, never-ending clamor of food orders and dirty dishes had propelled me and my colleagues into a heightened state of awareness, our frenzied movements synchronized by a surge of collective adrenaline.[5] Having weathered the rush, I felt I'd passed some unspoken test of belonging, which solidified as the team instinctually gravitated to the bar across the street to unwind after the shift. Liz aptly captured the vibe, comparing our experience to something she'd read in Tim O'Brien's Vietnam war classic, *The Things They Carried*: "You go into war with someone, and you build these unbreakable bonds where it's like you're going to be close for the rest of your lives because you face such hardship."

I explore this workplace phenomenon, which I call *communions of crisis*, through narratives from The Jones, DTC, and Disruption, using examples from each to illustrate its distinct dimensions. At The Jones, we see how the trust rituals of crises create a "trial by fire" through which workers' resolve is tested and status is bestowed accordingly. Delving into "the trenches" at DTC, we see how personal sacrifices bolster reputations and inform alliances. And then there are the "redemption narratives" at Disruption, which reveal how people draw strength from suffering, leading teams to rally around shared resilience. While I spotlight a specific aspect of communions of crisis at each work location, the three dimensions cut across the unique characteristics of their respective environments. Spanning all three sites, these patterns fostered flash intimacy, helping people achieve a sense of closeness at work not despite but rather *because of* the challenging contexts they found themselves in.

A pernicious politics underpins communions of crisis. Prevailing business logics govern what counts as a "crisis," consequently uniting teams around profits as opposed to human dignity and care. This dynamic exposes all workers (but especially marginalized ones) to potential alienation and isolation. Meanwhile, those in positions of power exploit the ensuing chaos. They utilize the temporary flexibility presented by a crisis to maneuver as needed in and out of humanity bubbles—spaces of intimacy within yet strategically differentiated from day-to-day business operations—to strengthen their influence and power. Trust-tuning, or the continual recalibration of trust's meanings, helps workers make sense of these emerging contradictions, while workplace cultures imbued by the morality of the fallen romanticize their suffering as a virtue, ultimately recruiting and ensnaring them in cycles of crisis.

Communions of crisis thus become self-generating and perpetuating, making them not just ad hoc inconveniences but chronic features of modern work environments.[6] Seized by the urgency of the moment, workers and managers focus on pressing needs at the expense of long-term sustainability, often running roughshod over protective protocols such as mandated breaks and safety measures. Immediate exigencies obstruct critical scrutiny of the broader business strategies (such as hypergrowth models and lean operations) that perpetuate crises, further shielding the flawed system from examination and change. Communions of crisis thereby contribute to the intensification of work in the US, helping to usher in a "new normal" of extreme working conditions, even in relatively mainstream occupations.[7]

TRIAL BY FIRE

"Have you seen a manager this morning?" server Margo asked as we sat together prepping silverware for Sunday brunch. I hadn't, and apparently no one else had either. Nevertheless, the morning unfolded with remarkable efficiency. As staff members filed in, we operated from muscle memory, restocking inventory and setting tables for service. Senior servers consulted the restaurant's floor plan, assigning primary sections to those scheduled as closers (who could not be cut early), while the rest of us signed ourselves up for the remaining sections on a first-come, first-served basis. "Boy, now that's autonomy in the workplace," someone quipped, admiring our unsupervised coordination. To an outsider, it might look like genuine autonomy—evidence of empowered workers running the show. But what appeared as freedom was in fact a disciplined orientation to crisis, shaped by unspoken norms and collective obligations that often exerted more pressure than a manager ever could.

Across The Jones, DTC, and Disruption, workers moved through a ritualized sequence—sharing the grind, crossing the threshold, and rehashing war stories—that helped them navigate the churn of high-pressure, unscripted moments.[8] In doing so, they framed these events as important rites of passage.[9] Ritualized crises became a testing ground for character, much like the ancient practice of "trial by fire," whereby one's reaction to boiling oil or a hot iron was believed to reveal their true nature. The modern-day workplace version of this trial secured workers' participation by treating performance under pressure as a test of trustworthiness—and thus a key entryway into workplace humanity bubbles.

The initial stage of the ritual, referred to as "sharing the grind," brought workers together in preparation for the accelerated pace of crises. This was the ritual that guided our autonomous cadence that morning as we prepped food stations, cleaned dishware, and filled coffee urns for the potential rush. During this stage, the mandate was to act in ways that supported the entire group, not just oneself. "If you see that there's one person still restocking knives in the back, help them finish that first [before setting up your own tables]," veteran server Amanda advised, underscoring the moral imperative of selflessness. Categorizing team members as "the strong and the less strong," she said it was important to socialize the latter: "It's the strong people's job to make the less strong stronger." Reiterating the importance of teaching and policing the rules of the grind, Amanda concluded, "It's all a flow. You have to trust everybody."

Sharing the grind culminated in a pre-shift meeting. More than just a briefing, this meeting was a performative display of readiness, marked by a blend of bravado and subtle encouragement. Veteran staff often excelled in displaying their menu and service expertise at these meetings, while newer members like myself felt the pressure, keenly aware that knowledge gaps would open us up to ridicule and corrective feedback. Managers also used the meeting to hype the shift ahead, often referring to data from historical sales and digital reservations to forecast the shift's volume and intensity. Not every shift was quite like Sunday brunch, but it was the restaurant's goal to pack the place to capacity as quickly and as often as possible, meaning almost every shift included some version of the rush. The pre-shift meeting was meant to psychologically prepare the team for the coming onslaught, and its end marked the beginning of the next phase of the ritual: "crossing the threshold."

The significance of crossing the threshold was clear from my first interview for the job. The general manager, Paul, grilled me with questions about the intensity of my last serving gig, trying to gauge my resilience amid stressful situations. Having drawn my cues from the company's website, I described the frenetic atmosphere of my previous restaurant, emphasizing how I enjoyed the energy and adrenaline of a fast-paced environment. Paul nodded approvingly and noncommittally offered to give me a shot. Clearly I could talk the talk, but could I walk the walk?

Both managers and workers approached crises through the morality of the fallen, perceiving adversity as a powerful revealer of truth. As veteran server Abigail observed, "Working in a high stress, crowded, fast-paced, hot environment—you know where it's really stressful—can make a lot of people do a lot of weird things." According to her, the pressure of crossing the threshold provided a unique window into a person's character and value.[10] Amanda agreed, pointing out how the intensity of busy shifts served as a natural filter, weeding out those not suited for the hustle and bustle. Indeed, people who couldn't keep up often left or were let go within just a few shifts, while those who thrived earned more lucrative shifts. In this way, crossing the threshold mirrored the experience of putting on the mythical Hogwarts's Sorting Hat, with the invisible hand of the crisis delivering verdicts on individual capabilities and designating future trajectories within the restaurant.

The belief in the evaluative power of crises made managerial decisions appear self-evident. Manager David, for example, described his personnel decisions in passive, exculpatory terms: "Before I know it, I subconsciously put [poor crisis performers] into tiny sections because I think that's what they can handle, without trying to be malicious or doing it knowingly." Over time, implicit assessments reified: "It just starts to ingrain in you that it's what this person can handle," David explained. "Anything more, and I'm going to have to be on them, be standing next to them all night, and I don't have time for that." Yet when I asked David what it meant to handle oneself well during the rush, he listed nebulous qualities, such as staying positive, being a good team player, and "persisting through the craziness."[11] The significance attributed to crossing the threshold lent a deceptive objectivity to evaluations that were, in fact, heavily influenced by subjective managerial perceptions and actions.

The trust (and distrust) forged through crossing the threshold was cemented during the third and final stage of crisis rituals—what I refer to as "rehashing war stories." At The Jones, this stage typically unfolded over drinks at a nearby bar, where team members bore witness to one another's feats and celebrated their communal grit.[12] These gatherings served as a platform for expressing judgments—commending the day's heroes and critiquing those who fell short. Through storytelling, people solidified the standing of team members and strengthened collective bonds.

Conjuring up a war story, veteran bartender Ryan scoffed, "There's bartenders I've worked with in the past who, they would literally just abandon you and just be on the other side of the bar, not helping you out." "[I'd be] getting my ass kicked," he recalled, "and the other person will just be at the bar, walking around, moseying around, or you know, having a twenty-minute conversation with a guest." Ryan was repulsed by the very notion of such seemingly selfish behavior. "That's an every-man-for-himself mentality," he said, shaking his head, "a little narcissism and a little bit of just not being good at his job—which is a *bad* combination." Ryan contrasted this image with those he trusted: "The ones that are the most helpful, good at their jobs, and they're there for you." "Matteo's a great fucking team player," he rattled off. "Noah, awesome team player. Phillip, great team player. Al, big goofy Al, great team player."

However, while trials by fire may appear to stand on their own, they do not exist in a presocial world. "God may be believed to speak," historian Peter Brown explains, noting the perceived role of divine intervention in ancient trials, "but the human group took an unconscionably long time letting Him get a word in edgewise."[13] As Brown suggests, ambiguities regarding the criteria for initiating trials and interpreting their outcomes affords substantial room for human agency. Today's workplace trials are similarly shaped by the subjective values and power dynamics of a capitalist system that venerates meritocracy over equality, resilience over sustainability, and able-bodied notions of individual strength over collective well-being.[14]

Perhaps most revealing of their inherent bias, trials by fire were only triggered by narrowly defined work crises: namely an influx of business at risk of being squandered. By contrast, incidents of harassment and disrespect tended to fall short of qualifying as a crisis, especially in the eyes of managers. For example, a Black woman server named Susan initially shrugged off an elderly white couple's standoffishness toward her but felt deeply disrespected later when they lodged an unwarranted complaint with Paul, the general manager. "Look at her," the couple said with disgust, without offering additional details regarding her offense. Several staff members who witnessed the incident understood the guests' behavior as racially charged, and what followed upended the restaurant's normally scripted commitment to inclusion.

When the situation escalated, Susan looked to Paul to stand up to the guests on her behalf. Instead, he immediately apologized to the couple and even took several items off their bill as consolation. Recounting the event, Susan initially empathized with Paul, whom she believed probably didn't have a lot of direct experience with racism as a white man. At the same time, she wished he'd handled the situation differently. "Even if you don't know what to do," she said, "I feel like you should ask someone for assistance or support." Susan experienced the moment as a crisis, but Paul's failure to rally around her at the time—despite the restaurant's zero-tolerance harassment and discrimination policies—resulted in a loss of trust. "Instead of other people building my trust by being an ally or helping me out, standing up for me, or creating an environment where I feel safe," she lamented, "I just feel that effort wasn't put in."

Susan later tried to engage Paul in a corrective recounting of the story—an attempt at constructing a shared war story. In their conversation, Susan sought to reframe the event as a crisis that threatened workers' well-being: "I told him [Paul] that it infringes upon how we feel in the workplace, safety in the workplace." She later conveyed Paul's failure to recognize the significance of the racist incident: "He was like, 'What do you mean you don't feel safe?'" Rather than a test of his character or an event worthy of drawing collective attention and resources, he saw what happened as a minor hiccup during an otherwise busy shift. Paul's inability to perceive the racism inherent in the customers' reaction was a turning point for Susan: "That was big for me, where I just, I lost all trust."

Notably, Susan was not alone in attempting to construct a shared war story around the incident. Several staff members were disturbed not just by the couple's behavior but also by the way Paul handled it. They wrote about the incident in the mandatory memos, known as communication reports (CRs), that staff were expected to complete at the end of every shift. May, a veteran server, explained how the team felt compelled to affirm Susan's value in response to Paul's dismissive handling of the situation. "Everybody wrote in their CR that day: 'I think Susan is important, and I think that she is a good human, and I think that her needs and her life are important.'" Yet May also acknowledged how the incident competed with the dominant view of the rush as *the* crisis. "I mean, I understand that that's a really tough situation, and it's brunch, and [Paul] is busy," she said. "The best way to make that situation go away is to give them a free meal. I get that." May summed up her assessment of Paul's actions with a relatively mild condemnation: "It was just a little disappointing."

However, for Susan it was more than a little disappointing. Not only did the incident make her feel unsafe, but Paul's inability to acknowledge customer racism as a significant problem led to a failed communion of crisis. Even as her coworkers rallied around her, Susan lost trust in her managers, and her sense of belonging within the restaurant began to wane. She quit a few weeks later, explaining, "It makes you feel like you're an outsider in your own world, and I don't want to feel like that at work."

The "strangely subjective objectivity" attributed to trials by fire made crises potent political instruments for employers.[15] Just as ancient trials pacified disruptive conflicts and consolidated consensus, modern workplace trials act like a cultural assembly line, bringing workers into a coordinated frenzy to support ongoing profit-making.[16] Like The Jones, many gendered and racialized organizations led by white men reveal important patterns in what and who are left out of the rituals of workplace crisis.[17] Disrespect and discrimination are often not seen by them as rising to the level of crisis, with those disproportionately affected by such acts particularly vulnerable to exclusion. As a result, communions of crisis tend to sustain profits and power as opposed to safe and inclusive work environments.

IN THE TRENCHES

DTC is in the business of experiential marketing—a strategy by which marketers create memorable, interactive experiences and live events to prompt and deepen consumers' connections with brands. Popular examples include the creation of Upside Down portals in big cities to coincide with the season premiere of *Stranger Things* and an in-store event at which people painted Adidas shoes to match the iconic blue-and-white trainers tennis legend Billy Jean King wore during her famous "Battle of the Sexes" match.[18] The execution of an experiential installation at DTC was a stressful and unsettled period, similar to the restaurant rush. According to a producer named Ronald, these crisis moments were "where the rubber meets the road" in terms of trust, with people coming together to do whatever was necessary to ensure the event's success.

When discussing crises, folks at DTC, The Jones, and Disruption often invoked the wartime notion of being "in the trenches." Viewed through the lens of the morality of the fallen, where authenticity was highly valued, the trenches became a sacred space where trust was forged. "In the trench is when you're down and dirty," mid-level DTC manager Wesley explained, while Creative Director Calvin described the ideal trench scenario as one in which "you're looking to the left or right, knowing that the people that are around you have your back." The military metaphor not only emphasized the raw character of crises but also raised the stakes of work, transposing the life-and-death consequences of war onto the job.

Two junior account workers, Marsha and Gabriela, vividly illustrated the all-out, no-holds-barred atmosphere of work in the trenches as they recounted an out-of-town promotional event they'd worked on together. "It was a fucking shitshow," Marsha exclaimed, her voice a mix of exasperation and pride. The two women found meaningful connection in their shared tenacity and passion to get the job done. "For a whole week straight," Marsha said, "we bonded because we were side by side through the most ridiculous. . . . I can't *believe* some of the stuff I did down there." Gabriela concurred, describing the humanity bubble that developed within the trenches: "I think that's definitely when we went from colleagues to friends."

The grueling conditions brought Marsha and Gabriela together in a communion of crisis, transforming their mutual recognition of work devotion into a deep trust that supported a sense of kinship. Gabriela laughed, recalling her and Marsha's battle-worn appearance: hair in buns, no makeup, dressed in sweatpants. "We would *fight,*" she explained, portraying their collaboration as a battle against all odds. "We'd fight with people to get the event how we wanted it to go." They were chuffed by their success in "achieving the impossible," even as doing so had pushed them to the edge of their endurance. Marsha beamed when recounting how someone would say, "'It's alright, don't worry. I'm going to give this to Marsha, and it's going to get done.'" "That's a home run for me," she admitted.

In the trenches of a crisis, no work demand was deemed over the top, because people expected each other to put the team's interests above their own. Lanie (from the introduction) articulated this expectation, saying, "[If] you're leaving everyone stranded, then I don't trust that you really care about this project." Noting the personal stakes involved, she added, "I don't really trust that you're totally sincere [and] that you care about us because you're ditching." But in high-pressure contexts where total commitment was venerated, individuals often sacrificed their personal time, health, and even basic hygiene to get the job done.

People come to jobs for different reasons and from different situations. Job motivations and commitments are complex and include constellations of passion, care, financial gain, status, and skill acquisition that vary across workers.[19] Outside of their immediate work environments, people's life situations are similarly diverse, with family responsibilities, health issues, and cultural values shaping and constraining individual work behaviors in different ways.[20] Put simply, not everyone wants to, or even can, demonstrate the all-consuming dedication required in the trenches.

Gabriela and Marsha traveled out of state for the promotional event that united them. The distance easily facilitated their undivided attention, as personal commitments were neatly contained back home. However, during more recent local events, Marsha noticed a difference between her approach and that of Gabriela. "[She] kind of more protects herself," Marsha observed, citing how Gabriela was often hard to reach late at night, even on the eve of important deadlines. Marsha contrasted this with her own engagement, saying, "I'm like, 'Holy shit, we have to get this stuff done. [. . .] I'm gonna stay up till eleven and send emails.'" Bemoaning Gabriela's violation of the ritualistic norms of crisis preparation, Marsha complained, "She doesn't get that whole 'share the grind' kind of thing," leading her to conclude: "That's where I also have had a problem now."[21] Their relationship was built on a shared commitment to the job, but when that commitment was put into question, the trust safeguarding their bond began to erode.

Just as people enter the trenches from differing life situations, they also do so from varying workplace positions, which shape how their participation is interpreted. Senior-level engagement in the trenches is often deemed optional, while junior-level participation is expected—a taken-for-granted logic that DTC CEO Adam alluded to one day while giving a presentation on the company's tumultuous history. "The front line might die," he noted, referencing pivotal crisis moments in DTC's past, "but you can still win the war." In the eyes of executives like Adam, junior-level workers—a group disproportionately made up of white women and people of color—were expendable, despite the major responsibilities consistently placed on them.[22] What mattered was that those at the core—themselves—would be there to carry on once the battle was won.

Thus, when high-level executives did enter the trenches, it drew the team's attention. Account Director Russ, for instance, called out senior management's engagement in the lead-up to a recent event. "These are pretty senior guys. They've earned their stripes," he marveled, "but it's just the mentality of, 'our clients are paying us to do something, and we gotta get it done. So, let's stay up all night and get it done if we have to.'" Understood as a choice versus a requirement, joining the trenches represented a gesture of humility and care by senior managers that temporarily leveled the playing field. "I think when they see that," finance executive Keith said of his willingness to pitch in during hard times, "people underneath me know that I'll do whatever. [. . .] They know if something's got to get done, I'm not going to shy away from doing—'Oh, this is beneath me!'—*I will do this*." Manager Wesley similarly highlighted the leveling tendencies of the trenches, recalling how he had jumped in to help out his direct report in the midst of the team's latest crisis. "We're both doing it," he said, "I'm not the senior account executive. She's not an assistant account executive." With his hands mimicking a scale in equilibrium, he said, "At that point, we're like same level, more of a team."[23]

Managers' entry into the trenches also provided them with a chance to tap into the deep reservoir of care that existed in the humanity bubbles formed there. For example, Gabriela recalled an evening when several senior managers stayed late into the night to help the team prepare for a new business pitch. "That showed me we were a team," she said, "and we work together." She explained how the gesture drove her to reciprocate further: "I see that you're staying late with me, then I'm going to do better than what you expected me to do because I see that you are trying to do the same." In this way, managerial presence in the trenches often bumped up the team's already intense pace. Describing how managers were really helpful in "keeping that team environment going," Wesley gave a typical account of what they expected in the trenches, saying, "You haven't eaten a full meal in however many days or whatever. And then no sleep. All that type of stuff."

Such sentiments contribute to the trenches becoming what feminist scholars critique as "workplace masculinity contests," in which public displays of heroism serve as a key mechanism for recognition and advancement.[24] When the trenches take on the atmosphere of such a contest, both workers and managers are incentivized to perpetuate crises. Jill noted this tendency among many of her managerial colleagues. She was hired a few months before I came to DTC as one of the most senior women at a company otherwise dominated by men. Despite her tokenized status, Jill was initially enthusiastic about trying to address some of the ongoing problems at the company.[25] Over time, however, she became increasingly disheartened by her colleagues in leadership, whom she noted had little appetite to address the company's root problems or to build more sustainable work processes. Indeed, some had even admitted to her that they enjoyed "fighting fires," noting the utility of crises for uniting teams, motivating workers, and demonstrating their own leadership.[26]

Nevertheless, Jill remained dogged in her pursuit, pushing for more honest conversations with clients and better strategic planning at the executive level. Unfortunately, her time spent designing and advocating such initiatives prevented her from joining junior- and mid-level workers in the trenches. "It makes me feel like a failure in a lot of ways," Jill admitted. "I'm ignoring [the team] in some ways because it's been so horrifically bad with the clients." She went on to explain, "It's almost like they're over *here*," gesturing toward one of her outstretched hands before then tipping her head in the other direction, "and it's like, I'm protecting you from not knowing how bad *this* is—and then trying to fix it."

Jill's dedication was not, in fact, evident to junior colleagues. "I don't think any of us have confidence that if the client was going to pull out of the company," said Ben, a mid-level member of Jill's team, "she's gonna fight for us." Another team member similarly described a lack of trust in Jill, noting she was "not very approachable." It was a lose-lose situation: Jill could either enter the trenches and acquiesce to the repetitive and exhausting cycle of chronic crises or endure the cultural stigma of abstaining from glorified communions of crisis, spending her time instead trying to prevent them from occurring. Reflecting on the consequences of her choice to date, senior leader Grady lamented, "She's lost quite a few people out there."

Like many women hired into leadership positions, Jill was on a glass cliff, tasked with turning around deep-seated problems within an organization but offered few resources and little support to do so.[27] I asked her whether she would do things differently if given the chance to start over. She paused and released a heavy sigh. "I would prefer to have all this headache removed from my plate," she eventually said. "I'd rather just be in the trenches all day long with these people to gain that trust." Instinctively, she understood what she'd given up in her attempts to tame the constant firefighting. When I checked in with her a few months after exiting DTC, she'd moved to a position at another company, leaving just one woman remaining on the senior executive team. Jill was at DTC less than a year.

The trenches served as crucibles of career building—sacred spaces where reputations were built and team building was fortified. Workers constantly found themselves on the front lines displaying their commitment and value, while managers occasionally ventured into the trenches to demonstrate solidarity and enhance their influence. But amid these communions of crisis where impromptu acts of heroism took center stage, unsung heroes—like those working diligently behind the scenes to develop sustainable systems and mitigate crises—remained invisible and were quickly marginalized. Consequently, companies like DTC, Disruption, and The Jones perpetuated a cycle of chronic crises, undermining long-term stability for short-term theater.

REDEMPTION NARRATIVES

"Look, I wouldn't have the perspective that I have now had I not gone through the last year and a half," Disruption CEO Shane told me after recounting the company's troubled history. "I certainly wish I could have avoided some of the *financial* challenges of that time," he conceded, before adding, "But, I mean, you kind of have to go through—you have to have lived the experience in order to get the benefits." Echoing Liz at The Jones, Shane continued, "It's like, you go through an experience with a group of people—like an *intense* experience with a group of people. [. . .] I think *that* helps build trust."

Within communions of crises, workers and managers often drew upon redemption narratives, or what psychologist Dan McAdams describes as stories that offer "deliverance from suffering to a better world."[28] At Disruption, The Jones, and DTC, these storylines provided teams with a common script for rationalizing their shared experiences of adversity. Embedded in the morality of the fallen, their accounts traced the trajectory of team building through grit, placing pain in the service of an ultimately redeeming outcome. In doing so, they gave workers a reason and a purpose for enduring hardship, helping them reconcile the harsh capriciousness of modern work with the stated (albeit aspirational) family-like values of their employers.[29]

The central redemption story at Disruption began with reference to its auspicious beginnings.[30] Describing the company's early days, Logan, who served on the operations team alongside Shane, said, "They hired a ton of people right away, and they had a ton of money." Shane elaborated on her description of the firm's beginning, explaining how they'd landed a major client through one of his former colleagues. "We grew to fifteen full-time employees over two years," he recalled. "By the third year, we got to our high-water mark of thirty-five people or so." He then laughed, confessing that "we didn't really try very hard—we didn't have to work to sell. The revenue, the opportunities were just coming at us." Veteran team members often reminisced about that early period, highlighting free happy hours and two early initiatives: Disruption Learning and Disruption Doing. Through the former, the company hosted industry talks and held knowledge-sharing sessions, while the latter served as an incubator for employees' own business ideas. A company vision that celebrated gumption, creativity, and social networking reigned over this "magical" era.

Unfortunately, the good times didn't last. "It turns out that it takes a lot of sales activities and selling success and really, really strong marketing to keep thirty-five people on billing," Shane said. "You start running out of money if you have too many people on the bench (working non-billable projects). You're paying too much overhead." As finances became more problematic, Shane's cofounder abandoned ship to pursue other interests. Shane filled the gap by hiring a new CEO, Palmer, as well as two other executives. As Logan put it, they were "brought in to kind of be the grown-up[s] in some way and put some order into the company."

Under the new leadership team, Disruption Learning and Disruption Doing were discontinued, and revenue-earning, client-facing consulting work became the sole priority. One consultant, Harold, recalled the shift with a sense of dismay. "When Palmer came in, it felt more like he was trying to move things in a direction I perceive as more corporate, as far as allocation, division of tasks, and sort of needing to appeal to the clients." Nylah, the consultant introduced in chapter 1, also remembered being deeply unhappy. "There's not any transparency," she told Shane at the time. "There's all this hierarchy going on, and it feels like there's two different levels of Disruption." She threatened to quit, as several other employees had done, but Shane didn't act, continuing to functionally endorse the revised strategy and structure.

A few months later, however, Shane deemed the executives' salaries unaffordable, and he let them go. The act marked a turning point for the team. "The feeling level changed, immediately," Reid, the third member of the operations team, told me. "The culture improved tremendously. It was like overnight." Nylah recalled the moment similarly: "My respect for Shane went up tremendously that day." "It's not because he became a different person," she explained, "but because he showed me the person he really was." Engaging in trust-tuning, workers reaffirmed their faith in Shane by reading the situation as a reflection of his renewed commitment to the company's original values and thus a testament to his integrity. This reading helped workers like Nylah move past their previous concerns about issues such as transparency, even as these problems remained unaddressed. While trust in Shane deepened, his decision to remove the executives was never openly discussed with the full group. Yet rather than focus on the lack of information, the team's trust enabled them to fill in the blanks with what they hoped to be the case: a return to better times.

The executives' departure served to transition Disruption's cultural atmosphere from a period of suffering to one of healing and redemption—a narrative that had fully congealed by the time I met the team six months later. "We started out very committed to that [original] vision," Reid told me in our first meeting, "and then we had a new CEO and other people in here that were much more committed to the bottom line and to a more 'old model' hierarchy." But then Shane saw the proverbial light and "phased those people out. Now, we are much more attuned to assuring that everyone is aligned and that we work toward our vision." Through this redemption narrative, the team not only decreed their suffering to be a thing of the past, but they also created a productive "us versus them" storyline that freed leadership of accountability and served to unite remaining team members.[31]

Crucially, this narrative required scapegoating the "phased out" executives.[32] Reid, for instance, attributed Disruption's problems to the previous CEO, notably omitting the inconvenient fact that Shane had appointed him: "Palmer was put into a CEO position. It was mainly him." Pressing the issue of accountability, I asked Shane why he'd appointed Palmer CEO in the first place. His response—"I was just burned out"—fit well with the team's trust-tuned perceptions. Shane hadn't lost conviction in the company's original values; he was simply overwhelmed. He emphasized how one of the other terminated executives "played a big role in convincing me that Palmer should run the company." Further offloading responsibility, he added, "When I had an opportunity to say, 'Here, take care of this for me,' I was all over it." But in never accepting responsibility, Shane (and the rest of the leadership team) bypassed the powerful stage of atonement that typically accompanies redemption.

With Palmer and others not present to justify their decisions, the team settled for vague explanations rather than investigating the root causes of the company's problems. "I don't really know what happened," consultant Mack admitted. "I've heard about how this is going to be a new year for us, like a new beginning. And Reid talks about, you know, moving on from whatever happened," he continued, "but I don't really have a good sense of what it was." As the team rallied around a narrative that made cultural conformity the cornerstone of trust, decisions enacted through the previously dominant business logic became alien. "I can't figure out some of Palmer's decisions," Shane declared. "We've talked about [those decisions]—Logan, Reid and I. . . . What was he thinking? I mean, some of it is really hard for us to understand."

By rendering past mistakes incomprehensible, the team embraced an oversimplified redemption story centered around "three bad executives." "So now, Palmer's gone," Logan summed up, "[and] everyone who really fits the kind of Disruption culture that we—much more of Shane's vision and certainly who me and Reid are—are here." Yet while the team galvanized around a trust-tuned emphasis on cultural conformity, all was not well. "The pains from the past are financially still there," Logan admitted. The team may have achieved a sense of seamless deliverance by coconstructing a narrative composed of "pleasant lies" and critical omissions, but this came at the cost of truly reckoning with past mistakes.[33]

Moreover, in their rush toward redemption, the group impeded their own ability to feel and express the full range of emotions experienced during the crisis. For example, both Shane and Logan recounted (separately) a difficult phone call they shared shortly after Palmer's termination—and one week after Logan had given birth to her first child. As Logan remembered it, "Shane called me and was essentially going to let me go," but Shane's retelling included more caveats and disclaimers. "I called her to let her know about the dire situation we were in," he said, adding ruefully, "I wasn't very sensitive to her situation. I said a lot of things that I regret in hindsight." He continued, "The truth was that I didn't know how we were going to pay her throughout her maternity leave." Although he didn't tell Logan that, what he did say was "something to the effect of, 'You know we really shouldn't have hired you in the first place.'" In his own defense, Shane contended that the company really didn't have the money to pay her. Nevertheless, noting that hindsight is 20/20, he acknowledged, "I didn't need to share that with her, and I shouldn't have shared it with her." Both Logan and Shane recalled the acute terror she felt in the moment, as she was the breadwinner for her family, which now included a newborn baby. "I really kind of threw her world upside down," Shane recalled guiltily.

Yet rather than linger in the complex and ambiguous emotions of the moment, Shane quickly pivoted to its purported benefits, describing the incident as a productive inflection point in his relationship with Logan.

"What Logan did after that [conversation] was essentially double down," he said, "showing me what she was made of, right? *While she's on maternity leave!*" He added, somewhat self-consciously, "It's not that I—I didn't expect, or even to some degree, want her to be active while she was on leave, right? I wanted her to actually be a mom for a while." Yet Logan—in a precarious position due to the fragmented nature of federal, state, and city parental leave protections at the time—did work throughout her so-called maternity leave, even hosting Shane and Reid at her home for operations team meetings.[34] Despite fleeting moments of guilt, Shane largely idealized Logan's "willingness" to work during her leave as a marker of her commitment and worth: "That was when I learned more about what Logan was capable of doing [. . .] where I started to realize that she was a lot more than she appeared to be."

In an organizational, and indeed national, context that celebrates redemption, Logan leaned into "silver linings" and "lemonade," relinquishing her personal story to the dominant narrative.[35] "I don't complain," she boasted. "I'm never like, oh, you know [feigns grumbling]." Instead, Logan took on extra responsibilities and even joined Shane and Reid in taking a temporary salary cut to keep the company afloat—an approach that required trust-tuning. Regarding the harrowing conversation with Shane, she said she understood that "the intention was not bad" and ultimately chalked up the whole thing to a misunderstanding. In effect, she made her pain productive and compensated Shane's mistreatment of her with greater trust. "By showing my trust and faith to Shane and Reid," she explained, "they know I'm all in, and that [sacrifice] provides strength to get through challenging times." In the process, Logan reaffirmed her commitment to the financially troubled company and doubled down on a CEO who at one point was deeply ambivalent about her value to the firm.

Relying on a morality of the fallen, redemption narratives romanticize suffering and treat trauma as training. These narratives contribute to communions of crisis by rallying teams in collective resilience and promoting the idea of post-traumatic growth.[36] At the same time—and in combination with trust-tuning—they also contribute to toxic cultures that exact unhealthy, even dangerous devotion from workers, ultimately rendering them martyrs to the organization.[37] Moreover, while the light shines bright on sufferers who prove their worth by rising heroically like a phoenix from the ashes, the catalysts of the fires that singed them persist. As McAdams warns, "The redemptive self sustains hope, but blind hope is naïve."[38] Sometimes suffering can't—or shouldn't—be redeemed, forcing organizations to contend with their pasts before bounding toward their futures.[39]

CONCLUSION

"I thought trust falls were just corny things," Shane chuckled. "But you know, in real life, who's gonna be there to back you up? It's easy to say that [you will back someone] when things are going great; it's hard to do that when they're not." Much like traditional trust falls, crises create unique environments of vulnerability and interdependency that prompt teamwork. Yet while the former are often seen as contrived and trivial, the latter enjoy an elevated status within the workplace. Through the rituals and narratives of trust that govern crises, managers and workers alike are drawn to the frenzied intensity, eager to step into the so-called arena to demonstrate their worth, commitment, and resilience. Consequently, rather than the skepticism that typically greets standard team-building initiatives, crises become highly anticipated and even welcomed moments of collective industry.

Business leaders may equate the near-constant energy and action driven by chronic crises with progress. But the stories at The Jones, DTC, and Disruption suggest something more akin to what literary legend Toni Morrison classifies as the "inertia, if not established paralysis" within classic tales of heroism.[40] Cycles of high exertion may produce short-term profits and offer teams the thrill of flash intimacy, but they also enable systemic issues such as inadequate strategic planning to linger, often even reinforcing those issues. All the while, frontline workers take the brunt of such workplace dysfunctions, regularly pushed to the brink of physical and mental exhaustion but rarely compensated for their discretionary efforts. Restaurant workers, for example, don't receive higher wages during peak hours, and most "exempt" employees don't receive overtime pay for extra time put in during a crisis.[41] These periods of high intensity are thus an ineffective and inefficient mechanism of upward mobility, particularly for lower-level and marginalized workers. Instead, chronic work crises may be more accurately understood as the axle on which the capitalist hamster wheel rotates.

In her essay, Morrison contrasts the spectacle of attending to crises with the more substantive potential of conflict, defining the latter as "a disharmony calling for adjustment, change, or compromise."[42] While communions of crisis fuel workplace cultures and intimacies, they simultaneously hide broader conflicts between workers and employers regarding pay and working conditions, and they alienate workers from potential allies (e.g., a slow diner or a colleague setting reasonable work boundaries). As a result, communions of crisis produce a misguided and depoliticized solidarity, with workplace actors unwittingly rallying around the pursuit of profit at all costs rather than a healthier and more equitable model of work.

In chapter 7 we'll see a different path to collective action in the case of the NYC ride-hail circuit. Rather than glorify their struggles, ride-hail drivers followed Morrison's advice in voicing a powerful repudiation of their suffering. They united with one another *against* their employers, forging a public conflict that brought attention to the industry's exploitative operations, spotlighting troubling business tactics and harsh working realities. In their collective quest, drivers sought to transform the relentless grind of modern labor into a true vehicle for ascent, thereby restoring the foundational promise of work. Meanwhile, at The Jones, DTC, and Disruption, the extremes of work were only one place where flash intimacy thrived. Less urgent but no less effective were the between-the-lines moments explored in the next chapter.

3 Between the Lines

BUILDING TRUST WHILE LETTING LOOSE

Any outing in Koreatown, Nylah declared, requires soju. "It tastes like vodka mixed with sugar," she explained, ordering several bottles for the Disruption team. Reid, the head of talent development, seized the moment as the bottles arrived. Raising his glass, he touched briefly on the start-up's recent hurdles before making a more prolonged tribute to the group's resurgent spirit and cohesion. Glasses clinked together, and a collective cheer went up—the starting bell of the night's festivities.

As the soju flowed, the conversations became livelier, and voices grew louder. Laughter erupted as CEO Shane shared whimsical stories from his youth. Consultant Lionel reveled in tales of his romantic escapades, prompting a spate of unsolicited advice culminating in a jovial debate about the pros and cons of dating in the city. All the while, phones circulated as people shared digital snaps of family members and vacations. I noticed a palpable camaraderie among team members, marked not only by mutual respect but also by a seemingly genuine sense of interest in and care for one another.

A couple of hours later, the collectively tipsy group migrated from the restaurant to a nearby karaoke bar. Everyone took a turn on the mic, belting out songs from across genres. There was Dawn, singing "Take Me or Leave Me" from *Rent*, and Lionel giving a strikingly accurate imitation of Nirvana's Kurt Cobain. Several coworkers offered renditions of their favorite Taylor Swift songs. Prompted by the team's insistence, even I joined in, delivering an enthusiastic if not exactly tuneful performance of Mary Chapin Carpenter's "I Feel Lucky." As the night wore on, singing gave way to dancing, infusing the private karaoke room with an electrifying energy. A newer consultant, Jay, cast me an uninhibited grin as he danced alongside Logan, the team's head of marketing. "This is so fun," he beamed, proclaiming a newfound appreciation for his colleagues. The night ended an hour or so later with a final toast and a series of warm goodbyes.

Booze-soaked events like this one were a staple of workplace sociality across Disruption, The Jones, and DTC. Alcohol was always on the agenda at Disruption's "all-hands" meetings, and happy hours peppered the team's schedule. At The Jones, post-shift drinks were standard, and the company's annual holiday party was a notorious bacchanal. For its part, DTC boasted a fully stocked in-office bar, and a beer cart wheeled around the open layout most Thursday and Friday afternoons.

Workers and managers referred to work-associated drinking sessions as *between-the-lines* moments. Drinking, they told me, signaled "a tangible way of clocking off from work," yet when drinking takes place in work settings or includes supervisors, peers, or subordinates, it is not true off-hours play. Drinks with colleagues represent a liminal space that blurs the lines between professional obligation and personal relaxation.[1] Analogous to first-time expectant couples who are no longer childless but not yet parents, people participating in these events are neither formally on the job nor completely off duty.

"Drinking" is one of three liminal acts analyzed in this chapter, explored through the case of Disruption. "Venting," in which workers express frustrations deeply rooted in underlying care for the job—thereby straddling the chasm between workplace loyalty and exit—is interrogated at DTC. And then I analyze "joking" at The Jones, where workers employed it to navigate feelings of belonging and marginalization, situating such interactional banter at the nexus of workplace inclusion and exclusion. Similar to the previous chapter, the three patterns documented here manifest across the different sites, but I concentrate on specific examples from a single site when discussing each to offer a clearer, more detailed exploration of their interactional dynamics.

Anthropologist Victor Turner describes the liminality characterizing between-the-lines moments as "ambiguous, unsettled, and unsettling."[2] On the one hand, these interstitial social spaces are liberating. Freed from the usual expectations and scripts, people unwind and forge connections that transcend everyday work roles while drinking, venting, and joking.[3] Dissonant cultural scripts and symbols converge, enabling people to improvise and cocreate alternative rules of interaction, forge new relationships, and look at their work situations from fresh perspectives.[4]

Trust is activated by the uncertainty of these moments, leading workers to embrace both the yin and yang of flash intimacy.[5] Opening themselves up to vulnerability, they enjoy the interpersonal benefits of "letting loose" in the form of intimate recognition and unbridled social connection. The beauty of the trust fall, after all, is in the sense of release it offers—which is rewarded by comforting reassurance and newfound fellowship when successful.[6] The risk, however, is in trusting the wrong people. And because trust guides perceptions of reality, misplaced trust at the wrong moment can blind workers to looming risks, potentially leading to psychological, financial, or even physical harm.[7]

Indeed, drinking, venting, and joking take place in dangerous gray areas where accountability is murky.[8] Drinking scenes are frequent sites of sexual harassment and assault, while venting sessions can regress into gossiping, bullying, or social exclusion, and jokes can become a medium of chauvinism and prejudice.[9] In these cases, people take advantage of lowered inhibitions and disrupted norms to indulge in offensive, hurtful, and other boundary-crossing behaviors, often drawing on a morality of the fallen that venerates the grittier and unvarnished aspects of work life to justify their actions. Unfortunately, risks are neither equally disbursed nor absorbed across people inhabiting between-the-lines moments. Those with the least social status and power are often burdened with the greatest likelihood of harm, and they have minimal resources for pushing back when things go wrong.[10]

As contested social terrain, the trajectory of between-the-lines moments toward emancipation or oppression relies substantially on configurations of trust. Trust-tuning, or workers' creative deployment of various trust meanings, is thus a determining factor in how these moments unfold. When workers connect with peers without employer interference, they are more likely to elevate notions of worker allyship and collective fairness when forging trust between the lines. With trust tuned to this frequency, acts like venting can take on transformational, even revolutionary vigor. Increasingly, however, employers recognize the potency of between-the-lines moments and therefore seek to co-opt them. When vertical relations of trust infiltrate humanity bubbles—the insulated spaces of intimacy that emerge in these liminal social spaces—not only do drinking, venting, and joking lose their revolutionary potential, but the dangers and risks inherent in them become more fraught.

BETWEEN OBLIGATION AND RELAXATION

"Honestly, it reminded me more of my old fraternity than a company that I work for," said Lionel, reflecting on his first year at Disruption. Describing company happy hours that began in the late afternoon and stretched into the early morning, he credited the gatherings for producing a "very strong sense of in-group belonging." Harold, another consultant, echoed this sentiment, detailing the role of happy hours in the formation of his key work relationships. "Nylah and I were part of the group of people who would stay really late," he recounted, "so we sort of got to know each other over that. Same with Lionel." He paused, shrugged, then added that he didn't have much else going on at the time. "It's like, I can hang around, [and] I like to drink."

Betwixt and between dominant institutions, collegial drinking sessions take place in what sociologist Ray Oldenburg calls a societal "third space" that exists "beyond the realms of home and work."[11] The relaxation of standard roles, duties, and agendas in such spaces, combined with the liberating symbolism of alcohol, creates a setting ripe for social experimentation and reinvention.[12]

Indeed, some workers leveraged the flexibility of drinking sessions to push back on normative workplace expectations regarding gender, race, and sexuality.[13] Recalling his previous workplaces as "sterile, corporate, buttoned-up," Reid described his existence then as "living in duality."

"I would play the part during the day and then, at night, take off the suit and rip off the tie," he said, highlighting the emotional labor of compartmentalizing his gay identity while navigating heteronormative professional spaces. Disruption happy hours, however, felt different. Reid explained how the laid-back, "anything goes" atmosphere allowed him to make previously hidden aspects of his identity visible among colleagues. Relishing the opportunity to express himself in more multidimensional ways, Reid characterized his frequent participation in collegial drinking sessions as a chance to "rebel against everything that was not me that I had dealt with in the past."

Reid was not wrong in perceiving subversive potential in drinking sessions. Notably, this between-the-lines time offered workers a chance to transcend instrumental scripts of professional sociality, extending their engagements into areas of personal and political interest. As Harold told me, "Whether it's languages or programming or politics, just sort of anything is on the table." In some cases, these conversations took on an explicitly radical tone, leading to workplace critique. In this vein, collegial drinking can be seen as continuing a tradition in which drinking venues have long served as arenas of democratic dialogue, countercultural expression, and political activism.[14] But at other times it simply gave rise to humanity bubbles in which people could express the full spectrum of their personalities and be valued beyond their productive output.

In a national context where exhaustion is often glorified as a status symbol, overt disengagement from performative displays of work devotion is itself provocative. As poet Tricia Hersey contends in reference to America's pervasive hustle culture, "We resist by crafting ease and invention. We resist by reclaiming autonomy and leisure."[15] Unfortunately, not everyone navigated these spaces with the same sense of ease.

Consider Hai, an Indian consultant who felt the sharp edges of cultural acceptance more acutely during informal company gatherings. Raised in the Midwest, Hai was well-versed in code-switching, adopting the Anglicized nickname "Henry" among white neighbors and friends in an attempt to avoid social friction.[16] However, when he relocated to the melting pot of New York, he saw an opportunity to openly embrace his identity: "You *can* still be Hai. You *can* still be American, and you *can* still go forward with that. People will accept that." He was therefore deeply disappointed during company happy hours when his colleagues responded to "Hai" with cool detachment. This standoffishness quickly drove him back to the safety of his alias, and his colleagues soon followed suit by enthusiastically greeting "Henry." Reflecting on the change, Henry observed that switching names helped him navigate the between-the-lines space with greater ease and led him to feel "a lot more free-er." At the same time, it extracted an emotional toll, requiring him to trade self-expression for professional survival.

Underpinning Hai's experience are the structural and cultural dynamics of gendered and racialized organizations. Companies like Disruption, DTC, and The Jones institutionalize social drinking to create "cool" workspaces, often in an attempt to compensate for poor pay and job insecurity.[17] For some, this is a worthwhile sacrifice. "I took a huge pay cut," Reid told me of his move to Disruption. "I just wanted to work with smart, young, hip people for a change. It's the first company in a long time where it doesn't feel like a job." But for others like Hai, the trade-off was more complicated.[18]

Professional cool has a distinct gender, race, and class, with *Mad Men*'s three-martini lunches and Anthony Bourdain's substance-fueled kitchens providing classic templates for their respective industries. While such paradigms often draw inspiration from the margins, they just as quickly revert to prevailing normative aesthetics that are both gendered and raced.[19] Nylah described the white, upper-middle-class "bro" vibe at tech start-ups like Disruption this way: "You're supposed to have craft beer. It can't be non-alcoholic because you're not part of the team, and it can't be hard liquor because you're not part of the group then. It can't be Budweiser because it *has* to be craft beer. There's this certain culture and expectation that goes along with that." While Hai had the gender and class "credentials" to participate in this environment, his ethnicity made him stand out in a way that inhibited a sense of ease.[20]

While Hai's story is unique, his sense of heightened vulnerability amid informal racialized contexts is not. These "white spaces," as sociologist Elijah Anderson describes them, require people of color to continuously ward off casual disrespect, something Hai understood intimately.[21] "When it comes to me being Indian, [the perception] is mostly negative," he said, highlighting several pejorative ethnic stereotypes he'd overheard while working in the tech industry (e.g., "*they* don't know what they're doing" and "*they* don't really understand how to engineer a problem").[22]

Indeed, employees across Disruption, DTC, and The Jones described drinking sessions as fertile ground for racism, sexism, and homophobia.[23] Just as Reid embraced the morality of the fallen to escape normativity and embrace his own authenticity in these moments, others simultaneously drew on their coded liberation to dabble in crude and distasteful remarks. Thus, for people of color, women, queer people, and other historically marginalized groups, the metaphorical trust fall that drinking sessions offered was heavily imbalanced, with the potential risks far outweighing the promised benefits.

Compounding the issue is how drinking, once institutionalized within workplace cultures and endorsed by upper management, morphs into something compulsory. Many workers I spoke with described how attendance at drinking sessions was essential to doing their jobs.[24] Not only did they offer an opportunity to gain crucial "face time" with leaders, but often important decisions and deals were made over cocktails. The bar, in other words, became an extension of the meeting room, and its obligatory nature was evident in senior leaders' view of nonattendees as ungrateful, apathetic, or simply unlikeable.[25]

Wade, a Disruption consultant, highlighted the perils of encroaching obligation to his colleagues who—invigorated by the team's night out in Koreatown—were calling for more frequent company happy hours. Bringing up his previous workplace as a cautionary tale, he described an environment in which drinking served as a prerequisite for workplace inclusion and mobility. As a light drinker, he felt unable to succeed at the company and left. "You're not only going to have problems with people like me," he warned CEO Shane. "What happens when you hire your first recovering alcoholic? What happens when you hire a Muslim, you know, someone who religiously doesn't drink?" The list goes on, from those wary of harassment to workers with pressing care responsibilities.[26] As Wade highlights, when drinking becomes intertwined with doing one's job, it's not an innocuous social gathering but a pernicious cultural tool for weeding out those who don't fit a particular mold.

As managers became more involved, there was also a palpable shift in how trust was tuned. Instead of nurturing authenticity and tolerance, reciprocity was prized, instilling a more transactional model of human connection. Managers framed drinking sessions as part of a social contract in which excess work was balanced by excess play, and sponsored indulgence should in turn be reciprocated with greater dedication to work. As manager Logan crowed, "I'll party to one in the morning, and then I'll come into work the next day." "I *always* show up," she emphasized, articulating the expectation for others. Celebratory tales like Logan's were often told alongside cautionary ones: the people who cut out of the party early or who missed work the next day. This "work hard, play hard" mantra transformed drinking sessions from a potential dissident salute to rest and leisure into a barometer of one's capacity to withstand and endure grind culture.

In the staged camaraderie of sponsored drinking sessions, trust was also strategically wielded by managers as a mechanism of control cloaked in the language of maturity: managers professed trust in their employees to "be adults" at these events. This manipulation of trust served two purposes. First, it shifted responsibility for any misconduct from the company onto individual workers. For example, Reid recalled a disastrous happy hour incident while employing strikingly singular terminology. "*He* drank too much," Reid said of the instigating employee, "and touched inappropriately and made comments to women and picked fights when *he* was rejected." Yet rather than the incident prompting a collective reflection on the company's culture and practices, the offending employee was simply let go. When drinking sessions were governed by a "trust" in participants to act like adults, issues that arose were easily chalked up to bad apples as opposed to a rotten culture.

Second, the governing mandate to be adults disclosed the fact that there was indeed an implicit script to which workers were expected to adhere in these more informal settings. Despite the invocation of trust, this script was enforced by subtle yet omnipresent peer and managerial surveillance. One worker shared a foreboding example conveyed to her by her manager, who said, "Don't ever cross the line too much because everyone does remember what you do, and, you know, it can come back to bite you in the future when it comes to like work-related things."[27] While the underlying script certainly rejected bigotry and sexual harassment, it also covertly demanded that workers maintain a veneer of positivity and gratitude while enjoying this so-called perk. Feeling the lingering weight of this mandate as the alcohol left their systems, workers sometimes lost sleep worrying over having said the wrong thing or seeming too negative in front of company leaders at drinking sessions. Self-censorship sparked by such concerns further undermined the possible revolutionary turn these between-the-lines moments could take.

Theorizing the potential of third spaces, Oldenburg described them as "the heart of a community's social vitality, the grassroots of democracy."[28] In rare cases, collegial drinking lived up to this potential, housing unrepressed self-expression and radical workplace dialogue. Unfortunately, much like straight patrons of gay bars trying to cultivate a cosmopolitan image, employers seeking to capitalize on "cool" through collective drinking rituals disrupt the sanctity of these spaces.[29] When made compulsory within structurally unequal industries and organizations, the risks of *not* participating increase for those who may wish or need to abstain, while the risks *of* participating remain high for those who are the most socially vulnerable. In short, as workplace drinking becomes an institutionalized form of team building, these social gatherings are converted into arenas of gatekeeping, where the stakes extend far beyond the next round of drinks.

BETWEEN LOYALTY AND EXIT

As a production manager at DTC, Sharon's life was tumultuous. She was charged with bringing creative campaigns to life, and the pressure to get it right was intense. Each new event setup entailed butting heads with vendors whose prices were too high, client services teams whose budgets were too low, and creative teams who wanted the expression of their ideas to be just so. Layered on top of these stressors were impossible timelines, understaffing, and sexist insinuations that a woman couldn't effectively do the job. When I asked Sharon whether she ever talked with her colleagues about these difficulties, she nodded enthusiastically. "As human beings, if you don't let a little bit spill out of your teapot," she shared, "how can you put more in?"

Employing metaphors like "spill" or "slip," workers like Sharon described venting as brief, almost involuntary interludes in their otherwise steadfast devotion to work. "[Sometimes, you] just need like ten minutes to spill all of your frustrations," Betty, a junior in client services, shared.

Framing venting as a buffer against more harmful, deep-seated resentment, she added, "[It's] important to be able to just word vomit a little bit." The choice of language is notable as it reflects the cultural tensions that can bubble up in the space between what economist Albert Hirschman famously called "loyalty" and "exit."[30] When workers vent—or express discontent and frustration with the job—they are choosing a third, sometimes thornier path: what Hirschman dubbed "voice."[31]

Historically, worker voice was bolstered through union participation, with disgruntled workers speaking in one collective chorus—a "strength in numbers" approach that helped offset the risks of challenging authority.[32] Today, workers navigate the choppy waters between staying and going largely on their own.[33] They must therefore carefully weigh the benefits and costs of venting against those of internalizing their frustrations or leaving the company.[34] By using vocabulary that frames their venting as accidental or uncontrollable in nature, workers can express unfiltered discontent without fully committing to it, testing the waters for mutual recognition.[35]

When such recognition was found, the trust that developed in these between-the-lines moments was tuned toward empathy and allyship. Venting became a forum for providing what Sara Ahmed refers to as a "feminist ear": "an invitation, an opening, a combining of forces."[36] It enables the expression of suppressed emotions, enhancing workers' acuity and collective resolve. "It's [about gaining] some mental clarity and clarification," Sharon explained, "like, 'Hey, am I going crazy, or are you witnessing this as well? Are we seeing the same thing here?'" The concerns about her sanity echo a common sentiment among workers, underscoring how normative workplace cultures—when misaligned with actual experiences—can act as a form of gaslighting, leading workers to question their own perceptions.[37]

Through venting, workers effectively counteract this subtle coercion, replacing feelings of isolation and alienation with a sense of solidarity. "I didn't realize anyone else was thinking [that]," graphic designer Kelvin recalled of the relief he felt upon hearing a coworker vent. "That made me feel comfortable to say the things that I was thinking," he admitted. DTC contract worker Trey similarly described how a colleague's sarcastic comment opened the door for a reaffirming hour-long conversation about problems they'd both encountered on the job. "What I was feeling, she was also feeling," he said. "[We shared] common ground of like, 'So, I'm not crazy to think that.' And they're like, 'Oh, now *I'm* not crazy to think that.'"

As workers became aware of the commonalities in their grievances, issues they once experienced as individual problems were recast as collective *workplace* problems, thereby creating the potential for collective resistance and change.[38] One mid-level manager, Josephine, articulated this galvanizing potential, telling me how through venting she'd discovered disparities in DTC's expense procedures. Armed with this information, she encouraged the informal coalition to approach management together. "The higher-ups wouldn't just think it was one person," Josephine claimed of a united approach. "They'd see the larger issue. Concerns wouldn't be able to be ignored."[39]

For their part, managers seemed both acutely aware of and threatened by the collective potential of venting. "Dwelling on things that are going wrong is a cancer," mid-level manager Jonathan proclaimed. "It will build. It will grow." Grady, head of the NYC office, was less dramatic but equally concerned. "There's some people who want that outlet of gossiping, bashing, and venting, which I don't think is wrong necessarily," he said. Telling me about an anonymous online chat forum on which junior employees were rumored to be airing grievances, he actively wondered, "What people are on it, and why [do] they choose to be part of it?" While Grady claimed no desire to "shut it down," he was keen to intervene in order to "change the conversation."

Grady was not alone in trying to infiltrate these between-the-lines conversations and redirect the discourse. Proclaiming emotions to be "data," human resources trained managers on how to elicit worker grievances through approachability and empathetic listening.[40] Regularly administered "climate" surveys also tapped workers for feedback. The goal was to convert worker voice into an asset rather than a liability, transforming employee grievances into tools for organizational improvement.[41]

Said differently, managers sought to make venting productive. Complaints about a lack of training? Suddenly, a new training program emerged. The culture is bad? A culture task force is formed. Although these managerial solutions rarely eradicated the underlying issue, by giving the appearance of caring, they often created emotional equity that could be traded within humanity bubbles' markets of reciprocity.[42] By "actively" listening to workers' concerns, managers signaled a commitment to employee well-being, which in turn nurtured feelings of gratitude and indebtedness among the staff.[43]

However, as venting was oriented "up" the hierarchy, entrusted problems were transmuted into opportunities for personal responsibility, with managers seeking to quickly pivot worker critique into action.[44] "People will come to me and vent, and I'm just like, 'Okay, well, how can we change things?'" mid-level client manager Felix explained. "What specifically needs to change in order to alleviate some of the stress. [. . .] What's a plan you can put in place?" Reflecting the disciplining nature of this discourse, junior brand strategist Lanie professed that before going to a manager, "I have to have a solution to my frustration, a suggestion on what should be done." In reality, Lanie had limited power (and few resources) to spearhead change efforts—especially for systemic issues like understaffing and underrepresentation—but nevertheless felt tasked with doing so whenever she raised concerns lest she be accused of indulging in "gossip."[45]

Lanie's fear of being seen as a gossiper speaks to how managerial discourse trivialized and devalued "unproductive" venting within a culture that esteemed displays of positivity, grit, and resilience.[46] "You need to be positive about things," Betty, who'd internalized the company's ethos, told me. "It makes people want you to be on their team because you're more productive." In this context, venting became a source of stigma. Felix, for instance, noted how "[venting] can kind of diminish your seniority," while others commented on how venting often led to derogatory labels like being "negative," a "complainer," or even "toxic." If a worker was identified as a troublemaker—or as having the wrong "mindset"—managers might be less willing to provide things like a promotion referral or future job reference. Venting in the wrong way to the wrong person could jeopardize workers' current *and* future job security.[47]

These dangers are even more pronounced for women and people of color, who are systemically susceptible to negative stereotyping.[48] Sharon's "let a little bit spill out of your teapot" metaphor thus did double duty, not only helping her stave off questions about her loyalty to the company but also limiting her exposure to this gendered vulnerability: "Because I am a female in production, I don't want to be the whiny chick that complains. So, I try to keep my venting to a minimum." In production work's overwhelmingly masculine culture, she feared her comments would be attributed to her gender and personality—*she* was too emotional or abrasive—rather than the problematic realities that prompted her to vent. Project manager Tiara shared similar concerns. "I don't want to have a bad day at work—or, let me make sure I'm always smiling so people don't think I'm the stereotypical spicy Latina who's got a bad attitude."

Indeed, marginalized workers were often more heavily policed by colleagues and managers during between-the-lines moments of venting. Upon hearing a male intern's sexist remark, Ruth, a mid-level client services professional, feigned shock, saying, "On International Women's Day?!" before lightly chastising the intern for not respecting women. In response, Ruth's peer, Ben, told her to be careful about what she said and where, while not saying anything to the man who made the remark in the first place.

This kind of oversight was particularly consequential when workers like Ruth were trying to point out subtle, hard-to-articulate issues like discrimination and sexual harassment. In another instance, human resources professional Lola recounted an inappropriate encounter in which a male leader placed his hand on her upper leg during a meeting. Days later he sent her an unsettling email, saying, "Anything to put a smile on your face." After sharing concerns about the interaction with a female manager, Lola received a perplexing response: "Oh, that's sweet!" Her feelings seemingly unintelligible to others, Lola spiraled into self-doubt and soon after moved to a position at another company.[49] Across DTC, The Jones, and Disruption, venting was often an attempt to bring marginalized perspectives into workplace humanity bubbles, but when the bubble was inadvertently (or deliberately) popped, the result could be alienating.

In addition to redirecting worker complaints and stigmatizing those who made them, managers' interventions in venting provided them with a useful means of deflecting their own accountability. This tactic was on clear display one day as I observed a conversation between Grady and another senior manager, Meraiah. Grady recounted an earlier meeting with mid-level manager Mona, who'd approached him about her overwhelming workload. While the conversation was productive, with Grady encouraging Mona to better prioritize her tasks and ask for help, the weight of these individual suggestions added to Mona's already high level of exhaustion, and she broke down in tears. Grady rolled his eyes at this, retrospectively calling the encounter "a meltdown." Rather than highlight the very real staffing concerns plaguing the company, he pathologized Mona's behavior. "[She] has a control issue. She can't let anything go," he claimed, adding, "It's a huge personality issue for her." Seeking validation, Grady turned to Meraiah and asked, "Are we doing something wrong here?" Faced with a choice of either calling out the leaking boat that was the company or throwing Mona overboard, Meraiah was quick to reaffirm Grady's characterization: "No, clearly the problem is her."

When managers closed ranks to protect one another against employee grievances, the concerns voiced by the less influential were lost in the webs of intimacy woven by the powerful, ultimately sustaining hostile and unsafe workplace cultures.[50] This was certainly the case when it came to the company's head of finance, Keith. The executive, who'd been at DTC for more than a decade, was known for having an explosive temper. His outbursts drew complaints, but little was done. Reflecting on management's inaction, mid-level account manager Manoj asked rhetorically, "What is this culture of middle-aged white dudes who are able to just ignore and just maintain the status quo because they don't want to do the right thing?" Talking to me about the issue, Meraiah provided some insight. "The running joke is that Keith must have naked pictures of Adam (the CEO)," she said, before she explained: "I think it's just they've been together a long time. Keith's protected Adam through some really hard times, and you don't want to get rid of your allies, right?"

Venting may be frequently described as a slip or a spill, but its visceral expression lays bare the everyday struggles of the modern workplace. When unfolding within what management scholar Katherine Kellogg calls "relational spaces"—social areas in which those with an interest in changing a system develop and nurture their ideas *apart* from defenders of the system—venting weaves a connective tissue among workers, fostering empowerment and solidarity.[51] As system defenders (usually managers) enter this between-the-lines space, however, venting gets folded back into neoliberal scripts, becoming a tool for policing employees and guarding against change. Thus, workers who spill their concerns are often the ones most likely to slip, finding themselves marginalized or penalized as their voices are distorted in a managerial discourse that prioritizes alignment over meaningful dialogue.

BETWEEN INCLUSION AND EXCLUSION

In my third week at The Jones, a guest handed me three $50 bills to pay their check. Lacking sufficient change in my apron, I went to ask the bartender, Matteo, if he could break the bills at his register. As I handed him the fifties, Matteo marked each with a counterfeit detector pen. Suddenly, he waved one of the bills in the air: "This one is fake." I was stunned. "What do I do?" I asked. He coolly advised me to inform the guest, causing me to break out in a nervous sweat. While I stood paralyzed, mulling over my next step, Matteo smiled. "Sorry, initiation," he shrugged, nodding to the other bartender. "Ken made me do it." I started laughing, realizing I'd been pranked.

That moment did more than add levity; it marked a subtle shift in my social standing. As comedian Trevor Noah explains, "If you laugh with somebody, then you know you share something."[52] Prior to this interaction, I'd watched workers and managers at The Jones make sarcastic quips, share funny stories, and regularly tease one another. Sitting on the sidelines of this banter, I'd felt like a server on the staff but not yet a member of the team. Matteo and Ken helped me bridge the gap. I was the butt of the joke—which reinforced my lowly position in the restaurant's social hierarchy—but they let me in on it as a signal of acceptance.[53]

Humor sits at the nexus of workplace inclusion and exclusion, offering people a way to overcome awkwardness, diffuse tension, and build rapport.[54] Shawn, a server at The Jones and an aspiring stand-up comedian, was a frequent interlocutor about this between-the-lines space. "I am like the only Black person," he told me of his experience at The Jones, before poking fun at the various racial categorizations he confronted in daily life. "I guess I should say *African-American* person of the *Negro* descent," he added, before provocatively saying, "But I am light-skinned, so I was probably raped by somebody white in the past." His eyes twinkled as he watched my reaction. "It's probably why I got the job at The Jones." When I failed to protest his joke, he smiled, saying, "If we can't laugh at our pain, then what's the point?"[55] Humor was both Shawn's spear and shield, helping him navigate the restaurant's racialized environment while also protecting his own vulnerability.

"I'm always performing," Shawn told me of his tokenized position, "for the guests, for the managers, for coworkers." He described what

W. E. B. Du Bois once referred to as a "double-consciousness," noting how his self-perceptions were continually filtered through the lens of others who might view him as different and even inferior. "I'm constantly analyzing. Did this person act like this because I am overweight? Is it because I am Black?"[56] He explained how humor helped him navigate this precarious position: "I'll use my charm. I'll use my wit. I play jokes with people and test people to see how they react," he said, adding, "Whoever sees through it and realizes it's just a joke, and it's just me being stupid, then I let them get close to me."

Aware that a comedian's power lies in the exploitation of ambiguity, Shawn's jokes leveraged his bifurcated social position to blur multiple social worlds and call out incongruencies between them—a tactic that often endowed his jokes with a subversive sharpness.[57] "I play the race joke a lot," Shawn told me. "I don't really mean it, but I *kind of* mean it." During a recent pre-shift meeting, for example, he jokingly raised a fist and declared, "Stay woke!" after pointing out that the menu item "monkey bread" might sound racially suspect. The joke called attention, with mock-seriousness, to how language can carry uneasy racial undertones.[58] "[Our] coworkers and managers try to walk around oblivious since they are all liberal and say, 'Oh racism doesn't exist anymore,'" he said. Shawn invoked the morality of the fallen to cut through to a hard truth: "I might pretend to be whitewashed, but I'm not whitewashed."

The success or failure of a joke, however, relies on a delicate negotiation among the jokester, their audience, the joke's subject, and the broader social context.[59] In cohesive groups, jokes aimed at "others" help define and strengthen boundaries, distinguishing those who belong from those who don't.[60] The Jones staff, for example, often parodied guests' mannerisms and food orders, building solidarity by casting consumers as outsiders and enacting the authority to judge them.[61] Within-group jokes like this typically went uncontested, with members endorsing the implicit elevation of their own status. Interestingly, so did within-group ribbings, such as when servers mocked one another's "table personas." Not taking offense demonstrated you were in on the joke and emotionally tough enough to withstand it—just as I had been expected to do during the counterfeit prank.[62]

But jokes typically become more fraught across lines of social difference. In her study of cross-gender joking in male-dominated workplaces, legal scholar Beth Quinn details how men's "chain-yanking" jokes—designed to get a rise out of their targets—ostracize and disempower women. The women targeted by these jokes face a cruel dilemma: laugh along and diminish themselves or protest and risk further marginalization as oversensitive "killjoys."[63] In these instances, most women opt to deflect. Participating in a trust-tuning that negates men's ill intent, they either proclaim "not to take it personally" (accepting women's denigration but exempting themselves) or chalk the joke up to "boys being boys" (upholding a gendered double standard). Such tactics offer provisional acceptance into the dominant collegial group but at the cost of implicitly reinforcing the existing gender hierarchy.[64]

I observed similar dynamics of cross-gender joking at The Jones, where women evaded rather than directly confronted male colleagues' crass comments and sexual innuendos. In fact, my reaction to Shawn's rape joke at least partially reflected this pattern, as I sought to remain unfazed in a moment that was sexually loaded. But the broader response to Shawn's racial jokes followed a different trajectory—shaped as much by his relationship to the audience as by the content itself.

While Shawn told me, "Black people get it; they laugh," his racialized jokes landed differently with his white colleagues. Al, a white bartender, singled Shawn out as a problem. "I feel [Shawn] sometimes goes over the line," Al said. "A lot of people joke around at work," he admitted, but "[Shawn] just makes people a little too uncomfortable." Similarly, a white server named Abigail said, "[Shawn] is a really good worker, [. . .] but on a personal level, I just don't quite understand him." "We've had some friction between us," she continued, "just because he makes a lot of racially charged jokes, which I don't necessarily know if they're jokes or not sometimes." Unsure of "how to respond," Abigail and other white colleagues were unwilling to absorb the discomfort of Shawn's jokes.

Unlike the dynamics around sexist jokes in male-dominant workplaces—where men punch "down," finding humor at women's expense and expecting them to deflect or endure it—Shawn's humor punched "up." He poked fun at his white coworkers' racial ignorance and privilege, making the Black experience the moral center of the joke. But because Shawn held a tokenized position on staff, his jokes didn't follow the usual patterns of between-the-lines trust-building. They surfaced racial tensions rather than smoothing them over. White colleagues refused to accept their own derogation as a basis for team bonding, and quite a few even reported him to management (a relatively rare response to sexist joking).

The protest over Shawn's humor underscores the asymmetric power relations that shape trust-building in between-the-lines moments. While sexist jokes exploit women's structural vulnerability, Shawn's jokes flipped the script. Rather than seeking safety within the dominant order, his humor exposed it. By refusing to flatter white sensibilities, he alienated himself further from the team, even as he sought to find bridges.

The role of power was even more salient when managers participated in interactional banter with the aim of adding levity to tense situations.[65] Those who did so successfully charmed workers. Liz, who detailed the horrors of Sunday brunch in the last chapter, described one playful manager, Matt, as "the most popular manager . . . the goofy one." Much like getting in the trenches, engaging in interactional banter reduced the hierarchical distance between managers and workers, making them appear more approachable and understanding.

Joking could also help "soften the blow" of exerting authority or calling out worker indiscretions. Server Fiona articulated how this worked between her and Paul, the general manager. Explaining how the two jokingly referred to one another as "Cap't" and "Mate," Fiona told me, "It's turned into this whole scenario where when I'm in trouble or when I do something wrong, he's like, 'You're in the boiler room right now. You're in the bottom tier of the ship.'" In these situations, Paul would do something like mime a shoveling action, sparking light-hearted laughter between them as they dealt with the situation at hand.

Banter went the other way, too, with workers using jokes to test the boundaries of acceptable behavior or to call out rules with which they disagreed.[66] Despite frequent physical contact between staff members, for instance, workers would often dramatically pull back their arms from touching one another and shout "HR, HR!" in the presence of managers, making a mockery of The Jones's formal policy banning physical interaction among employees. Affirming managerial reactions to such jokes helped guide restaurant behaviors, enabling workers to experiment in order to find a middle ground.

Joking with managers, however, could prove dangerous territory, as jokes were often policed "down" hierarchies but rarely "up." This dynamic was exemplified by a series of jokes targeting an Indian manager named

Ashley. After Shawn called Ashley a "spicy curry dish," David—Ashley's peer and a white man—reprimanded him. "You cannot say that to her," David told him, highlighting how Shawn had crossed a racial boundary. As Ashley put it later, "[Shawn] doesn't get the immigrant struggle."[67] "My parents worked really hard to come here to make sure I *wasn't* a spicy curry dish," she said.[68] As a woman and person of color, Ashley was also infuriated by how white men in positions of authority were never the target of such jokes. "[He] would have never spoken to Paul that way." David summarized these sentiments to Shawn, saying "[Ashley's] a South Indian woman, and she's a woman, and she's your boss. [. . .] apologize!"

While the managerial response to Shawn's joke was certainly warranted, its impact as a deterrent to inappropriate and hurtful racial commentary was complicated when DJ, a white manager, made a joke about Ashley's race the following week during one of the team's pre-shift meetings. Introducing a new beer called the "Brown Bird Ale," he laughed and said, "also known as Ashley."[69] The team responded with an awkward silence, and Ashley, who was coleading the meeting, quickly moved on to the next topic. While DJ's remark didn't carry the same overt racial and cultural connotations as Shawn's joke, it still objectified Ashley and potentially diminished her professional status. But because DJ was more senior than both the staff and Ashley, the reductive nature of his joke was simply ignored rather than directly confronted.

The unequal dynamic that emerges through managerial participation in banter has at least two significant implications. First, because most managers at The Jones were white men, they became the arbiters of sanctioned joking. In this context, humor like Shawn's that provokes their racial or gendered anxieties (e.g., white fragility, fragile masculinity) is more likely to be shut down, blocking a potentially useful mechanism for calling out social inequities or managerial contradictions. By contrast, jokes that don't offend a white male sensibility are less likely to be challenged, even when they are offensive to marginalized workers. As a result, those jokes often slip through the cracks.

For example, banter about how The Jones would "lose the whole kitchen" if Trump were elected became so routine it was treated like a running joke—despite the very real threats migrant workers faced. In this case, humor didn't ease tension; it dismissed it, offering those with privilege a way to laugh while others stayed silent. Eventually the joke became so pervasive that a group of immigrant workers approached management to explain how hurtful it was to hear their US-born colleagues make light of the intense fears they were experiencing daily.

Second, the envelope pushing that occurs within improvisational spaces of interactional banter could become dangerous if and when managers changed the rules of the game. "I don't know if I'm like friends or we're just, you know, whatever," one bartender said tentatively of his joking relationship with a manager, "'cause he can flip a switch and change." Liz was similarly unsure of whether manager Matt was usually joking or serious, and imagined confronting him: "If you're deadpanning, I have no way of knowing. You're my authority—you can't fuck around with me like that."

Such concerns were not hypothetical; I witnessed several coworkers get reprimanded as a result of misinterpreted humor. But rebuffing managerial joking also risked weakening the relationship, leading many workers to feel coerced into consent. For example, bartender Shannon told me she didn't trust DJ, but nevertheless engaged in banter with him. "I'll play along with his bullshit," she explained, "just to not cause controversy [and] get through the day." Ultimately, the ambiguity of this between-the-lines space served those with the most power.

"Done well," novelist and essayist Roxane Gay writes, "comedy can offer witty, biting observations about human frailties. It can force us to look in the mirror and get honest with ourselves, to laugh and move forward." Workplace humor holds this potential, helping people overcome relational barriers and prompting employers toward self-reflection and even change. Yet, as Gay warns, "done less well, [humor] leaves its targets feeling raw, exposed, and wounded."[70] And when humor intersects with power, it's often those with the least of it who are left out in the cold.

CONCLUSION

Between-the-lines moments open new possibilities for workplace relationships, creating humanity bubbles in which people can communicate and connect in ways that transcend their typical workplace roles and identities. At Disruption, DTC, and The Jones, these moments fostered opportunities for self-definition, worker solidarity, and even the development of an oppositional consciousness, but at the same time, the trust fall they require via the shedding of normative scripts and institutional structures exposes participants to the risk of emotional and even physical harm.

Unlike work crises, which emerge as almost exogenous shocks to the system, between-the-lines moments are seen as more willful opportunities, embraced at one's own discretion. Rather than being pushed into the trust fall, workers elect to participate. The calculation for marginalized individuals, however, is a tricky one. These individuals suffer daily from systems of oppression enacted through "standard operating procedures," making the potential of between-the-lines moments particularly enticing.[71] However, to the extent that normative ideas and hierarchies infiltrate these moments, the risk of confronting interpersonal indignities and disrespect is elevated when the safeguards of formal accountability structures are subverted.[72]

This chapter highlights the tension between consent and dissent within drinking, venting, and joking, and it also reveals how the flash intimacy fostered within—regardless of whether embraced by workers as a means of coping or resistance—becomes a resource for employers.[73] When employers co-opt between-the-lines moments, the activities within are converted into commodities in a market of reciprocity, with employers selling them back to workers as perks, "good" management, and a "fun" culture in return for their dedication and commitment to the job.

Moreover, when the trust nurtured within between-the-lines moments is reconfigured along hierarchical versus peer relationships, employers use it to explore the otherwise inaccessible critical undertow of their workforce—and do so with a clear agenda. As French sociologists Luc Boltanski and Eve Chiapello illuminate in their analysis of capitalism, successful systems require opposition and critique to "find the moral supports [they] lack and to incorporate mechanisms of justice whose relevance [they] would otherwise have no reason to acknowledge."[74] By identifying opposition within between-the-lines moments, employers find new justifications that either filter out or recruit workplace skeptics while assimilating the critique.

Thus, it may be more advantageous for workers to connect in settings beyond their employers' grasp—spaces that lie "outside the lines."

In chapter 7 we'll see how platform labor practices inadvertently isolated ride-hail drivers from management while simultaneously congregating them together in airport lots. In these settings, drivers connected with one another without employer interference or surveillance, and the resulting autonomy helped nurture critical dialogue and forge a broad and diverse coalition that was more immune to employer redirection. Consequently, they were able to mount a more meaningful challenge against labor practices that didn't benefit them. As the next chapter will demonstrate, maintaining interpersonal distance from management can also minimize the influence of charismatic personalities, reducing the risk of cults of personality that some managers create in the workplace.

4 Maverick Management

BUILDING TRUST TO SUPPORT CHARISMATIC LEADERSHIP

The announcement should have been handled more tactfully. Jonathan's managerial promotion coincided with DTC's implementation of austerity measures, including a delay in merit-based raises for the rank-and-file. But Donnie was brimming with pride in his mentee's accomplishment. Buoyed by a few drinks on a long flight back from Dubai, the senior leader impulsively sent out a company-wide email to share the news.

DTC's head of communications, Lark, accepted the bulk of the responsibility as she and I debriefed the ensuing firestorm. It was a mistake, she told me, to grant Donnie company-wide email privileges. But then again, how could she have guessed the highly accomplished executive would be so careless? He apologized after the fact, blaming it on jet lag, but Lark thought he failed to fully appreciate the trouble he'd caused.

In truth, Donnie prided himself on going against the grain, especially when it meant valuing people over process. He was not afraid to occasionally ruffle feathers and even enjoyed it. When he met people who "put on airs," Donnie couldn't help but poke at them, asking, "What's the matter with you? Why are you acting this way?" He explained, "I'm just used to people kind of being who they are," telling me about how he'd grown up in a farm town that smelled of cow manure half the time. Donnie believed in a kind of homegrown, real-world grit; being himself was not always diplomatic, and it entailed a certain acceptance of his shortcomings, but it was "authentic."

Workers were drawn to this unconventional approach. Lanie, the junior brand strategist who in the introduction cited Donnie as a mentor, described him as "a visionary." When I asked graphic designer Kelvin if he trusted senior leadership, he pointed to Donnie, saying, "He seems really good. I would definitely trust him. If he suddenly made huge changes, I would feel like he knows what he's doing." Donnie's following went well beyond his own team, with workers from multiple departments seeking a direct reporting line to him.

Donnie's influence was grounded not so much in his bureaucratic authority as in what sociologist Max Weber called "charismatic legitimacy." That is to say, Donnie commanded admiration and fostered deep loyalty from workers as a result of their belief in his exceptional *personal* qualities.[1] "Just being in that one meeting with him, I kind of feel more comfortable now," one DTCer explained after a one-on-one meeting with the executive. She described him as "a better fit for a boss for me" because of his "personality type" and hoped she'd be moved under his purview. People followed Donnie not merely out of obligation but because they trusted who he was deep down and believed in his approach.

This chapter examines how managers like Donnie develop trust and establish charismatic legitimacy through performances of what I dub *maverick management*. Through specific actions that foster a personal connection, these leaders present themselves as atypical in ways that separate them from the rationalization of normal work life.[2] Maverick managers' distinctive, person-centric aura elicits flash intimacy, compelling others to invest care and loyalty, often against their better judgment or self-interest.

I observed three facets of maverick management in action. As in the other chapters, I delve deeply into each by focusing on its expression at one particular site. However, all three were observed across the three sites, and they often intersected in their performance. Focusing first on DTC, I unpack maverick managers' *plain talk*, by which they distanced themselves from executive administration by adopting an unpretentious affect and blunt speaking style. At The Jones, I analyze maverick managers' *endearing incompetence*—an unapologetic embrace of their shortcomings and flaws that ironically positioned them above the minutia of everyday business life. Finally, I highlight how maverick managers at Disruption engaged in *discretionary rule-bending* to demonstrate their anti-bureaucratic leanings and personalized approach.

While maverick management effectively elevates some managers, its scope is limited by inherent biases. Historically, white (cis) men—from Henry Ford and Walt Disney to Steve Jobs and Jeff Bezos—have been elevated as the template for leadership.[3] At DTC, The Jones, and Disruption, the same demographic numerically dominated positions of power.[4] This combination often made them appear as a "natural" fit for the role. Consequently, when they enacted maverick management to set themselves apart from the status quo, their individual personalities came to the fore, effectively making them appear more personable.[5] This dynamic made it easier for cis white men enacting maverick management to establish humanity bubbles, cultivating relationships that transcended standard business interactions.

Unlike their white male counterparts, traditionally marginalized managers—such as white women and people of color—could not rely on their individuality as a basis for trust. They were already conspicuous, not because of *who* they were but because of *what* generic categories they were seen to represent.[6] For these managers, enacting maverick management (if they dared) required careful calibration. Cultural narratives about gender and race meant that distinguishing themselves on their own terms risked triggering harmful stereotypes.[7] At the same time, workers struggled to trust-tune with marginalized managers, as bias distorted how such managerial actions were read. Even the term *maverick*—derived from Samuel Maverick's unbranded cattle—carries the weight of a lingering racialized and gendered history, evoking a cowboy masculinity steeped in white supremacy.[8]

Beyond these disparities in the success of maverick management, the charismatic leadership it fosters breeds instability. Charismatic leaders must continually replenish their emotional connection with followers in order to maintain their legitimacy.[9] To do so, they often promote discord and chaos, peddling hard truths and adversity within the morality of the fallen.[10] This pattern not only enables them to performatively uphold their heroic image, but also simultaneously weakens systems of accountability that would otherwise provide a check on their power.[11] Consequently, followers become increasingly entrenched due to their affective connection to these leaders and the growing costs—emotional, social, and strategic—of investing in one figure over others, ultimately making them highly dependent on the charismatic leader's individual whims.

PLAIN TALK

Donning jeans, a plaid shirt, and a Patagonia vest he wore like a second skin, Adam sat on a lone stool in the open foyer of DTC's bustling office. A crowd of employees gathered round, eager to hear the details of their CEO's journey from Midwestern roots to NYC success. He broke the ice with a self-deprecating joke about his receding hairline before launching into a vivid description of an adolescence punctuated by soccer games and summers spent laying sod and manning the McDonald's drive-thru for extra cash. After recalling a major setback—losing both parents within mere months of one another while in college—Adam described finding an easy fit coming up through the ranks of corporate event marketing. Eventually, however, he grew restless. He bet everything—literally mortgaging his house—to stake a claim in his own venture, the company that had since become DTC. Surveying the hopeful faces before him, he ended with a key kernel of advice: trust your instincts and chart your own course. This was, after all, the unspoken mantra that had brought him from those humble, sod-laden beginnings to the front of that room.

Adam's talk was a masterclass in the kind of "plain talk" maverick managers at DTC, The Jones, and Disruption used to set themselves apart from the corporate mold. By sharing his story of hard work, unexpected challenges, and bold decision-making, he humanized his status and success, making himself more relatable to staff members across every level of the organization. Further, the narrative framed his sometimes brash, forthright communication style as a personal idiosyncrasy shaped by earnestness and deeply held convictions. Filtered through the morality of the fallen, Adam's unfiltered interaction style was not callous or malicious but courageous and admirable, the embodiment of what Brené Brown calls the "audacity of authenticity."[12]

This kind of plain talk resonated strongly with workers. "I thought [the presentation] was awesome," mid-level production manager Ethan told me afterward. "I'd heard variations of his story before," he noted before adding, "but it's nice that he'll put himself in front of everyone and open up like that." Junior account executive Marsha agreed. "I like that he tells his story," she said. "It makes me feel more comfortable when people are completely open." Revealing the root of her admiration, she confided, "I actually feel like a lot of things Adam's been through in life, [. . .] I just feel like we have a lot of things in common, so I just really like him as a person." Adam's talk helped recast workers' relationship with their CEO into the realm of the personal, fostering a humanity bubble in which they saw him not as a distant corporate figure but as a person with whom they had a special bond.

In the context of this intimacy, workers like Marsha were willing to interpret even distressing news and questionable managerial decision-making in a positive light. For example, she recalled when Adam informed the team about significant problems regarding the piece of business on which she worked. "He came in [and] was like, 'I wanna be transparent. I'm not gonna keep secrets. We're basically giving the client a million dollars back.'" In a striking display of trust-tuning, Marsha digested the news—which arguably put her job security into question—through a personal lens that focused on Adam's straightforwardness. "I didn't know. He just told us. I was like, 'That's pretty cool!'" she explained. "I'd much rather have that than hear it through the grapevine. [. . .] [I]t was cool that they were open about all that."

Other managers sought to emulate Adam's plain talk. Grady, the head of the NYC office, distinguished himself from more "guarded" and "rigid" executives, telling me, "I'm holding myself [accountable] to just be out there more and just let people know who I am more and, as Adam would say, be more vulnerable." Grady further highlighted a similarity with Adam in terms of directness. "I'm very candid and honest and straight with people. I don't try to talk around something. There's not a lot of flowery language around it or HR language about it," he shared, differentiating his style from feminine-coded bureaucratic forms of communication. "Just really direct and honest."[13] Finance director Keith adopted a similar stance, describing himself as "pretty straight." "I don't hide my emotions," he said. "You always know where I stand."

This purported transparency, however, entailed a notable sleight of hand. While maverick managers championed openness and honesty as virtues, they simultaneously benefited from the cover provided by their power and privilege. For instance, Adam enjoyed the privacy of a closed office, while the rank and file were subject to the blanket gaze of an open-plan layout. Exposure for leadership was therefore the exception, not the rule—a distinction adeptly obscured by their conspicuous broadcasting of selected disclosures.

The limits of leadership's transparency came into view when Lola, a human resource professional, requested access to a high-level strategic meeting. She was summarily denied by Casey, the head of sales, who explained, "I'm all for inclusion, but we just need to get this worked out on our own." Later, in another meeting, Casey advised mid-level managers on maintaining "transparency within reason." The phrase served as a telling reminder that in a context where omnipresent worker monitoring was taken for granted, managers maintained a tight grip on what information trickled down.[14] For the critical reader, such paradoxes of visibility eerily resemble Orwell's Big Brother, underscoring the power of doublespeak and the manipulation of transparency as a tool of control.[15]

White managerial men were particularly well-positioned to execute this subterfuge as their "unmarked" race and gender shielded them from the scrutiny that often befell tokenized colleagues, granting them unmatched interactional freedom.[16] Women and people of color, in contrast, felt uncomfortably conspicuous. "It's just not a very diverse office at all," Latina project manager Tiara told me, "I stick out because of that." Tiara's colleague Gabriela affirmed this sense of a racialized spotlight. She recalled her manager's strange reaction when she recommended Tiara for a position on their team: "Oh yeah, you guys are always speaking in this Latino language." Beyond her dismay at the obvious disrespect toward her native tongue, Gabriela was disappointed by her manager's narrow perception of Tiara through a racialized lens. Even more disconcerting, she felt like Tiara's ethnicity was viewed as a disqualifying trait, which left Gabriela insecure about how her own Latina identity—which she saw as an asset given their client's focus on Latinx consumers—was perceived by the team.

In the harsh glare of tokenization, managers from traditionally marginalized groups found it harder to embrace the plain talk of maverick management.[17] Indeed, several women brought this issue up in a managerial training that occurred shortly after I left the company. "They *wanted* to 'show up' as their authentic self," the facilitator Lola recalled the participants saying, "but they had a hard time doing that because it's such a male-dominated environment." In direct contrast to maverick management, the women said they found it necessary to "sound meaner than they really are" or "come up with this front" to protect themselves. In a similar vein, senior creative director Calvin described how enacting plain talk risked triggering racial stereotypes. "When I need to be frank and straightforward and brutally honest or demanding or any of those things," he said, "it's very easy to tip the scale from a passionate leader to an angry Black man." "It's like," he paused, then snapped his fingers in the air. "It's super delicate."

In this environment, marginalized workers with managerial ambitions had to learn distinct "feeling rules" to appease and appeal to colleagues with a more naturalized status in their workplaces.[18] I saw this play out one day while sitting in the office with human resources professional Edith and her junior colleague Odell. Edith was advising Odell to calm down in the wake of a confrontational interaction with a colleague. "You can't just go in guns blazing all the time," she explained. "You can't do that here and be successful." Citing a confrontation of her own earlier in the day in which a male colleague stood over her chair and yelled at her, Edith recalled her blood pressure rising and her ears turning red. But outwardly, she told Odell, she remained very calm. Echoing Calvin, she referenced the specter of the "angry Black man," telling Odell he'd have to learn to control his emotions if he wanted to get ahead at a company like DTC. "Unfortunately, you show your emotions on your face," she continued. "You can't let other people see you like that." Edith, herself a Black woman, offered to remind him to "fix his face" whenever she saw him showing too much emotion.

As noted by management scholars Ella Bell and Stella Nkomo, environments rife with double standards and discrimination compel marginalized workers to "armor up."[19] Doing so is an effective means of self-preservation in such contexts, but it requires a meticulous and circumspect approach to social interactions. Take, for example, the Obamas, who were at the center of the first Black presidential administration in the US. Talking to Stephen Colbert in 2018, Michelle Obama articulated the administration's hypervigilance, explaining, "We couldn't afford to make a mistake, we couldn't afford to look cavalier, we had to watch our language. [. . .] We had to speak carefully and intelligently and clearly, and we couldn't just say things off the cuff."[20] While warding off stereotypes and other threats to legitimacy, this strategy simultaneously betrays the down-home, authentic appeal of plain talk. That's not to say marginalized managers never enacted plain talk; rather, this dynamic simply complicated the process, making it harder for them to build the kind of personalized trust that supports charismatic leadership.

Yet even among white managerial men who successfully performed maverick management, charismatic legitimacy could be elusive. Needing to continually recharge their connection with staff, some leveraged truth telling for its shock value.[21] Managers like Grady and Adam appeared to relish the opportunity to share "bad news," such as lost business or market downturns, in ostentatious displays of transparency. Explaining his underlying logic, Grady told me, "If people just share good news all the time, it's a horrible idea. It becomes—it could almost create a trust issue, like 'What is he not telling me?'" Workers' responses offer validation of this strategy. Following a meeting in which Adam warned the team about financial turbulence at the company, junior event coordinator Carly echoed Marsha's earlier reaction to similar news, saying, "Even though it wasn't the nicest information [. . .] it made me feel safe because [. . .] if there are problems, he will let us know."

While maverick managers championed their candid delivery of hard truths as a testament to their candor, this strategy could sometimes take a toxic turn. This was the case with Jonathan, who prided himself on his direct and open communication style. "Whether I'm communicating something bad or something good," he told me, "the fact that communication occurred, and I'm being honest in that communication [. . .] that is going drive trust." As an example, he recounted a contentious interaction with his colleague Katie during a recent project debrief. In disagreement with Katie's version of events, he cut her off mid-sentence: "Stop talking. You're lying." "It needed to be said," he said self-righteously before justifying any discomfort Katie may have felt as a result. "I'm less concerned about the forum and embarrassing her. She *should* be embarrassed because she's lying. At this agency, we have a very hard time with accountability." In cases like this, maverick managers wielded the "truth"—itself always partial—as a formidable tool of dominance, strategically centering their own perspectives while casting dissenting voices as untrustworthy.[22]

Plain talk, for all its appeal, often operates on uneven terrain. Leveraging the ease of their social privilege, white managerial men use plain talk to build and sustain humanity bubbles that bolster their managerial legitimacy. Through the intersecting dynamics of the morality of the fallen and trust-tuning, plain talk helps maverick managers extend the boundaries of normal communication, sometimes enabling them to cross into the realm of carelessness and disrespect in the name of truth. Meanwhile, women and people of color who attempt plain talk do so at the risk of distinguishing themselves in unintended ways that ultimately undermine their legitimacy. Thus, what serves as a parachute for successful maverick managers—upholding their credibility via the exhilaration of freedom—can become a straitjacket for marginalized managers who need to convey enough personality to express their humanity while taking care to not upset normative (white, masculine) sensibilities.[23]

ENDEARING INCOMPETENCE

In my first few weeks at The Jones, colleagues advised me to avoid seeking help from Paul, our general manager, when things got busy. Paul would offer assistance, they explained, but he lacked urgency and follow-through. Gary, who helped train me, explained, "Paul means well, but oftentimes he's not really that helpful." "Like, he doesn't know how to enter orders in," Gary laughed. "Often, I'm like, 'What are you doing here? How did you get this [job]?'" When I asked server Abigail if she trusted Paul, she joked about his inability to complete the quotidian managerial task of voiding mistakenly added items from a customer's check: "I trust that Paul won't do three of the voids that I give him." Another server, Jenna, admitted that she didn't trust Paul to "do things like mess with the side work [. . .] take an order at a table [. . .] have a conversation [about] things that need to change [. . .] get things done."

Nevertheless, these liabilities did not detract from Paul being valued by the staff. Much like Michael Scott from *The Office*, Paul cut an ineffectual but lovable figure. Jenna gushed, "Paul I trust on a *human* level." In a culture infused by the morality of the fallen, his mistakes were an asset. They not only signaled his authenticity but also showcased a humility that seemed to lessen power differentials, helping him connect with workers on a personal level.[24] "Paul is remarkable," busser Pete told me, emphasizing how he felt personally recognized by the manager. "Paul sees every person as a person." Server Danielle even described how Paul would be her top priority if there were ever a shooting at The Jones. "I'd be, 'Paul, hide!' You know what I mean?" she laughed. "I would make sure Paul was safe. [. . .] I would worry about what happened to Paul."

As an archetype of "endearing incompetence," Paul's fumbling manner set him apart from the typical manager and helped lay the groundwork for personalized relationship building. Yet he wasn't alone in using fallibility as a means of connection.[25] "Every time I've had a conversation with upper management," Jenna told me, "you believe them. Because they're human too, and they admit their mistakes." She spoke particularly fondly of Evan, the head of operations: "Every time I've ever brought an issue to him, he's so genuine and honest. [. . .] He's like, 'I didn't do that well.' He always admits to, 'I did that badly.'" Evan's willingness to openly acknowledge his imperfections made him seem more honest and trustworthy to Jenna, opening the door to a humanity bubble where intimate connections could thrive unimpeded by business operations.

The contours of endearing incompetence come into sharp relief when looking at DJ, another manager at The Jones who took a markedly different approach. DJ reveled in the inner workings of the restaurant, knew the ingredients of every menu item by heart, and had a flair for charming disgruntled guests. While he was often incredibly helpful on the floor, most staff members resented him, interpreting his attention to detail as petty and his by-the-books approach as a grab for power. "When he's training someone," server Nelly explained, "he'll just like tell you to do things because he can." "I feel like DJ betrays my trust," server Cecilia told me, highlighting his obsession with how things *should* operate versus the often messier reality: "It's like, 'Why is your ego more important than the truth?'" While some like server Jasmine defended DJ—suggesting others disliked him simply "because he does his job"—the consensus was more critical. "He just feels skeezy," server Kate observed. "He tries to *act* positive [but] it's a put on. It's just a face. It doesn't feel genuine."

As a white man, DJ exposed the steep interpersonal costs of eschewing endearing incompetence and consequently maverick management. But for women and people of color, the stakes of embracing or rejecting this approach were doubly complex. On the one hand, overt displays of expertise could lead to accusations of being like DJ: an egocentric know-it-all devoid of the human touch. Yet in a workplace defined by gendered and racialized inequities, the perception of marginalized managers' competence was perpetually under attack.[26] Ashley, a South Asian manager with extensive bartending experience—so much so that she'd been featured in magazines for her skill—spoke to the doubt that constantly surrounded her performance. "I probably know 20,000 times more about beer than the average guy," she remarked before noting how, in others' eyes, she'd never "know enough about beer—because I'm *not* a guy."

Indeed, the gendered dynamics of endearing incompetence were particularly pronounced in the context of bar management—not because of Ashley, who strategically avoided what she saw as a no-win situation, but rather through the experiences of Donele, another woman manager who often found herself the target of bartenders' ire. Bartender Ryan, for example, was highly critical of Donele's staffing decisions. "This is someone who has never bartended in her life, never comes behind the bar, just doesn't understand the rhythms of a bar," he claimed, disregarding the fact that Donele, like all managers, had undergone extensive bar training and was one of the longest-tenured managers at The Jones. Al, another bartender, echoed this sentiment, adding, "She doesn't understand how we do our job. She doesn't understand the flow of the bar." Given their perception of her as unqualified, any attempt by Donele to embrace incompetence was likely to solidify rather than challenge their negative views.

The bartenders' perception of Donele stood in sharp contrast to their view of David, a white man who'd also never tended bar and had only become a manager earlier that year. David took his lack of knowledge in stride, owning it with a sense of honesty and good humor. "Everyone looks at me, 'Oh, how do you make a drink,'" he laughed. "I'm like, '*Girl*, I don't know!'" Articulating the utility of endearing incompetence as a managerial strategy, he described using such moments to build relationships, inviting workers to look up the recipe and make the drink with him—a tactic that sounded good in theory but that I imagined would be highly annoying in the middle of a rush. When I asked David if he was comfortable with "driving blind" like that, he again spoke of his ignorance in utilitarian terms: "I'm fine with that because I've figured out a way to kind of handicap myself in a sense." "I'm not a bartender," he said, lifting his hands in a gesture of candidness as if to lay bare his lack of expertise without pretense. "If you asked me if I was a bartender, I'd straight up say 'No. Like, hand to God.'" For David, embracing his shortcomings didn't present a threat to his legitimacy; rather, it demonstrated his sincerity and helped him build stronger, more relatable connections with the team.

His ability to do so was shaped, in part, by workers' trust-tuning. Matteo, another bartender who'd been critical of Donele, acknowledged that David also occasionally kept too many bartenders on shift—a decision that meant the tip pool would be divided among more people. But Matteo chalked up such decisions to David's lower managerial rank: "I try to look at it also from the other side," he said. "I feel that sometimes the managers' hands are tied with certain things—from what comes down to them from above." In this framing, the issue was not intent or knowledge but an externally situated constraint on power. Similarly, Ryan conceded that David wasn't the best "in terms of being an actual manager where he is back there understanding everything, all the needs that we have and how to be there and how to help [bartenders] during a shift." Still, Ryan identified other bases of trust on which to ground his relationship with David, emphasizing (for example) how he was not a micromanager. Through trust-tuning, both bartenders found ways to minimize David's shortcomings while their distrust of Donele persisted.

Endearing incompetence is more than a passive trait; it's a deliberate performance that serves the maverick manager well. Crucially, it allows them to sidestep accountability. This shielding effect was laid bare in the aftermath of a confrontation between the general manager Paul and Amanda, a veteran employee at The Jones with an impeccable service record. Amanda was an aspiring actress with a vibrant and positive demeanor, and she was well-regarded by both her peers and management. So it was striking one day to witness her sobbing openly during our opening side work duties and throughout the shift meeting—an unusual display of distress from someone who was normally so cheerful.

When I later spoke to Amanda, she recounted the incident. A disgruntled customer had sent a scathing letter to corporate, criticizing her service. But it wasn't the letter that upset her—it was the management team's reaction. Led by Paul, they called her into the office and berated her. "This was the most traumatic thing that's ever happened to me at The Jones," Amanda recalled. "Paul was yelling at me." "That hurt my feelings a lot," she shared, explaining that her anguish was not driven by the customer's complaint, which she fully disregarded as a ploy for a freebie. Rather, it was the feeling that her years of experience and discretionary efforts in training new employees and managing the restaurant's annual charity drive seemed to mean nothing at that moment.

But only weeks later Amanda and Paul were as close as ever. When I asked Amanda about it, she wrote off Paul's behavior. "[He] just can't handle confrontation, and he can't listen. I love him, but he can't listen . . . so, he explodes with this rhetoric that's this preconceived script." Paul himself had told me as much, admitting, "I'm not a confrontational person. I don't like it. I run away from it." Attributing his behavior to incompetence, Amanda forgave him. "I wasn't mad at him for saying the things he did in the moment because I knew that those are the things he says in situations, regardless of what's true, what's false, what's right, what's wrong," she explained. "So, I sort of, I was prepared for him to be emotionally unavailable. . . . I expect that from him because I know him well." Paul's perceived ineptitude became a protective shield, insulating him from the fallout of his actions.

While incompetence suggests a sense of naivety, Canadian sociologist Linsey McGoey argues that ignorance is often a strategic tool, willfully deployed to protect or advance one's interests.[27] Kate, another veteran server who'd been with The Jones for five years, insinuated this when talking about Paul. "When he is on the floor," she said. "I just feel like he is a little fumbly or doesn't really know how to be hands-on or do something quickly." Initially giving him the benefit of the doubt, she mused, "Maybe he's in his own general manager world," but then offered a more pointed observation: "But it's just a little like 'I'll just let you—the quick floor managers—help me out.'" Kate laughed to soften the accusation, which at its heart suggested that Paul played up his incompetence as a form of Tom Sawyering, tricking others into doing his work for him.[28] This "strategy of incompetence" mirrors tactics scholars have also observed among heterosexual married men seeking to avoid housework—an intentional helplessness designed to shift the burden onto others.[29]

In another case of playing dumb, Paul fumbled through the introduction of an arbitration agreement we were being told to sign, holding up his ignorance of the legal system as a shield against meaningful questions.[30] Conveying what the owner of The Jones had told him, Paul framed the agreement as pragmatic: "They have a lot of money, and most of us would never be able to match them in court if we filed a lawsuit." In doing so, Paul shifted responsibility for the document's implications away from himself and onto those above him. More importantly, he helped to reinforce a collective ignorance about the negative implications arbitration agreements can have for workers, such as smaller rewards, limited appeals, and protecting the company's confidentiality.[31] As a result, the endearing incompetence on which Paul forged interpersonal trust with workers ultimately upheld the status quo at their expense.

As a managerial strategy, endearing incompetence disarms workers by reducing power differentials and elevating the common thread of human fallibility. Yet this strategy isn't equally accessible to all managers; women and people of color, in particular, must tread carefully, toeing the line between demonstrating a humility that makes them more approachable and reinforcing deep-seated biases they already face. Beneath the surface, what appears as harmless vulnerability may well be a calculated maneuver. Like the pool hustler who downplays their skill to gain an edge, maverick managers who adopt this tactic are sometimes seeking to deceive others for personal gain, whether that be shirking work or offloading responsibility to sustain their own charismatic legitimacy. Thus, endearing incompetence is far from unconventional; rather, it's one of the oldest tricks in the book—an age-old con that leaves those who fall for it holding the short end of the stick.

DISCRETIONARY RULE-BENDING

In an early blog post outlining his vision for Disruption's culture, Shane wrote, "Some rules are necessary for any organization to function, but too many rules can create drag that slows down the team and stifles innovation." He idolized figures like Jack Kerouac and Andy Warhol, admiring their iconoclastic approach. To think big, he surmised, one had to view existing frameworks not as guideposts but as obstacles to be overcome. His goal was to build a workplace environment that liberated human creativity from the confines of bureaucracy. "Innovation comes from not being constrained," he told me, "from *not* following rules."

Like other maverick managers at DTC and The Jones, Shane took an ad hoc approach to formal policy and procedure, engaging in what I call "discretionary rule-bending."[32] As he'd written in that early blog post, he tolerated rules, but he favored value- and trust-based approaches that enabled flexibility within and across them. "I trust people's intentions, and they trust mine," he explained, "and we deal with it when the realities don't meet up with the expectations." Indeed, I observed this philosophy at play during "all-hands" meetings, in which Shane actively adjusted operating procedures on topics like remote work and vacation policies as issues arose.

In this way, Disruption embodied what sociologist Alvin Gouldner famously called a "mock bureaucracy," in which "indulgent" managers like Shane acknowledged rules but enforced them selectively.[33] This decoupling of informal practice from formal procedure contributed to the development of humanity bubbles, in which workers enjoyed a sense of autonomy and rule exceptions made them feel as though their personal needs were a priority. As consultant Norman told me, the focus on trust meant that workers were given the benefit of the doubt, and managers were "willing to ignore some flaws" as long as the ends justified the means.[34] In this way, maverick managers' use of discretionary rule-bending served to differentiate them from the stultifying and sometimes dehumanizing character of rising workplace rationality, creating space for meaningful connections to flourish.[35]

Shane's skepticism of rules also fostered an in-group mentality at Disruption that further strengthened team relationships. Through the embrace of discretionary rule-bending, the team distinguished themselves as smarter and more daring than outsiders. Consultant Nylah, for example, told me she rejected job candidates who were "too academic." Their steadfast devotion to standard programming processes, she believed, led them to miss the opportunities found through more pragmatic problem-solving. Similarly, consultant Destiny derided one of Disruption's clients as being "married to the process," describing the client team as "more interested in just like being factory worker(s) than actually getting better." Through such contrasts, the team forged a collective identity that served to build group cohesion and reinforce trust.

Yet rule-bending did not occur on a level playing field, and there were unspoken norms about who could break what rules and when.[36] For example, Nylah recalled how a white male colleague admitted to her that he'd padded his résumé, adding a false layer of managerial experience. She was impressed he was "able to pull that off" but felt that if she "tried to make the same leap, it wouldn't work." As a transgender woman in the tech field, Nylah already stood out and thought it would be harder for her to sneak through the cracks of typical workplace surveillance in the same way as her colleague.

The close link between rule-bending and one's location in existing social hierarchies crystallized one morning as I sat in a café with consultant Jay. We laughed about how often drug use surfaced in office interactions. The employee referral program, for instance, was cheekily named "reefer madness," and after meeting with a cannabis industry representative, Shane brought back THC edibles for the team—even though such products were legally restricted to medical use.[37] Jay appreciated what he saw as leadership's laid-back, progressive stance, noting how "Shane and Reid and Logan are very conscious, woke people."

Despite this permissive atmosphere, Jay never told them he'd been arrested in college for selling weed—a moment he described as "earth-shattering." "It makes up a huge part of who I am," he said, explaining how the arrest, which led to his expulsion from college, eventually pushed him to enroll in a coding boot camp. "It's this big part of my life that really defines how I got into tech." The information was publicly accessible through a simple Google search, but he deliberately chose not to disclose it to his colleagues.

As a Black man well-versed in the racialized history of the drug war, Jay recognized the stark cultural inequities between his colleagues' casual drug provocations and his lived experience.[38] "It's like, damn fit the stereotype, Jay," he said, berating himself. "There's not a day that goes by that

I don't recognize I am a man of color," he reflected. "I love it. [My identity] is not anything I'm ashamed of or upset about, but it definitely affects my experience, daily." Working as a Black man in tech meant constantly "proving I can contribute and add value at the same level anyone else can."[39] In this context, sharing his drug-related arrest felt fraught, even in a supposedly progressive workspace. "I do realize that people, once they have that knowledge, they might look at you kind of differently," he sighed. "People will judge you and draw conclusions and be prejudiced against you."[40] Unlike his white male colleagues, Jay couldn't rely on trust-tuning to modulate his rule-bending toward originality without risking distortion.

In addition to disparities in the act of rule-bending itself, there were also inequities regarding who picked up the loose ends that were left when standard operating procedures were bent or overlooked. As the only woman on Disruption's leadership team, Logan often felt obligated to step in to help consultants who felt lost amid the lack of clear direction from Shane. Recognizing her dependability in this way, consultant Wade told me, "I now realize that my way into the operations team—like who I should be communicating with—isn't Shane or Reid. It's actually Logan. She has a much faster way of responding and is on top of the stuff better." Speaking to this essential yet undervalued labor, Logan groaned, "My whole life is, like, Mom," enclosing that term in telltale finger quotes. To be sure, Logan's efforts helped her build strong relations of trust with the consultants, but it did little in the way of bolstering her career as a marketing professional.[41]

While traditionally marginalized workers were burdened by the biased judgments and surplus work that often came with rule-bending, there was little that constrained white men with authority. Indeed, those who successfully performed maverick management through rule-bending actively struggled to determine where to draw the line.

Wade, a white guy being groomed for management, wrestled with the ethical boundaries of his unorthodox approach to leading organizational change for his clients. Having been emotionally abused as a child, Wade admitted to using "the same techniques to create change in companies," highlighting how he employed lies and bullying tactics to achieve his objectives. He described, for example, how he'd brashly called out a member of the client team as "fucking stupid" during a recent meeting and explained how the interaction cast doubt on the team's taken-for-granted assumptions, creating space for new ideas.[42] But he admitted, "I don't know if this is capital-G good or right to do to people." "I'm not comfortable with the idea," he continued, "and I've been living with it for years." Despite his unease, Wade justified his methods as effective, highlighting concerns about the seeming lack of limits to rule-bending for white men in power.

The question took on greater relevance when Shane sent the team a copy of a presentation drafted by his mentor (a white man). The presentation adopted the ethos of the morality of the fallen, unapologetically casting the world in raw and sordid terms. Industry success, the slides argued, required capitalizing on societal taboos, using technology to help people engage in "forbidden behaviors" while obscuring the consequences of doing so. Companies like Google, Facebook, and Reddit served as exemplars, each tapping into primal human desires such as gluttony, self-aggrandizement, or unfettered malice. It concluded by attempting to reassure readers that "you don't have to be evil" in following this advice. Technologists can "satisfy your users' deepest desires without making your users into monsters"—the key was simply in "building limits and safeguards."

Yet in mock bureaucracies where everyday life operates autonomously from formal policy, necessary "limits" are often not discovered until it's too late.[43] Sociologist Diane Vaughan brilliantly demonstrated this dynamic, detailing how a culture of normalized rule-breaking at NASA contributed to the *Challenger* space shuttle disaster, with millions of viewers watching the devastating consequences in real time.[44] At Disruption, the blurred lines of discretionary rule-bending were apparent as the team discussed new business opportunities. Despite Shane's repeated assertion of a "do no harm" policy when making decisions about which clients the company would serve, the policy proved remarkably fluid.

Despite ethical concerns about two potential clients, the team—led by Shane—ultimately chose to accept both. The first company was a drone operator that assisted construction project managers in simulating demolitions to save money and improve safety, but a member of the team raised questions about potential military applications of the technology. Shane and Logan dismissed these concerns, noting that the scope of the work Disruption would be doing for the company was quite limited. Later, the team discussed a company building a digital breastmilk market. Consultant Lionel voiced demographic concerns, noting that the company's leadership team was composed entirely of men and that most of the breastmilk sellers were projected to be low-income women, while the recipients were generally expected to be wealthier. Shane acknowledged these concerns but ultimately reframed them in a positive light, arguing the platform would provide a meaningful way for low-income women to make money and applauding the men's interest in a traditionally feminized industry.

The scene brings to mind a passage from Hernan Diaz's Pulitzer Prize–winning novel *Trust*, in which a powerful financier explains to his biographer: "My job is about being right. Always. If I'm ever wrong, I must make use of all my means and resources to bend and align reality according to my mistake so that it ceases to be a mistake."[45] Maverick managers like Shane—and those on the rise like Wade—may not present their actions in such explicit or deliberate terms. Yet at the end of the day, they aren't just bending rules as an expression of the human condition—they are bending reality to their will, leaving everyone else to navigate a precarious trust fall that requires them to rely on the fickle whims of those with the most power.

CONCLUSION

Donnie, the DTC manager who sent the controversial email, compared trust to an amusement park ride. "If you're going to ride a roller coaster, you're scared the whole time it's about to happen," he said, "*until* it's happening. Now, I'm not operating on fear anymore. I'm operating on exhilaration. I *trust* that all the fears that I had are allayed. It's like that." Bringing the conversation back to the workplace, he explained that people wanted a sense of security about their overall career trajectories, but claimed "day to day, I'd rather be *uneasy*." When things were too safe, he explained, life was too familiar and predictable. "If it gets to that point where everything's like that," he continued, "[then] why am I here? What good am I? I offer no agitation, you know? And in some respects, that's what living's about."

When successfully executed, maverick management provoked trust by disrupting established systems. By exploiting professional taboos, managers infused the workplace with a sense of spontaneity and ambiguity, offering a counterbalance to the banality of bureaucratic processes and establishing the sweet spot for trust as articulated by Donnie. Drawn to maverick managers' self-proclaimed outsider status, workers often interpreted their behaviors through a morality of the fallen, heralding crudeness as authenticity, buffoonery as humility, and deviance as courage. Thus, the foundation for charismatic leadership—built on personal attributes as opposed to hierarchical status—is laid.

The great irony, of course, is that the tension and chaos maverick managers evoke are not aberrations to the system but inherent within it. As sociologist Randy Hodson and colleagues have pointed out, organizations rarely operate as idealized, smooth-running bureaucracies; instead, they are characterized by Kafkaesque characteristics such as contradiction, confusion, and absurdity.[46] Moreover, those who perform maverick management most successfully—white men in positions of power—are not outside of the system but atop it. They are false foes of the establishment whose embrace of plain talk, ignorance, and insubordination *is* the system at work, and their charismatic leadership is based on a fabricated duality that frames them as the exemplar of what it means to be "human" in the workplace. However, white managerial men's personification of "humanness" in their own self-image undermines the true diversity of the workforce, and workers' trust in them serves to perpetuate entrenched patrimonialism as opposed to disrupting the status quo.[47]

Chapter 7 reveals a potentially different reading of maverick managers. Distanced from management via their independent contractor status, restricted communications, and automated decision-making, NYC ride-hail drivers were less willing to give such managers the benefit of the doubt. Indeed, their antics were seen as indications that they were out of touch and exposed their tyrannical tendencies. Instead of rallying around the illusion of tearing down systems, drivers rallied around ideas and people interested in building up more effective frameworks. This stood in stark contrast to Disruption, DTC, and The Jones, where workers' willingness to accept false dichotomies not only glorified the underbelly of the human condition, but also hid the more sinister aspects of business. We'll delve into the implications of the former in the next chapter and the latter in chapter 6.

5 Heavy Ties

TRUST IN UNEQUAL CONTEXTS

I sank into the couch, satisfied after finishing The Jones's new hire paperwork earlier that day. My brief moment of peace was interrupted by a text from an unknown number—someone asking if I could cover their shift the next morning. The restaurant's weekly schedule must have dropped. Sure enough, my email was also flooded with messages:

> "Hey guys, I REALLY need Wednesday night off! I'll release it if anyone can pick it up, or I can swap for any Monday AM shift! Even BROC! I'll swap for any annoying OC shift you have this week!"
>
> "Hey friends, my mom is coming to the city, and Wednesday night will be her last night here. I don't know what happened since I requested it off a long time ago. Please take it off my hands."
>
> "[I]t turns out I have strep, too, which has complicated the flu virus still in me. [. . .] I can't work tonight's REGPM shift or tomorrow morning's AMCL shift. If you can help out in any way (particularly those who are on call. I'm so sorry) to pick up either shift, it'd be a tremendous help."
>
> "Hey guys! I'd love to work your Monday PM or (preferably) trade my PM OC on Tuesday for any other PM shift."

Brow furrowed, I tried to make sense of my new colleagues' cryptic shorthand. I guessed OC meant an on-call shift, but terms like REGPM (regular dinner shift), AMCL (a lunch closing shift), and BROC (a lunch shift with the possibility of also being called in for breakfast) would take weeks to become second nature. It would take even longer to decode the complex social choreography—the informal rules and unwritten contracts—of swapping shifts.

Although I was initially clueless as to their meaning, the sense of urgency in the messages was evident from the outset. Sociologists often talk about "strong" and "weak" ties—how closely we're connected to each other based on factors like proximity, duration, emotional intensity, intimacy, and/or reciprocity.[1] But the relationships in these messages didn't fit neatly into that framework.[2] Instead, they carried a unique weight that led me to view them as *heavy ties:* interpersonal connections that demand social investment and carry meaningful consequences.[3] Some were rooted in friendship or mentorship, others in convenience. But all involved significant risks and rewards shaped by power dynamics and social context, affecting not only workers' current job experiences but also their future employability.[4]

This chapter explores how The Jones, Disruption, and DTC relied on the cultivation and maintenance of heavy ties. For example, at The Jones, the "bartering" of shifts helped workers gain control over an erratic schedule, but it did so on the backs of peer support. At Disruption, workers engaged in "bridging" to navigate precarious networks and create relational footholds in an uncertain landscape, but they constantly worried about how even small missteps might be amplified or weaponized against them. And at DTC, seasoned employees—many from marginalized backgrounds—shouldered the burden of "buffering" their colleagues from dangers that were deeply interwoven yet rarely acknowledged within ostensibly supportive workplace cultures. As in previous chapters, these distinct patterns surfaced across all three sites, but I home in on one dynamic per site to offer deeper insight into each.[5]

Considered holistically, heavy ties form the connective tissue of humanity bubbles, crafting delicate spaces of intimacy where people find meaningful attention and support. These relationships are a vital lifeline for workers, helping them manage unpredictable schedules, stay afloat amid job insecurity, and endure challenging, even hostile work environments. But heavy ties are equally beneficial for employers, often acting as conduits for trust-tuning, by which workers conflate the reparational work of key individuals with the intentions of the broader company. Heavy ties are thus the faces of care that make indifferent work environments appear warm and inviting.

Yet as sociologist Alejandro Portes reminds us, "sociability cuts both ways," with opportunity and obligation tightly intertwined.[6] If heavy ties are the interlaced arms catching individuals in the trust fall, those arms become battered and bruised over time. They require continual attention, which can be depleting, especially for those with greater vulnerability and less power.[7] Nevertheless, opting out is ill-advised, as doing so risks exclusion and stigmatization.[8]

Heavy ties also sit within a broader hierarchy of trustworthiness, one that casts workers as inherently suspect. Employers, ever wary of worker malfeasance, protect themselves with institutional safeguards: on-call scheduling, surveillance systems, and legal contracts.[9] Workers, in contrast, have little more than the fleeting promises of flash intimacy, cobbled together through the often undervalued labor that sustains heavy ties. But under enough strain, these ties begin to buckle and groan. When they do, employers fall back on their institutional supports, while workers are left adrift in a cultural current governed by the morality of the fallen. With dysfunction reframed as authenticity and resilience celebrated as a virtue, workers' instincts toward individual self-reliance are activated, preventing the ripple effects of betrayal from spreading through the system as trust once did.[10] The upshot is that heavy ties uphold workplace systems that fail to value or protect workers, offering them a paltry return on their emotional and social investment—while employers reap the benefits.

BARTERING

"I can almost always pick up or give up a shift if I need to," server Jenna explained, "even if it comes down to bartering with individuals." Another server, Shay, echoed Jenna's view, noting that instead of making a formal schedule request, "It's easy—well, not always—but sometimes easier to swap shifts." Both acknowledged that schedule favors among coworkers weren't always returned, which could create drag within workplace relationships. With a knowing look, Shay said, "I'm kind of learning who I can trust to do that, to help each other out."

The Jones's weekly schedule was posted via a mobile app every Thursday or Friday, detailing the following Monday through Sunday workweek. Requests for time off were required two weeks in advance—two months in advance during the busy November to January holiday season—along with a written explanation for the request. Even then, not all requests were granted, and permanent accommodations (like having every Thursday night off) were strongly discouraged in favor of maintaining "open availability."[11]

Despite these constraints, workers found ways to manage their schedules alongside other significant responsibilities. Some juggled two or three hourly jobs to make ends meet, while others tried to balance restaurant work with artistic or academic aspirations.[12] The majority sought to maintain an average of at least thirty-five hours a week—the threshold required to qualify for health benefits—while not crossing into overtime (over forty hours), a situation management actively discouraged. As a result, The Jones's digital communications—app messages, emails, texts—resembled the Grand Bazaar, where the trading of shifts among colleagues extended beyond simple swaps to include favors and even gifts, from baked goods to cash—all in a bid to secure a workable schedule.

Bartering transformed what could have been a volatile and even dehumanizing schedule into a negotiable asset and a means through which workers sought to reclaim autonomy.[13] Server Nelly, for example, highlighted the appeal of working at The Jones: "I can choose to work morning shifts or night shifts, and [. . .] it's not very difficult to get a shift covered for you if you really try." Similarly, busser Pete cited "a schedule I can play with" as a key perk of the job. This flexibility, made possible through coworker cooperation, sustained a humanity bubble in which individual needs for flexibility were seen and addressed. For some, such as server Michelle, malleable work arrangements outweighed other job benefits. "That's why I like working in a restaurant. [. . .] I'd rather make half [the income] and have my own schedule and have my own life."[14]

But as communications scholar Sarah Sharma argues, individuals do not control their experiences of time in isolation. Instead, their time is always intertwined with the demands of others and shaped by institutional structures.[15] At The Jones, the rhythms of NYC diners dictated the weekly schedule, with managers using projected customer traffic levels to determine staffing needs for each shift.[16] Shift end times were also tied to consumer demand: while start times were strictly enforced (and tardiness the most frequent cause of termination), end times remained unpredictable.[17] Workers might be sent home after just a couple of hours if business was slow or be required to stay ten or more hours if it was busy. The on-call system added another layer to this "web of time," requiring several employees per shift to stand by, unpaid, for hours—an insurance policy against absenteeism guaranteed at workers' expense.[18] Bartering may have given workers a sense of agency, but much like turns in improv, this performance was highly influenced by the stage and available props, fellow performers, and the given audience.

Moreover, the agency workers exerted was offset by the weight of responsibility. "Every week I have to fix my schedule," senior server Tracey sighed after reviewing her upcoming hours. Her remark was met with a chorus of "Me too!" With the formal schedule rarely meeting their needs, workers were left to beg, bargain, and borrow—a dynamic that not only was time-consuming but also trapped them in cycles of dependence. Each favor or shift swap placed them in debt to others, leading to the need for more bartering down the road.

Moreover, the bartering market was a site of moral policing, placing each engagement under high levels of scrutiny. "If someone ever switches a shift with me," server Jasmine told me in a display of her own honorability, "I'm like, 'Hey, I have a raincheck for you. Whenever you need something picked up, and I'm not working, I'm there.'" Reflecting a common complaint about coworkers' freeloading, she added, "I don't think that a lot of people do that."[19] Indeed, workers who repeatedly failed to reciprocate exchanges or who took more than they received from the bartering network experienced reputational damage. "[She] is consistently trying to either call out or get rid of shifts," server Lynn groaned about our colleague Annie. "It doesn't make me trust that [she was] truly genuine or really needed that shift covered if [she's] doing it all the time." Annie was eventually blacklisted on the bartering market, leading to her being fired when she couldn't rearrange her schedule and subsequently showed up late to several shifts.

Given the burdens associated with bartering, some workers—like bartender Drake—tried to opt-out entirely. Drake refused to share his phone number with other bartenders and almost never requested shift changes or accommodated others' requests. By stepping away from the bartering system, Drake removed himself from the social fabric that held the team together, leading not only to his own isolation but also to stigmatization. Bartender Shannon spoke for many when she shared, "We're all pretty good about coverage for the most part, except for Drake. [. . .] He's not a team player at all." She added, "I would say pretty confidently that nobody behind the bar has a good relationship with him. [. . .] It's not him as a person, but it's him as a coworker." Drake was affable, and he was good at his job, but his failure to participate in bartering made him a bad colleague.

These peer-to-peer tensions often overshadowed managerial responsibility for the schedule—a dynamic that became especially pronounced when someone couldn't get a shift filled and was forced to call out. "I think [the system] causes the staff more grief than me," manager DJ shrugged, "'cause it's not me getting called in." His detachment reflected how the emotional burden was shifted downward onto workers. Manager Donele agreed: "As soon as you have someone that calls out for a reason that is clearly not legitimate, it instantly causes friction between the staff—way before it will cause any issues with management." In the end, Donele said there was little concern at the manager level about absences, "'cause in reality, we're gonna always be able to cover."

Because management's primary concern was ensuring coverage, which the system practically guaranteed, they cared little about the extra burdens any given callout placed on workers. Colleagues, however, were firmly trapped within the system and, as a result, set somewhat unreasonable expectations for their peers. During one lunch shift, for example, my coworkers Mike and Shawn began deriding two servers who were emailing the group asking for coverage for their night shifts because they were sick. "I mean, your nose is running," Mike said. "I don't think that is worth calling out. We all feel under the weather sometimes." Shawn agreed: "Those two are always sick. I mean, you gonna call out because you have the sniffles?" Tellingly, both Mike and Shawn were on call that evening, meaning if the sick workers called in, they'd be forced into a double, which could entail twelve-plus hours of nonstop work. Facing that potential outcome, almost no reason for calling out seemed valid to them.

These sentiments fed into a morality of the fallen, in which enduring hardship, including working through illness, became a badge of honor. Cecilia, a veteran server, boasted, "Back in the day, you had to be, like, *dying* to call out." "I only called out twice in four years," she added, "and once was because I was in the hospital because I *was* dying. And I was texting them pictures of the IV in my arm." Consequently, my coworkers frequently stumbled through shifts with hacking coughs and fevers. Gary, a server who religiously avoided the practice of calling out, told me, "I just feel like if I call out, I'm letting the team down. It's one more headache for them, and that's not what I wanna be." When people did call out, there was pressure to quickly atone for missing their shift by not only apologizing to those affected but working to pay back the debt through favorable shift swaps or other tokens and gestures. "It is this sense of, 'Oh, I owe these people something,'" Jenna explained.

Despite managerial detachment, the schedule was in fact a nexus of managerial power and control. Managers not only issued the schedule, but they monitored and oversaw all bartering, with the right to approve or reject any initiated swaps. Speaking to the surveilling lens scheduling provided, DJ professed: "I see it all, like, I see *everything*." He listed out all the variables they regularly monitored—schedule requests, switched shifts, tardies, missed shifts—commenting, "It's literally in front of me on the screen in a graph." Yet while DJ and other managers emphasized the operational challenges of scheduling—limiting overtime costs and maintaining a certain skill level among the staff on shift—they largely stayed above the fray when it came to the real-life consequences scheduling decisions had on workers.

Their ability to do so reflected and reinforced the hierarchy of trustworthiness that underpinned the restaurant's temporal infrastructure. By this logic, workers were unreliable and fickle, and thus their schedule requests held little value. As one cook, Malik, put it, "You work in a restaurant, you get whatever shifts [they] give you." Admittedly, managers did take human limits into account, rarely scheduling workers for marathon work hours, such as a double (lunch and dinner shift on the same day) or a clopen (a closing night shift followed by opening the next morning). Yet they had no problem allowing workers to switch into such schedules on their own—often the collateral damage of workers' logistical gymnastics in coordinating their schedules. Thus when in the middle of these marathon stretches, workers rarely blamed managers, instead pointing the finger at themselves or a peer who'd somehow let them down on the bartering market.

In this context, when managers did make schedule accommodations for workers, it was seen as a gesture of generosity—a gift instead of something the worker had a right to ask for. Senior executive Deanna explained the value of such gestures: "If we make an agreement as to what your schedule is and honor that—that's a great carrier of trust." Far from a pain point in their relationships with workers, schedules became a resource managers used for building trust and intimacy. Labor scholar Alex Wood explains that such schedule gifts "bind [workers] to the manager through an emotional debt and sense of moral obligation" because workers' lack of power and control ensures that such gifts can never be fully reciprocated.[20] Despite a structural inability to repay their "debts," workers nevertheless often took on extra tasks—everything from drafting menu descriptions to planning events—in an attempt to acknowledge schedule gifts and stay in managers' good graces. Exemplifying the kind of loyalty schedule gifts could forge, manager and chef Kevin boasted how his staff "would die" for him: "Not because they're scared because I'm the boss, but because every time they ask me to do something for them, I will always do it."

Yet managerial generosity had clear limits. When I asked Kevin if he was usually able to accommodate workers' schedule preferences, he laughed, noting that some workers needed a "reality check." Most workers were satisfied if he simply entertained their request. They "just appreciate the conversation. Even if I don't end up doing it, they just know that I tried." That distinction turned out to be key. Just trying was enough to maintain trust in management, illustrating how trust-tuning works in unequal contexts, with the less powerful willing to bend and reshape the meanings and bases of trust to keep the relationship intact. For example, despite often lending a helping hand to management, server Jenna's schedule still required significant bartering each week—a frustration she frequently brought to management, but which rarely led to substantive changes. Regardless, Jenna was grateful: "I do always feel like it's a conversation," she said, revealing the low bar managers had to pass to keep her trust. "It's not a 'just deal with it' kind of thing."

Bartering is not, in and of itself, problematic; indeed, there are many examples across cultural and historical contexts that demonstrate how the practice can nourish and sustain community life.[21] At The Jones, however, this dynamic was distorted by a parasitic element: employers feeding off peer reciprocities, extracting shift coverage with little concern for workers' well-being. Rather than supporting the collective, bartering in this context primarily served the needs of capital accumulation, ensuring that operations would continue uninterrupted. Though workers depended on one another, their exchanges lacked mutual care, warped by the demands of survival and the pressures of managerial indifference. Navigating an inflexible system through bartering thus became a transactional, emotionally taxing process—the ties forged burdened by anxiety, guilt, and resentment, hindering worker solidarity while leaving management comfortably detached.

BRIDGING

"Tech in general is this huge bubble," Disruption consultant Nylah explained. "I feel like this is especially obvious when you go to a place like Google," she continued, recalling her own interview experience there, where they'd asked, "Do you know anyone at Google that could help your case?" The idea that *who* you know matters as much as—if not more than—*what* you know in the labor market is so commonly expressed it risks becoming trite. Yet its constant repetition doesn't make it any less true. In fact, the importance of social networks is deeply embedded within the labor market, visible in employers' reliance on referrals, reference requirements in job applications, and even the prominence of ratings on digital labor platforms.[22]

In this context, the labor of *bridging*—cultivating and sustaining connections beyond one's immediate social network—is essential for accessing new opportunities and advancing mobility.[23] The right bridge, forged at the right moment, can provide not just job leads but also the personal endorsements that separate someone from the pack.[24] However, bridging isn't only about construction; it's about maintenance.[25] As the adage "don't burn your bridges" warns, a spoiled connection isn't just a missed opportunity but also a liability. In a networked economy, the gravity of pathways created or blocked bears down on each relationship and interaction, making the bridged ties heavy.[26]

Much of the popular conversation about bridging tends to center around extracurricular contexts like after-hours events, conferences, clubs, and social media. Yet anthropologist Ilana Gershon argues that connections made on the job are the primary carriers of our labor market reputations.[27] In this environment, bridging efforts are not just about making connections but about carefully managing perceptions. Interactions with managers, coworkers, and even customers can profoundly impact one's career trajectory, where even minor mistakes can carry outsized consequences. Because negative impressions tend to stick longer than positive ones, maintaining these ties can feel like a perpetual high-stakes audition, with the true impact of a misstep often becoming clearest in hindsight.[28]

Mack, a newer consultant at Disruption, described the delicate balance required for successful bridging. "This is the first time I've been employed full-time as a programmer for a consultancy," the twenty-nine-year-old said, explaining that his previous experience came from freelancing and working for friends. He occasionally struggled with impostor syndrome, worrying he might not meet the team's expectations. "It certainly lends you a sense of legitimacy to be connected to a consultancy," he shared, but noted, "there's a sense of responsibility that the work you're doing isn't just representing yourself; it's representing this company."

He was therefore relieved when a senior-level client executive praised his work, but that relief soon became fraught when the executive followed up with a job offer. Mack had heard cautionary tales about consultants who'd left the company to work for clients. CEO Shane, for example, described one consultant's ultimate departure as a personal betrayal. After a serious motorcycle accident had left him unable to work for three months, Disruption had continued to pay the consultant's salary and benefits—an act of care that aligned with the team's constructed humanity bubble. He eventually returned to work and delivered an outstanding performance on a major client project. But once the project ended and the consultant found himself between assignments, he accepted a job offer from the former client. "It was an insult," Shane fumed, exposing the emotional yoke placed on the relationship. "It was, in my opinion, unethical." The perceived betrayal remained an open wound, transforming what could have been a valuable professional resource for the consultant into a potential obstacle.

With stories like this weighing on his mind, Mack said the offer put him in a tight spot. "On one hand, it's very flattering," he admitted, but noted how that personal recognition existed in tension with his duty to the company. "[The client] doesn't think of me as what I'm supposed to be, which is a consultant." His role was to bolster Disruption's reputation and expand their sales opportunities, not his own worth. To Mack, the offer felt like a signal he might have inadvertently prioritized his own interests over those of the company. But would accepting the offer really be a betrayal of the trust the team had shown by hiring him with such limited experience? "I just had to kind of dodge that question a little bit," Mack confessed.

Mack understood that alienating Shane or the client could trigger a butterfly effect, with consequences rippling through his network for years. In this way, heavy ties outlast individual work assignments or jobs, binding workers to relationships that have the potential to shape future opportunities. The client's offer wasn't just a kind or flattering gesture; it was also fraught with risk. Accepting it could trigger ill will in his relationships with Shane and the Disruption team, but rejecting it might lead the client to pull away from Mack and perhaps even jeopardize the team's engagement with the company.

Such dilemmas reflect the emotional labor involved in navigating power imbalances, where those with less power are forced to carry a disproportionate burden of bridging relationships.[29] While Mack agonized over the implications of the offer, the client likely did not, underscoring how even casual or well-meaning gestures can feel like tests or traps amid asymmetrical power dynamics. In these contexts, bridging demands more than tact; it requires constant negotiation, balancing personal ambition, political considerations, and interpersonal decorum. In this way, bridging imitated a game of Jenga, with workers maneuvering among precarious relationships to build themselves up but with the constant (and seemingly inevitable) risk of tumbling down.

This state of flux was particularly challenging for tokenized workers, as their historical exclusion from robust networks made bridging essential, while their conspicuousness within homogenous environments exposed them to increased scrutiny, making every move potentially incriminating.[30] For example, Nylah, who identified as transgender, came face to face with the high-stakes consequences of on-the-job bridging when she angered Logan, one of her managers. In an attempt to expand her professional experience, Nylah volunteered to take on extra work to assist Logan on a design project. However, the initiative backfired when Nylah's other work responsibilities and a miscommunication on the timeline led her to miss Logan's expected deadline.

Logan's negative reaction, which included a series of angry emails over the weekend, took Nylah by surprise. However, when I spoke with Logan, I realized she saw Nylah's missed deadline not merely as an operational oversight but as a personal affront to the time and emotional energy she'd invested in their relationship. "She's somebody that I took shopping, got her a makeover, got her hair [done]," Logan recounted. "I've taken her out to dinner when I was *nine* months pregnant, and I was hot as fuck and tired, because *she* needed some support." When Nylah failed to meet the deadline, Logan felt disrespected and betrayed.

What's notable was Logan's decision *not* to engage in trust-tuning and reinterpret or rationalize the offense, as was often the response when confronting managerial disappointment. Logan could have framed Nylah's offense as the result of being overextended due to her inexperience or lack of support within a cis-masculine industry. Instead, she reverted back to a normative, one-size-fits-all perspective that cast Nylah as personally problematic, saying, "I think I've let my sensitivity to—being perfectly frank—to some of her needs as a diverse employee cloud a little bit of what I normally would do."[31] Rather than leveling the dynamics between her and Nylah, Logan chose to reassert her relative power and status.

While the women eventually debriefed and resolved the situation, Nylah's experiences afterward reveal how the moral weight of heavy ties extends beyond the immediate situation. Months after the incident, I noticed Logan dismissing Nylah's requests to participate in decision-making, commenting, "I think she wants to be a leader, and she's not one." The reputational stain also bled into others' perceptions, which were already shaped by a cisgendered environment that devalued both trans and feminine statuses.[32] Nylah relayed the dynamics of a recent meeting with

Shane, Logan, and Reid, at which they used pejorative terms like "petty" and "dramatic" to describe her professional orientation.[33] These labels, which emerged after she lost Logan's endorsement, forced Nylah into a double bind. To counteract the feminized stereotypes undermining her leadership competence, Nylah would need to enact normative masculinity, yet doing so threatened to undermine her identity as a trans woman.[34] These tensions made Nylah wary about her future at Disruption: "I'll be valued, but then someone else will zoom past me and get the cool projects because in their head, they're like, 'Oh, Nylah's a little bit weird.'"

What was telling was that Nylah felt responsible for repairing the strained relationships in order to preserve her career prospects. Essentially dropped in the trust fall, she didn't wallow in the hurt but used it as a source of motivation, embracing the ethos of the morality of the fallen. Over the subsequent weeks, she sought to increase her "face time" with Shane, initiating a series of one-on-one meetings, taking on a high-visibility operations project, and contributing regularly on the team's internal communications platform (Slack).[35] She also experimented with different, "more professional" office attire.[36] By attempting to solidify her workplace relationships and reputation, Nylah hoped to increase her chances of being assigned important projects and securing her managers' endorsements when she went up for new opportunities at the company or needed future job referrals.

While Logan had firm footing in the heavy tie with Nylah, she had to tread more carefully in her other ties, which required more delicate bridging. For example, she approached her relationship with the company's former CEO—who'd been fired—much more tentatively. "That one's a much more strategic relationship," Logan said, speaking to the influence the former executive, Palmer, could still have over her career, "because he was my direct boss for a while. I need him to be able to appropriately refer me at one point. He knows a lot of people I know." Just as Nylah's misstep created a moral breach in Logan's eyes, Logan understood that failing to maintain her connection with Palmer might compromise her future prospects: "I just never know, particularly with the state of this company," she sighed. "It's good to have your business relationships strong."

Nevertheless, maintaining a relationship with Palmer while still working at Disruption was tricky and required careful diplomatic maneuvering.

"[Palmer] thinks this place is stupid," Logan said. She trod carefully when talking with him, seeking to display an appropriate sense of empathy while not betraying her continued alliance with the Disruption team. "I haven't been like, 'Yeah, it's ridiculous,' by any means, but I'm just more like, 'They're changing it up, and it is totally not the right place for you.'" Logan's relationship with Palmer required not just interpersonal skill but considerable emotional labor in the form of trust-tuning to maintain the sense of security it provided.

At the same time, her relationship with Palmer threatened Logan's ties with the other Disruption leaders, whose support Logan viewed as a critical resource for success within the company—not to mention if she ever left.[37] Shane and Reid could interpret Logan's continued contact with Palmer as self-serving and a violation of workplace humanity bubbles that would brand her as disloyal.[38] To preempt any misunderstandings, Logan divulged the continuing connection, saying, "I'm trying to have a good relationship with [Palmer] so I can play the good cop." But Shane interpreted her remark as a criticism: "I don't think I've been the bad cop. No one here has." Logan therefore had to carefully backpedal and explain that despite the lack of wrongdoing on the team's part, Palmer held a grudge about being fired. "It's just that he doesn't think of me as a decision-maker," Logan finally concluded, "so he doesn't see me as one of the responsible ones."

Pitching her bridging efforts with Palmer as beneficial for the team and noting that Disruption still owed Palmer back pay, Logan framed her communications with him as a valuable shield. She could keep the team abreast of Palmer's state of mind and potentially identify and deflect legal liabilities as they emerged. "He texted me to ask how things were going," Logan recounted. "I was trying to be transparent and honest, but also not say the company was great because then he'd want his money faster, and we don't have it." It was a move I'd observe Logan make again when she told her colleagues about meeting with two other terminated executives, Hallie and Leah. "I think there might be business opportunities there," Logan proposed, explaining how the women seemed open to referring Disruption's services to their new employers. "Wow, I had no idea," Shane responded. "I would have never even thought there was a slight possibility for a bridge there." Aligning her personal bridging with the company's goals, Logan responded, "Well, I think the bridge is me."

However, her alignment strategy—which itself was a form of bridging—made it hard for Logan to fully maximize the personal benefits embedded in heavy ties. For instance, after Shane and Reid agreed that Logan's relationship with Palmer was advantageous for everyone, Logan tentatively shared a more contentious piece of the conversation. She divulged that "[Palmer] asked if I was looking to do freelance work." The offer was enticing for Logan, who was her family's breadwinner and had recently taken a pay cut to help Disruption stay afloat. In choosing to bring it up with Shane and Reid, she was not only protecting herself in case someone else told them, but was also testing the water, trying to determine whether such an arrangement might be deemed acceptable.

The room quickly grew silent, and looking uncomfortable, Logan decided to cut bait. "I am telling you this not because I considered it, but because can he even ask me that? Was that in his contract?" Smoothing over the interaction and repositioning her relationship with Palmer solely as a resource for the team, she emphasized her desire "to be transparent." Having done the extra leg work of providing her colleagues a basis for trust-tuning on her behalf, the tension dissipated. Shane said they'd released Palmer from his contractual obligations, making the request technically legal, although still underhanded in his view. Shane said he'd email Palmer with an update on the timeline for financial repayment, and the team quickly pivoted to the next item on the agenda.

The labor of bridging—of empathizing, coordinating, translating, and facilitating—already places a disproportionate burden on workers, who must maintain these connections while employers freely harvest them for institutional gain. The introduction of anti-poaching and noncompete policies during my time at Disruption demonstrates how bridging is becoming even more lopsided, with employers insulating themselves from risk while workers remain vulnerable to the vicissitudes of others.[39] Although workers might be tempted to act on the words of poet Kate Rushin, who gives voice to the unspoken weight of bridging—"I've had enough; I'm [. . .] [s]ick of being the damn bridge for everybody"—they also know that they depend on bridges for professional survival.[40] These connections are fraught with peril, where a single misstep can trigger cascading damage to one's reputation and opportunities, leaving individuals adrift while employers remain safely anchored by their institutional protections. In short, bridges offer tempting passages, but when these connections falter, they threaten to drown individuals in the undertow of broken expectations and lost opportunities.

BUFFERING

When DTC production manager Sharon arrived on-site to lead an annual promotions tour, her gut told her something was wrong. "I didn't think it was safe," she said. Each event demanded the promotions team essentially build a two-story house from the ground up. But promotions teams typically focused on brand representation and attendee engagement at events, not construction. "This was too much to be putting on this team," Sharon explained, clarifying her concern was not about the team's ability to perform, but the dangerous overreach of their role. Determined to change what she saw as an exploitative and risky status quo, Sharon vowed to remove the builds from the team's workload, telling them, "Whatever I have to do, I'll go to the mat, make sure this happens." Initially, workers were skeptical, and upper managerial support was shaky. But Sharon pressed on, eventually securing funds for a professional construction crew and negotiating a complete overhaul of the tour's structure. The team "started to see, 'Alright, wait a minute, maybe this chick has our back.'" By the following year, morale was steadily on the rise, and retention rates later followed suit.

Sharon's intervention exemplifies the labor of "buffering," through which more tenured workers—most often middle managers who identify as women and/or people of color—absorb workplace risks that employers should have dealt with. These seasoned workers fill the gaps left by institutional failures, acting as intermediaries, protectors, and advocates for more vulnerable employees.[41] They help make workplace cultures feel more welcoming to those with less power and status, even as the institutions that house those cultures are not. In short, buffering supports the creation and maintenance of humanity bubbles.

The relationship between Lanie and her supervisor, Constance, offers an illustrative example. Prior to joining Constance's team, Lanie worked in the client services department. "[They] never protected me," she said, recounting how her previous colleagues kowtowed to a client who frequently and publicly berated her. "[They] just brushed [the verbal attacks] off because it's a client." In contrast, Constance put Lanie in positions of high visibility, working to strengthen and empower Lanie, and carefully coached her through those situations. "We will always talk," Constance explained, "when we come back from a meeting. Things that went right. Things that went wrong."

Constance's role as a buffer extended beyond coaching; it also involved shielding Lanie from harm. When a senior leader harshly criticized Lanie's work, Constance not only defended her output but later debriefed the situation with Lanie. "She made me realize why he might have said that," Lanie said, noting how Constance reframed the leader's actions through the lens of workplace inequities and politics. "Like, where I am, my position, my gender. And the stars kind of aligned as to why he would say that," Lanie observed, explaining that "it was more of a power play on me."

Later, when she received a random email from a senior man that read, "I don't know if it's your tan or your shirt, but you look so pretty today," Lanie again went to her supervisor. Constance talked her through the situation, assuring Lanie it wasn't her fault, and sought to ensure Lanie was never in a position to be alone with the man. Unfortunately, neither woman trusted the formal system to handle the situation; I myself had heard that a male employee *bit* a woman the year before, but nothing was done after it was reported.[42] "I understand my position within the company. I understand that person's position," Lanie sighed. "They would let me go over him."

In an interesting manifestation of trust-tuning, Lanie allowed Constance to become a proxy for the company's trustworthiness. "The reason I'm still at DTC, to be honest, is because Constance is here," Lanie admitted. She trusted the institution only insofar as Constance was present, interpreting her supervisor's personal efforts as a stand-in for the organization's goodwill. Lanie stayed not because the company earned her trust but because Constance embodied it.

But the gendered inequities built into the structure and culture of the company made the ties Constance and Lanie forged heavy for both women.[43] While Constance's support helped Lanie find her footing within a challenging environment, it also underscored the heaviness of buffering as a gendered, often racialized labor that can weigh down the careers of minoritized employees.[44] As a South Asian woman who'd navigated unequal workspaces for over a decade, Constance was highly attuned to the vulnerabilities of minoritized workers. "I see it because of work, just because of . . ." she shrugged, "I don't know, life as a whole." It felt immoral to her to stand by and simply watch mistreatment play out: "[It's] ingrained in how I just treat people and how I relate to people." Enacting a version of the morality of the fallen, Constance felt compelled to help others navigate these systems, flawed as they were.

Her labor made her a beacon among vulnerable workers, who frequently sought her out for support. There was Valerie, a junior client services worker, whose male colleague was taking credit for her work. "She was so junior," Constance recalled. "She didn't know what to do. She had no one to go to." Constance advised her and followed up a few times after to make sure the intervention was effective. And then there was Cain, who worked in Constance's department but reported to someone else. He approached Constance after a new creative manager, Grey, began harassing him. Grey mocked Cain's Puerto Rican identity, consistently making condescending remarks about his intelligence and asking offensive questions like "Don't you like tamales?" Once again, Constance stepped in to help.

Although Constance found fulfillment in supporting her colleagues, she was keenly aware that the company neither recognized nor valued this relational labor. "It's invisible work," she said. "None of that stuff is appreciated. None of that stuff is valid." Buffering labor never showed up in her performance reviews, even as senior executives occasionally noted improved outcomes among those she mentored, but it added to her workload.[45] Consequently, Constance seemed to work around the clock, frequently sending work emails late into the evening and coming into the office on weekends seeking uninterrupted time to complete her other tasks.

She also stayed at DTC longer than she may have otherwise, afraid of what might happen to the workers who depended on her if she left. Indeed, workers were quite vulnerable to disruptions in buffering relationships, whether stemming from their buffers' own career decisions or through company restructures that shifted people around. Matilda, for example, described the dramatic change in her work life when her trusted supervisor, Harper, was transferred to another team. In an event coordination role that often felt unappreciated, Harper worked hard to protect Matilda from unreasonable demands. She also went outside of DTC's formal policy to let Matilda rearrange her hours and occasionally work from home, making the fertility treatments she was undergoing easier to manage.

But Matilda felt much more exposed under the regime of Jane, her new supervisor. Jane didn't filter requests and was quick to assign blame. "You get that feeling that nothing's ever good enough," Matilda said. When she needed time off for a medical procedure, Jane demanded a doctor's note.[46] "I don't feel comfortable with them knowing I'm going through this," Matilda winced, feeling her desire for motherhood might be interpreted as a lack of job commitment.[47] Without Harper's buffering, the stress mounted. "I know there's no future for me," she said. "I don't feel I have the support at all." Her voice cracked as tears began to well. "It's like, why am I having this stress, when it's not even worth it?" A few weeks later, Matilda approached me in the office kitchen, a look of resignation on her face. She'd learned she was being laid off in the company's latest restructuring. The shelters provided through buffering were ultimately only a temporary refuge, and when they collapsed, the stark realities of modern employment often bore down on those least equipped to withstand it.

While buffers were a vital lifeline for vulnerable workers, maintaining those relationships could nevertheless be fraught. For Lanie, her sense of comfort became tethered to what her mentor could—or was willing to—do on her behalf. While Lanie was inclined to link her struggles to capitalism's inequalities, Constance embraced a more pragmatic, access-focused approach that sidestepped structural critique.[48] "I am really proud that I am part of [the] conversation, whatever that conversation is," Constance said, highlighting instances when she and Lanie were often the only women in the room. But she was reluctant to take a more forceful approach focused on systemic change, explaining, "There's only so much I can do. I'm not the policymaker." Instead, she preferred individualized "solutions" that aligned with a morality of the fallen by helping workers persist within rather than challenge the structures that constrained them. This pragmatism gave Lanie valuable tools to navigate an oppressive system, but it required her to reshape herself to fit within the given mold, subtly prioritizing assimilation over transformation.[49]

Lanie—grateful to but increasingly dependent on Constance—also carried the emotional weight of her mentor's inferred expectations. Although Constance rarely asked Lanie to stay late or take on extra tasks, Lanie spoke of wanting to "work harder" to make Constance proud, driven by a desire to prove herself worthy of the care and attention she received. This dynamic speaks to how buffering relationships can easily slip into paternalism, where compliance is subtly nurtured through affection and persuasion rather than force, a phenomenon sociologist Mary Jackman calls the "velvet glove."[50] In this instance, Constance and Lanie's shared struggles as women navigating a masculine-dominated workplace meant their interests were often closely intertwined, limiting the potential for exploitation. However, when the lived experiences of those offering buffering—commonly thought of as allies—diverge from those they seek to support, the risk becomes more acute. In these cases, even well-meaning allies may unintentionally perpetuate the dynamics they purport to disrupt, and at the worst, these relationships can become a site of abuse.[51]

Meanwhile, the very institutions supposedly set up to protect workers often betrayed them. Cain's experience is illuminating in this regard. With Constance's encouragement, he filed a complaint against Grey through Human Resources, but they responded with a slap on the wrist, sending Grey to a "sensitivity training" session that did little to rein in his behavior.[52] Making things worse, Grey somehow found out Cain had lodged the complaint. No one could say exactly how the information got out, but it wasn't the first time confidential reports slipped into the hands of powerful managers. Indeed, the presumed confidentiality of employee conversations proved quite tenuous in practice.[53] "I'll take it to the grave," HR professional Edith told me, before admitting the opposite: "I'm not really going to say anything *unless* it's going to be detrimental to [the worker] or like the larger organization."

Edith of course didn't actively identify as a henchwoman of management. Rather, like many HR professionals, she was trapped in the contradictions of her role. Often cast as the guardian of workers' rights, HR ultimately doesn't answer to workers but to leadership.[54] Moreover, weak labor laws and the relative marginalization of HR within the realms of corporate power leave HR professionals little armor with which to defend workers.[55] Thus, when management knocks, they answer—not out of malice but out of compliance. In the case of Grey, he retaliated by making Cain's work life unbearable, pushing the latter to consider quitting without securing another job.[56] Luckily, Constance and several other team members stepped in, threatening to quit if Grey wasn't fired. Within a few weeks, Grey was terminated—not because institutional safeguards shielded Cain from harm but because of the buffering enacted by a particularly motivated group of workers.

Ultimately, the issue is that institutional safeguards are rarely designed with workers' safety and well-being as the top priority.[57] Workplace surveillance offers a paradigmatic example.[58] Lanie saw little use in DTC's cameras and email monitors as defenses against harassment. Her harasser, she explained, had no fear of being caught. "That's what blew my mind most," she said. She kept copies of inappropriate emails but felt sure these "receipts" wouldn't be enough to trigger action. Meanwhile, Grady, the head of the NYC office, had a different view of surveillance altogether. He gleefully recounted to me how he'd used the office video cameras to identify a thief in their midst: an employee taking more than his "fair share" of company-provided snacks. He didn't take action right away, but the culprit was let go a few weeks later during a restructuring initiative. Grady laughed, recalling how the person turned ghost white on his last day when he vindictively told him, "I know you stole the nuts."

Perceptions of supportive workplace cultures often rest on the emotional and relational labor of buffering. Yet those who shoulder this burden are seldom recognized or rewarded, and those who benefit from it cannot rely on its fragile protections. Rather than addressing systemic inequities, organizations exploit these relationships, allowing individual workers—predominantly women and people of color—to absorb institutional responsibilities and risks. Further, the commitments forged in buffering relationships often keep both parties tied to less-than-ideal workplaces, where employers preach the value of trust but fail to practice it. Though buffers and those they protect form meaningful bonds, these connections are warped by institutional neglect and survival demands, creating dependencies that serve managerial interests while hindering collective action. In the end, buffering is a patch that covers holes and tears in the institutional canvas, creating an illusion of smooth functionality, while the underlying social fabric quietly erodes, and management stays safely above the fray.

CONCLUSION

Heavy ties are like trapeze partners, offering their counterparts just the right mix of thrill and security to sustain flash intimacy. Amid the dizzying, high-wire act of modern work, we rely on such ties to navigate an otherwise vast labor market and to pull us through complicated workplace environments. The labor embedded in these ties transforms the rigid into something flexible, the unreachable into something within grasp, and the threatening into something almost exhilarating. Heavy ties don't just help us survive; they give us reason to hope and feel alive.

But the magic of the circus comes at a steep personal price. Individual performers, like trapeze artists, must continually stretch to new heights and contort in unimaginable ways to satisfy the insatiable appetite for spectacle. As the twentieth-century circus proprietor Henry Ringling North observed, "[The circus] is a ravening hag who sucks your vitality as a vampire drinks blood—who kills the brightest stars in her crown and who will allow no private life to those who serve her; wrecking their homes, ruining their bodies, and destroying the happiness of their loved ones by her insatiable demands."[59]

Today's labor system isn't so different. Employers regularly depend on the relational labor of heavy ties to maintain (and indeed enrich) their workplaces. Yet they seldom invest in the very people who perform this indispensable work; instead, they rely on workers' passion and sense of obligation to carry the load, expecting them to stretch ever further without support. Inevitably the burden becomes too heavy, and when these ties begin to fray, there's no safety net beneath. Workers are left to fall alone, while the enterprise moves on without missing a beat—much like the circus packing up for the next town.

The ride-hail drivers discussed in chapter 7 also navigated heavy ties amid minimal institutional supports. However, they used the spectacle of their labor to recruit others to their cause—to build awareness around the danger, degradation, and dehumanization they experience on the job. While their efforts are a work in progress, they nevertheless shed light on a means of exposing the humbug tales of modern work. Before examining their case in chapter 7, however, I explore how "cryptocorporations" create illusions that prevent workers from advocating for themselves.

6 Cryptocorporation

THE MARGINS OF WORKPLACE TRUST

People exchanged anxious glances as they gathered in DTC's main foyer, their unease palpable in the hushed silence. By now, most had read the news article, the one reporting that many marketing conglomerates, including DTC's parent company, were planning to institute cost-cutting measures in response to "ongoing market challenges." No one seemed to know what exactly this meant for the team, with some hypothesizing it wouldn't affect them at all and others predicting layoffs. Today's afternoon meeting promised answers.

As he kicked off the discussion, CEO Adam announced the company would be freezing travel, hiring, and—most painfully—raises for six months. He framed the decision as a "favor" to DTC's parent company, emphasizing how leadership had "good intentions" when making the call. Nevertheless, he acknowledged it was "a hard pill to swallow." This pill was especially bitter given that raises had already been delayed once, despite what seemed by most accounts to be steady profit growth at the company. "Being part of a holding company," Adam explained, "requires putting the collective good over individual interests sometimes." He thanked the team for their "sacrifice" and noted that future requests like this would "personally be an issue" for him.[1] The meeting ended with the opening up of the office bar and Adam promising to stick around to answer any lingering questions.

The friendly, communal tone of the discussion sharply contrasted with its content. Equally significant were the things Adam left unsaid. He didn't specify the market challenges the company was facing, nor did he offer any guarantees about future job security. He also didn't mention that most of the cost-cutting initiatives only applied to those under the director level—a nuance I would only learn later from private conversations. For now, as drinks were poured and the space filled with chatter, Adam casually made the rounds. At one point, he even joined my conversation with junior account executive Rufus as we recapped the previous night's softball game. While I excused myself after a few minutes to further meander around the room, Rufus enthusiastically told me later they'd chatted for over an hour; his beaming expression made it clear the CEO's personalized attention overshadowed any negative feelings he had about the announcement.

That afternoon encapsulated a broader pattern I observed across DTC, Disruption, and The Jones. Managers consistently downplayed the "business" side of work when interacting with junior staff. They obscured operational systems and power structures—what I call the *cryptocorporation*—by studiously avoiding details about the company's financial transactions, bureaucracy, outsourced contracts, and plans for automation.[2] By keeping the cryptocorporation at the margins of employee understanding and experience, leaders could emphasize company cultures rooted in democracy, inclusivity, and care.[3] The result was a workplace defined by flash intimacy, in which interpersonal relationships floated freely above lurking structural issues.

This chapter examines the processes through which the cryptocorporation shapes workplace life. We begin at DTC, where managers sought to elevate humanity against a backdrop of commodification and digitalization, but still used a "hands-tied" narrative to justify instrumental decision-making. Then at Disruption, we examine how managers fostered a "partner mindset" that muddled employer-employee distinctions in ways that encouraged workers to sacrifice their own needs for the good of the company. And finally at The Jones, a case of "frayed trust" reveals what can happen when the cryptocorporation unexpectedly emerges from the shadows. In continuity with other chapters, I draw specific examples from each site to highlight a particular theme, but the individual themes were observed across the three sites.

Taken together, these processes demonstrate how workplace relationships governed by a logic of care and commitment—humanity bubbles—flourish when power dynamics and conflicting interests are concealed within the cryptocorporation. The sense of belonging, recognition, and being valued that exists within humanity bubbles is deeply comforting, providing a reprieve from the often transactional nature of professional life. Workers like Rufus made it clear: it wasn't the job itself that kept them at companies like DTC, but meaningful workplace relationships that made those companies inviting and vibrant places to be. Indeed, the allure of intimacy was so strong that many workers were willing to swiftly move past painful experiences of betrayal, creatively trust-tuning their definitions of trustworthiness to restore workplace harmony.

As sociologist C. J. Pascoe has shown through her provocative ethnographic study of a close-knit American high school, it's often difficult to address structural issues like inequality and exploitation in environments that stress interpersonal amiability and kindness.[4] The same dynamic was present at DTC, Disruption, and The Jones. With organizational problems pushed to the margins, workers found it difficult to make their material needs visible, and raising issues like understaffing or fair pay often felt inappropriate or confrontational. Instead, excessive strain, personal setbacks, and enduring inequities were naturalized and viewed as unfortunate but inevitable characteristics of modern work, and as such had to be stoically endured—particularly in workplaces underpinned by a morality of the fallen that valorizes hard truths and individual resilience. As a result, the depths of the trust fall turn out to be much deeper than they appear at the outset.

THE HANDS-TIED RATIONALE

At first glance, DTC's cost-cutting announcement seemed like an isolated, albeit intriguing, moment. But like those Magic Eye puzzles from the 1990s, a closer look reveals the deeper dynamics embedded in the image. Indeed, as I spoke to DTCers, it became clear that most teams were chronically understaffed, with overburdened employees often waiting months, if not years, for promised help and career advancement. Take Ben: after nearly a decade at the company, he was in the position of senior account executive, only two modest half steps up from entry level. "It's been a very, very slow process," he confessed, noting that he was essentially "three years behind . . . where [he] should be" in his career. Ben's slow progression was puzzling, given his strong reputation among senior management as a hardworking, dependable team player. Indeed, for six months he and another junior employee managed an account usually handled by a team of five—all by themselves. Ben chuckled self-consciously as he acknowledged that his loyalty and dedication weren't particularly self-serving. Still, he claimed to stay at DTC for "the people."

The managerial neglect of Ben's career was out of sync with a culture that prided itself on its human-centered values. When I asked Ben about the disconnect, he attributed his advancement delays to the organization's client-driven structure. "Every client is its own silo [and] the funds are built into that," he explained. "So, it's not like the company as a whole is gonna be like, 'Oh yeah, you deserve [a promotion].' We're funded by our client. So, it's a different bucket of money." From this view, his career trajectory was not under the purview of managers. Ethan, a manager at DTC, shared a similar story, noting that several members of his team were overdue when it came to advancing to the next rung on their career ladders. "What's funny, too," he said, acknowledging the decoupling of career progression from company growth, "is I'm saying this as the biz is doing pretty well. It's just that *our client* is so up and down with their seasonal investments." He conceded, "It's like, 'Oh, I think XYZ deserves a raise,' but I can't do it because I don't know what the client's gonna do."

Narratives like these represent what I identify as the "hands-tied" rationale, a classic example of a thought-terminating cliché captured by dismissive phrases like "boys will be boys" or "it's all God's plan" that stifle further inquiry into a topic.[5] In this case, the hands-tied rationale shut down discussion and deflected dissent to contentious business decision-making by making operational choices seem immutable. At workplaces like DTC, Disruption, and The Jones, the hands-tied rationale maintained surface legitimacy by exploiting the fractured and fissured nature of the contemporary economy.[6]

Specifically, managers used dispersed operations to strategically transform unpopular decisions into external mandates, positioning themselves as powerless intermediaries. Sociologist Gabriel Rossman calls this "obfuscatory relational work," noting how subjective experiences of enacting it can vary widely, "from lucid culpability to compartmentalization or dual consciousness to fully internalizing the [underlying] premise."[7] Regardless of the degree to which managers fully believed in the hands-tied rationale, it was useful. By obscuring their control of workplace rewards (in this case), managers were free to demand the moon from workers while only paying for a streetlamp and blaming the discrepancy on external parties or factors.

While the hands-tied rationale trapped full-time workers like Ben in career purgatory, it imposed a different kind of burden on DTC's contract workers. The company frequently delegated legally and morally ambiguous tasks to these workers, who were provisional team members, making them easily detachable proxies for blame when things went wrong. Peg, a contracted brand ambassador for one of DTC's alcohol clients, knew this role well. Her job took place in "gray areas," she explained, where the legitimacy of her work was often suspect.

For instance, to secure placements for her brand at local bars and restaurants, Peg regularly spent large sums of money at those establishments in a bid for reciprocity. "That's technically illegal," she admitted, distinguishing between how things were spelled out on paper and how they really went down. "You're not allowed to do that. But that's the fucking business. That's how we're *meant* to do this." Peg had a keen grasp of how she and other contract workers served as shields for companies like DTC and their clients. "[Our job is to] do the things that the client needs to get done without it being them doing it—to be kind of in the middle, to be a scapegoat," she explained. "They need somebody to go in there and kind of do the shady shit that they cannot physically have their hands dirtied with."

Peg felt the strain of being caught in the crosscurrents between the demands of the cryptocorporation and DTC's humanity bubbles. She appreciated the company's personal gestures, like the custom vodka bottle with her and her wife's picture on it that the team designed for NYC Pride, but these acts increasingly felt hollow as she navigated the gray areas of her job without support. Her sense of being unmoored was especially pronounced when it came to handling on-the-job expenses. Peg and her colleagues often paid these costs out of pocket, regularly waiting upward of three months to be reimbursed. The real stress, however, came when submitting expense reports, on which every line item required careful justification. Too vague, and finance might reject the report; too detailed, and she risked exposing the off-the-books nature of her work.

Although her boss was fully aware of Peg's predicament, he would merely point her to the formal policy whenever she asked for guidance. The message was clear: if an audit flagged one of her reports or if a client questioned her spending, her boss's hands were tied, and she'd take the fall. "This company doesn't care about me and my day to day," she concluded, "because I am not a real person. I feel like I'm a ghost sometimes." DTC thrived on the energy of workers like Peg, yet it reduced them to ever-present specters designed to absorb fallout while shielding the real power brokers behind layers of plausible deniability.[8]

In the 1970s, Rosabeth Moss Kanter described a "shadow structure" in which organizational power circulated through informal, invisible channels.[9] While it was a hidden and stratified system, rank-and-file workers nevertheless could gain influence and career mobility when they were able to effectively navigate it.[10] The cryptocorporation is a modern evolution of this shadow structure, shaped by contemporary outsourcing practices that create layers of obfuscation. Given the fragmentation of workplaces, contract workers charged with "getting things done" are unable to leverage those actions to advance their careers. Instead, they act as the public face of a shell company, shouldering risk and liability while the true beneficiaries enjoy anonymity and immunity.

Workers like Peg were not the only ones to observe the tensions, gaps, and inconsistencies between humanity bubbles and cryptocorporations. Middle managers, who often gave the hands-tied rationale to their teams, were also aware of its contradictions, frequently finding themselves on the receiving end of the excuse as well. Event coordinator Sigi explained, "I certainly trust my manager, Ernie, but I find myself in similar situations [to him] as a manager. And the way I'm handling it, he's probably doing that to me." She recalled asking for a raise only to be told Ernie's hands were tied, and later she gave the same response to her direct report. Sigi recognized how the hands-tied rationale perpetuated a cycle of passivity: "I'm not doing much to figure out what's the root of this: why can't we get more money? I'm kind of depending on Ernie to do that," she said, adding, "He's probably not doing much on his own for me, and he's probably depending on someone else." But rather than confront the cryptocorporation, Sigi saw it as more pragmatic to simply toe the company line, a move she acknowledged let the effects of inaction simply "trickle down."[11]

Another middle manager, Hugh, took a harder line—at least rhetorically—telling me, "You see how easy it is where your senior manager goes like, 'There's nothing I can do. My hands are tied.'" He called this a "cop-out," explaining that if a manager truly valued an employee, they would find the money or make it work. "I understand there's a level of expendability to all employees," he added, taking the logic of the cryptocorporation as a given. "I get that because I get business." Reflecting on instances when his managers should have done more for him or his team, he sighed. "It makes me look at senior management in a different light." Yet Hugh, like Sigi, saw little value in resistance, offering an analogy of a cracked tooth that captured the danger of dwelling too much on the issue. "You keep touching the tongue to the tooth," he said. "You keep festering it until eventually . . . that crack will degrade the entire thing."

Yet Hugh wasn't wrong in his assertion that at least senior managers had more control than they let on. Adam, for example, spoke with me at length about how change was a constant in business and how good leaders made strategic decisions to maximize agility. As an illustration, he told me about how he'd invested several months earlier in technologies that would allow DTC to automate parts of the labor process. Thus, when the company's largest client began expressing budget concerns, management was able to quickly reduce costs by laying off about two dozen workers whose roles overlapped with the new technologies. While Adam insisted their commitment to "stay human" in the digital age was a distinguishing feature of the company, he (privately) viewed these automation-driven layoffs as a taken-for-granted cost of doing business.[12]

Notably, Adam's role in the layoffs was obscured for most workers, including those laid off. Carly was one such worker. She'd been working as an event coordinator at DTC for seven months when her boss Ernie called her into his office. Having been in attendance for Adam's cost-cutting announcement a few weeks before, she was aware of the purported market headwinds, but she hadn't really thought her own job was at risk. She described his tone as "very apologetic." "I didn't wanna do this," he told her, enacting the hands-tied rationale: "It has to all do with the client's restructuring plan. [. . .] [Y]our position didn't move over." Carly described a similar conversation with her lower-level supervisor, Jane, immediately afterward. "We talked a little, but there's nothing really to talk about. It was our client's decision," she shrugged. "Our client decided to make the change, and obviously, since they're our client, we have to listen to them."

Carly's termination violated the communal logics that characterized life within DTC's humanity bubbles, exposing the harsh reality of worker expendability. Yet through the hands-tied rationale, her managers distanced themselves from the moral consequences that hovered around the dismissal and threatened to disrupt the team's carefully crafted bubble. Although the groundwork for layoffs was laid months earlier, the client's efficiency demands became a convenient catalyst that allowed managers to offload blame. This scapegoating was instrumental, severing potential alliances between workers and clients by making the latter the face of unpopular decisions. Thus, rather than turning to clients (with whom DTCers often collaborated closely) as a potential ally or advocate, workers came to see them as minions of an impassive, profit-obsessed machinery.[13] In fact, Carly condemned her client's constant cycle of "cuts, rehires, cuts"—which arguably also defined DTC's operations—noting how the devaluation of human labor was not only unconscionable but also shortsighted.

Her ire targeted elsewhere, Carly sought to retain strong relationships with her soon-to-be ex-managers, even agreeing to stay on for a few weeks to help with the restructuring process that was taking her job. In doing so, Carly creatively reinterpreted the details of the situation in ways that bolstered trust in her direct supervisor, Jane. "She was looking out for me when this whole restructuring happened," Carly told me. "Obviously, I don't know the nitty-gritty, but I think she was very stressed knowing that my position was getting cut." As evidence for this claim, Carly recalled observing Jane's troubled demeanor following a private meeting with Ernie about a week before she was laid off: "[Ernie was like,] 'guys, I'm really sorry,' [and] Jane was like, 'This isn't fair. This isn't fair at all.'"

Through trust-tuning, Carly used Jane's visible frustration in an ambiguous moment to cast her as an ally.

By embracing the hands-tied narrative, Carly stayed resilient. She didn't take the dismissal personally, framing it as "simply how it is," and she quickly applied for other roles within the company. "I don't wanna sit there and mope," she said, embodying the hardy ethos of the morality of the fallen. "You can't dwell because that's when you lose out on opportunities." Despite several agonizing weeks of uncertainty, Carly was one of the few people laid off who secured another position at the company. While her sustained trust and loyalty likely contributed to her success, it also papered over the broader reality of the precarious position she found herself in.

DTC worked hard to present itself as a caring and human-centered company, with inspirational quotes decorating its walls in handwritten fonts and branded keychains and stickers emblazoned with the word "human" scattered throughout the office. Yet there is something oddly perverse about humanizing people who are already human. Perhaps if managers didn't erase their own fingerprints from workplace operations, they would feel more compelled to treat workers like Ben, Peg, and Carly with the dignity they deserve. Instead, akin to the Wizard of Oz, they draw on the all-powerful imagery of Adam Smith's "invisible hand" while they keep pulling the levers behind the curtain.

THE PARTNER MINDSET

"The number of times when I didn't know how to make payroll a day before payroll was due was extraordinary," Shane recalled, his voice heavy with the past year's financial troubles. The CEO credited the team's dedication for Disruption's survival, saying, "They were acting like my partners, not employees of the company." Envisioning the alternative, he imagined how they could have responded: "They'd be worried about their paychecks [or] negotiating a better deal because I didn't pay them on time [and] pressuring management to get what they deserve." He was proud of the team for treating the company as their own and making personal sacrifices to keep it afloat. "[It] kinda makes me feel like, okay, I can do this," he said, before correcting himself: "Not *I* can do this, but *we* can do this."

Shane's description of the team's approach reflects what I call the "partner mindset," a set of worker beliefs, values, and ideals promoted by managers and adopted by workers (to varying degrees) across Disruption, The Jones, and DTC.[14] Specifically, the partner mindset merges entrepreneurial values—proactiveness, risk-taking, and passion-driven zeal—with a communal ethos, encouraging workers to see themselves as vital contributors to the team's collective success.[15] Empowered by the perceived significance of their individual impact, their dedication becomes intertwined with their reputation, fostering a sense of accountability that can often transcend more immediate self-interests. In today's insecure economy, the partner mindset threads a fine needle between workers' commitment and vulnerability, binding them to the team through a sense of personal indispensability, even as their jobs remain highly unstable.

Employers like Shane promoted the partner mindset by obscuring structural dynamics that differentiated actual company owners from workers. For example, Shane compared his managerial approach to asking a friend for help moving, recounting a study that found the promise of a collective beer afterward was more effective in securing help than offering payment. "The direct line that I directly see in how we work now is that people are willing to do more out of loyalty, feelings of belonging, just liking you, professional courtesy—all of these sort of hard-to-quantify things," he explained. "They are much more likely to help you out then than when you want to structure a business relationship and put a dollar value on it." His team offered a case in point: "There is no way most of our consultants would have gone through what they've gone through had we not created *what we have*. We wouldn't have the money to keep them, right? It would all be about dollars, benefits, vacation time."

By "what we have," Shane meant the company culture, and he was right. Many consultants described the culture as their primary motivation for working at Disruption. Lionel spoke for many when he shared, "I mean, what's the point in working here when we can work somewhere else, you know, if we don't have that culture?" Interestingly, when I asked people at Disruption to describe the culture, they most often did so by outlining what it was not: namely, corporate. Reid, the head of talent, explicitly described the culture as "not corporate-y and old school, but quite the oppo—more cutting edge and current," while consultant Mack praised the company for "not trying to be a buttoned-up, nine-to-five consultant kind of [place]." This image aligned with Shane's emphasis on the interpersonal over business. In effect, he'd fostered a humanity bubble, in which people experienced a sense of interpersonal care that felt unique and special. Logan, the head of marketing, put it to me this way: "The difference here [compared to other places she'd worked] is that there is just a much more genuine . . . I genuinely like everyone a lot. I'm not trying to make it work, you know?"

The subtle vilification of business operations that underpinned the team's embrace of the company's culture became more pronounced whenever the conversation turned to their previous CEO, Palmer. Consultant Wade noted with disappointment how Palmer had tried to turn Disruption into a "body shop"—a derogatory term referring to tech companies that serve as temporary staffing providers to clients. Wade explained the issue he had with Palmer's approach: "It took the humanity out of the work team and introduced a higher level of control, which, to me, isn't the desire of making the world better. It's making the world profit." Palmer was moving things in a more "corporate [direction] as far as like allocation, division of tasks, and sort of needing to appeal to the clients," offered Harold, another consultant. "It's [the] part of business I don't like." Nevertheless, workers viewed this side of business as necessary, with Harold referring to it as "a means to an end."

Framing the impersonal and financially driven sides of business as a necessary evil, the team sought to actively conceal the visibility of those realities within everyday work life. Instead of traditional business terms, they often used euphemisms—for instance, rebranding the management team with the more nebulous title of "operations," and softening firings into the language of "phasing out." Visibility was even more constrained when it came to routine transactional tasks like payroll and client billing, which was outsourced to Adrienne, a contractor so physically removed from employees that she admitted, "I don't even know what [team members] look like."

Yet perhaps the clearest example of this dynamic was the contrast between the company's "all-hands" and "operations" meetings. The former, held in a sunny conference room, featured the team gathered for topline discussions, often with cocktails in hand—painting a picture of open deliberation and cheery optimism. Meanwhile, I watched as the operations team—the cryptocorporation at work—literally huddled in dark, closet-like spaces, hunched over laptops as they worked diligently on a shared spreadsheet detailing company projects.

Amid the clandestine cryptocorporation activity, a sense of collaboration and unity flourished. This emphasis on teamwork and collective identity, however, obscured deeper issues. As social scientist Melissa Gregg explains, when leaders frame everything in the language of teams, they "conveniently [remove] status distinctions or questions of wealth and equality," moving people "from 'me' to 'we.'"[16] This insight illuminates why the partner mindset is so effective: by subsuming and subordinating workers' needs under the rubric of company goals, it deftly sidesteps thorny issues of hierarchy and equity in fostering a collective identity, making it difficult for the rank and file to advocate for what they truly want and need.

As Harold and I wandered around Greenwich Village one afternoon, I observed him wrestling with this tension. Although management had yet to tell him directly, he'd heard through the grapevine that his project assignment was being extended another six months. But he was restless for change. "Ideally, there would be something else in the pipeline I could go to, but there's not," he explained, before asking almost hopelessly: "How can I justify saying, 'No, I don't want to do that?'"

Beyond the lack of vocabulary to assert his interests, Harold knew raising the issue would go against the morality of the fallen's dictate to tough things out, potentially jeopardizing his standing in the company. "I'm not sure what would happen," Harold said, hypothesizing management's reaction: "They might decide 'If he can't sort of suck it up [. . .] then even if we do find work for him now, [in the future,] there might be a similar situation, and he's sort of putting his own needs in front of the company.'" Reflecting on the consequences, he added, slipping again into their imagined voice: "That might be a problem, and we might need to just say goodbye to him."

Of course, the obfuscation of the cryptocorporation contributed to Harold's challenge. He didn't know enough details to make an effective business case for his position. He didn't know, for example, how consultants were selected for specific projects, and whether he might be particularly well-suited for a different project.[17] "There's not really much that I can work with as far as that conversation and sort of pushing things toward my wants as far as the company's needs," he explained. Like Theseus in the labyrinth from Greek mythology, Harold was fumbling his way through a purposefully convoluted maze, while powerful forces loomed in the shadows, threatening to devour him if he took a wrong step.

In addition, the opacity of the cryptocorporation naturalized its operations, making them seem impermeable to intervention. "It's sort of the constraints around what someone can and can't do with a business," Harold told me in a resigned tone. Yet he didn't apply the same taken-for-granted instrumentalism to his own career decisions. When I asked him if he thought about leaving Disruption given the crossroads he was at, he replied bashfully, "This is dumb, but I sort of feel a bit of indebtedness." He recalled how Reid had helped him transition from a part-time to a full-time role a few years before, when others were less confident in his abilities. He now felt like he owed Reid—and by extension, the company—a degree of loyalty, particularly given Disruption's recent hardships. "With the company being really small right now and struggling," he said, "it's like I'd be sort of leaving them out to dry." He shook his head. "I don't know what the right thing is," he said. "I feel like no matter what I do, I'll feel bad."

Logan grappled with a similar dilemma. She'd taken temporary salary cuts in the past to help the company stay on solid ground. But she was the primary earner at home, and money was important given her family's recent welcoming of a new baby. Regarding her sense of obligation, she explained, "It's kind of hard because I'm not a partner in the company, but I feel like I am." To be clear, this wasn't something she wanted: "I don't want to be a partner. When you're a partner, you don't have to pay yourself. There's a lot of things that you give up." And yet she said, her voice softening in surrender, "I do feel the same." Indeed, rather than directly address her need for higher pay with Shane, she actively debated taking on additional contract work to supplement her income. Lacking the words to express her complicated emotions, she simply offered, "It's interesting that I kind of feel the sense of responsibility I have for the team."

Harold's and Logan's sense of unease reflects what Freud would call an encounter with "the uncanny."[18] In such moments, they recognized the inherently familiar sentiments of their own needs, but those needs felt foreign in a company culture that sought to repress them under the universalism of the partner mindset. The glimpse of their own alienated interests was unsettling, not least of all because it hinted at the exploitative dangers of workplace intimacy.[19] Indeed, the jarring nature of these encounters with their estranged desires marked an important inflection point for workers, with some prompted to reclaim and assert their interests, while others sought to restore a sense of comfort and safety through trust-tuning.

Jay, a newer consultant at Disruption, took the former approach when the team's ongoing diversity discourse sparked internal ambivalence. As a tokenized worker in the field of tech—and the only Black person at the company—Jay didn't want to participate if talk about inclusion was simply performative.[20] "I think a lot of times companies say they want diversity," he explained. "I think you also have to be very aware of the reasons and motivations behind it." He confronted Reid, the head of talent, asking, "Do you just want [diversity] because it's good for business?" Reid flatly rejected the accusation, but an awkward silence ensued. In a subtle act of defiance, Jay refused to break the tension, allowing it to linger uncomfortably until the drumbeat of work attracted attention elsewhere. As a lone diversity representative in the workforce, he felt compelled to make his needs visible; otherwise, they were likely to be subsumed under those of the company.[21]

Others, like Harold, dealt with the tension by instead tuning their trust to render the company as only unintentionally at fault.[22] "I do get frustrated about some lack of communication," he admitted, referring specifically to the fact that management hadn't told him about the project extension. He added, however, "I think [it's] oversight, not malice," reconfiguring the neglect of his need for information—and the underlying professional need to expand his experience—as an issue of incompetence as opposed to a lack of care. Doubling down, he said, "I don't think there's anyone who would intentionally do something against my interests at Disruption." While he didn't always agree with management, he believed that they "have people's interest at heart."

It's not clear why some workers were mobilized by the experience of the uncanny to advocate for themselves while others were more willing to resolve the situation through trust-tuning. It may be that Harold, who'd invested more time at the company, had internalized its values, making it harder for him to challenge management or acknowledge his own unmet needs. Alternatively, it could be that Harold, as a white man, saw himself better reflected in leadership, potentially making the partner mindset's claims of universality more believable.[23] Or it could be a combination of both.

The partner mindset blurs the lines between employer and employee, empowering workers to "take ownership" of their work while framing personal sacrifice as part of a shared mission. Yet companies like Disruption are not worker owned and operated.[24] True participatory environments require mutual recognition, in which both worker and employer interests—and the inevitable tensions between them—are openly acknowledged and meaningfully addressed.[25] Without this, the emotional leash of loyalty and sacrifice keeps workers tethered to a mission that isn't truly theirs, masking exploitation behind the guise of shared purpose.

FRAYED TRUST

"In the beginning," busser Pete told me, "you know exactly what you're doing. You are there for the money." Four years later, having just won The Jones's "best employee" award, he was less sure. "[Winning the award] made me cry so badly," he said while showing me a picture on his phone of him smiling and holding the certificate: "It's a good thing—but it shouldn't be." Pete reflected fondly on the strong relationships he'd built with colleagues and managers. Yet, with a hint of foreboding, he added, "You might lose your way after a few years working in a restaurant." He went on to describe his once thriving career as an artist, a pursuit to which he wished to return full-time. He'd taken the bussing job for utilitarian reasons to cover costs. But over the past four years, he'd become fully immersed in restaurant life. Returning to the award, he said, "I was really pleased, like 'thank you very much.' But I was devastated, right? What am I doing?" The recognition was a painful reminder that he'd lost sight of his priorities along the way.

Pete's predicament reflects how The Jones, DTC, and Disruption cultivated workplace communities in which friendships grew and thrived, people were encouraged to take care of one another, and rituals like "family meal" recreated a sense of home.[26] In this humanity bubble, a purely instrumental approach to the job was rendered problematic, making it difficult for workers like Pete to stay focused on their personal goals. Or as The Jones's manager Donele put it, "People that come in and are super money hungry [. . .], they're not going to be a team player because they're focused on *their* tables, *their* money."

Yet money is the purpose of having a job, and for tipped front-of-house workers at The Jones, good wages were never a given. While NYC enacted a $9.00 hourly wage floor for these workers, a lack of guaranteed weekly hours and the high cost of living made this pay barely sustainable; in reality, such workers survived on tips.[27] Nevertheless, managers took a hands-off approach, refusing to even print recommended gratuity guidelines on guest bills (except for parties of six or more).[28] "Remember," the employee handbook read, "the guest has the right to make the final assessment and leave whatever amount he or she chooses." Consequently, managers were conveniently shielded from wage complaints.[29] This was the case even as they drew on tipped funds to cover wage minimums, credit card processing fees, and family meal expenses—all of which impacted workers' take-home pay.[30]

Typically, misalignments between workplace intimacy and business operations were resolved through trust, protecting workplace relationships by providing the flexibility for cryptocorporations to act independently of everyday work life. But a case of "frayed trust" at The Jones strained the mechanism through which people normally compartmentalized their personal and business expectations in the workplace. This moment exposed a fundamental tension between how managers and workers believed intimacy and business should coexist, ultimately revealing sharply contrasting expectations of workplace relationships.[31]

The issue began one night when Ken, a veteran bartender, had one of his regulars—a blue-haired bartender from a nearby staff hangout—order appetizers and drinks at the bar. When manager DJ, who was suspicious of the chumminess between the two men, looked at the check later, he found that "seventy dollars' worth of things" had been taken off. To be sure, "comping"—offering valued guests complimentary items—was standard practice at The Jones and was even acknowledged in the employee handbook. It was an especially common practice at the bar, where regulars were viewed as more likely to reciprocate with return business.[32] "It's part of [bartenders'] play with the bar guests," DJ explained. "It's sort of like, 'I'm gonna get you this round.' It's just part of the flow at the bar." Still, comping rules—as part of the cryptocorporation—were intentionally left ambiguous, and practices varied depending on the manager, the worker, and the guest.

DJ recalled Ken's reaction when confronted that night. "Ken basically said that he was comping all sorts of checks because he was angry at us for how we're scheduling, and he wanted to make more money." DJ was incredulous: "I was like, 'You literally just told me that!?' Like, just say you didn't really understand the policy!" In explaining his actions Ken had gone off script, failing to follow the logic of the morality of the fallen, which would require him to take his poor earnings in stride and repress his own self-interest in the process. Moreover, he didn't attempt to invoke the accepted rationale: the taken-for-granted opacity of the cryptocorporation, which as DJ intimated, could have offered him an escape. DJ took the issue to senior management, and when Ken arrived a few days later for his next shift, he was accused of theft and fired.

Economic sociologist Viviana Zelizer argues that intimacy and business are never truly separate, despite cultural practices—like those at The Jones—that treat them as "hostile worlds" that must not overlap.[33] She notes the ongoing work people do to manage the interconnectedness of these two spheres: establishing relational expectations by defining economic transactions and media (e.g., money) in ways that align with specific relationships and social contexts.[34] In the case of Ken's comping, both managers and workers engaged in such work as they interpreted the situation. But given the multiple interconnected relations between the parties—manager, mentor, friend—and the negative consequences at stake, these negotiations were especially fraught.

Managers, for their part, framed Ken's actions as *theft* and the comped funds as *stolen profits*, reaffirming the dominance of the *employment* relationship between managers and workers typically obscured within the cryptocorporation.[35] In this view, intimacy could be useful for motivating workers, but it was also a threat to business, requiring careful monitoring and control.[36] This incident wasn't the first time there'd been discrepancies over comping policies at The Jones. Indeed, the ambiguous nature of the policy and the varying levels to which managers enacted oversight made it a frequent point of tension. Yet DJ chose to make an example of one of the restaurant's most beloved employees and escalated the issue directly to senior management rather than handling it through the general manager Paul. In doing so, DJ demonstrated to senior management that he understood the restaurant's priorities and would not let relations of intimacy "pollute" his business judgment.

Workers didn't disagree that Ken messed up. Pete conceded that "DJ had a point. He sadly did have a point," while Ryan, another veteran bartender, acknowledged, "I think Ken did comp too much." But workers took issue with management's interpretation of the situation, with Ryan dismissively describing it as "corporate deductive reasoning." In contrast to the managerial view that Ken acted purely in self-interest, they highlighted a mutuality between his interests and those of the company. "Ken just meant, 'If we don't treat people well, they're not gonna come,'" server Jenna said, explaining Ken's logic. "'*We're* not gonna have a business, and they're not gonna come back and tip me, and that's how *I* make money.'"

Rather than viewing the comped funds as stolen profits and Ken as a thief, workers defined the funds as Ken's *livelihood:* money essential to his survival. Ryan, for example, interpreted Ken's statement in this way: "Ken was just like, 'Look man, the way you guys are staffing, if I don't take care of my regulars, I won't make enough money to live.'" This reframing, which foregrounded the *communal bonds* between workers and managers, presented Ken's comping as a *rightful claim* to his earnings (see table 3 for a side-by-side comparison of the interpretations). Notably, this perspective didn't sidestep the material and structural forces that shape the job but confronted them directly. Workers insisted that true care for employees could not be divorced from their financial well-being but was woven into the very fabric of doing business. In the words of Beyoncé, they were calling on their employers to "put some respect on my check."[37]

Management's failure to recognize their framing of the situation as legitimate left workers reeling. "They treated [Ken] like he was a thief," Jenna exclaimed. "It was like, 'You're not welcome back here. You're terminated. We will mail you your last check. You cannot go out the server door. You have to go out the regular door.'" Ryan was equally surprised by management's reaction: "This is a smaller restaurant. . . . I feel like

Table 3. Managerial and Worker Interpretations of the Comping Incident

	Managerial	*Worker*
Characterization of relationship	Employment	Communal
Characterization of transaction	Theft	Rightful claim
Characterization of media	Stolen profits	Livelihood
Perceived business/ intimacy relationship	Intimacy, while a useful resource, threatens business	Intimacy is interwoven into the fabric of doing business
Implication	Ken broke the terms of his contract, requiring the relationship to be severed	Ken was trying to balance his needs with those of the company, requiring flexibility within the relationship

it's the type of situation where you pull Ken aside and you're like, 'Look, this is way too much; you can't comp like a dozen oysters.'" Server Cheryl offered an analogous situation as a model for how she thought Ken should've been treated, recalling how manager David once helped her out when a large party left her only a couple dollars as a tip. "He definitely comped things off so that the tip was bigger." In recounting the incident, she specifically challenged the notion that such acts of care threatened business (in this case, David's authority): "I'm not gonna step all over him, and be like, 'Do this again. I know you did it one time.' I just respect him more."

As trust frayed, workers began to poke holes in the company's humanity bubbles. "If we're talking about trust in the workplace," Jenna said, "Ken brought such a great level of that. He just brings such a great energy, and that's what upper management talks about." She added flatly, "I guess that was just missed by the certain people that happened to be around at the time." Ryan also expressed a growing wariness: "Having seniority, I have a little bit more trust toward management—maybe cut them a little bit more slack—but there's still a line." Using his relationship with Paul as an example, he explained how Ken's situation had shifted his perspective:

"I like Paul. I like him a lot. I know he likes me. But, if push came to shove, he would fire me in a heartbeat if the higher-ups said."

The incident involving Ken wasn't just a case of personal betrayal; for many workers it brought the dominance of the cryptocorporation to light. In response, they began to distance themselves from management, prioritizing instead their bonds to each other. They made a conspicuous display of collecting funds to support Ken, even after learning he'd found another job. Emphasizing the livelihood perspective, bartender Shannon explained, "It's near the first of the month, and rent is coming up." Later, when Shannon worried to a group of servers that Ken might view the collection as "pity" money, Jenna cut in: "No! Tell him we are mad, and we think this is stupid! This is our way of showing our support and standing up for him." The money became a symbol of their resistance and collective power—a way to show they still cared about Ken, even if management didn't. It also sent a message that just as workers could be replaced, so too could sources of income.[38]

Workers also began to talk more openly of their restaurant work as a "survival job." The term had been subtly bandied about beforehand, often as a way for those also pursuing other passion-driven careers to signal their focus on those ambitions.[39] But the conversation grew louder after Ken's firing, with a notable shift in tone. It was no longer just a way to describe the job as a stepping stone, but also a direct challenge to the expectation of enduring commitment to the restaurant. As server Michelle, who'd been at The Jones for two years at that point, put it: "It's just right now—very temporary."

These changes caught managers' attention, and they quickly sought to restore the peace. DJ approached staff members, asking ruefully, "Do people hate me? Do they think it's my fault Ken got fired? Don't I even get to defend myself?" While DJ's attempts to heal the rift were largely unsuccessful, other managers made greater headway. "Donele had this list of seven of us," server Amanda recalled, "and she individually sat each of us down to explain why they fired [Ken]." Amanda was still frustrated, but her feelings softened when she realized Donele "thought she owed me an explanation." Several weeks later, when DJ was promoted, Paul met with several servers individually once again, saying, "We need you guys to be calm and be on board with our decision, because we didn't make this choice lightly, and we need your help with the rest of the team." These managerial trust-tuning efforts made a difference; while most workers still didn't like DJ, they accepted his promotion without complaint, ultimately trusting other managers' discretion.

Sociologist Laura Adler argues that many people avoid or quit well-paying, secure jobs with opportunities for growth out of fear this employment would distract from their efforts to pursue their vocational calling.[40] The Jones offered none of these temptations; the vast majority of its positions were neither lucrative, stable, nor upwardly mobile. Still, humanity bubbles drew workers in, often leading them to overcommit, sometimes at the expense of their own dreams.[41] They were reminded that companies like The Jones were first and foremost a business only when Ken inadvertently crossed an invisible line, disappearing through the cryptocorporation. But by then, many were in too deep, vulnerable to a managerial discourse that guided them back to an illusion of safety.

CONCLUSION

The opacity of the cryptocorporation enables thriving workplace cultures in which people connect across divides of power, status, and access to resources. While the relationships forged are often emotionally rewarding, there are legitimate questions to be raised about the costs of these connections. Are people connecting in ways that acknowledge their differences and meet their needs for mutual recognition, or are those with lower status and power being asked to sacrifice their priorities and needs in the name of harmony? In the latter case, these connections risk becoming tools that reinforce, rather than challenge, existing inequalities.

Such questions about who controls—and who benefits from—the terms of intimacy have long been central to sociological critiques. Arlie Hochschild, for instance, explored this issue from a different angle, interrogating what she called the commercialization of intimate life. With her signature poignancy, she asked, "Are we okay with the fact that baby may say his first word to the childcare worker, and grandma her last word to the nursing home aid?"[42] Hochschild's work captures how familial relationships can become mediated or dominated by economic structures, often at the expense of those directly involved. Yet critiques of this kind—which uphold a binary between intimate and economic life—have been challenged on historical and empirical grounds, with examples like family-run businesses, childhood allowances, and the economic dimensions of weddings revealing that intimacy and economics have long been intertwined.[43]

This chapter takes up the concern about the terms of intimacy but points to a different dynamic specific to workplace relationships. The issue is not one of "contamination"; workplace intimacies are not cheapened by their economic context, nor are businesses corrupted by the relationships they foster. Instead, the problem lies in a deliberate misrepresentation: employers attempt to "decorporatize" work by appropriating intimacy to mask how relational dynamics in the workplace are intertwined with business processes. This misdirection reframes structural inequities and power imbalances as interpersonal problems, making it harder for workers to recognize, articulate, and act on the systemic forces shaping their lives. As a result, workers often experience confusion, guilt, and burnout due to the pressure to prioritize interpersonal harmony over their own material needs. Ultimately, they lose not only visibility into the systems that govern their work lives but also the tools necessary to advocate for better conditions and hold management accountable.

The case of "frayed trust" at The Jones offers a peek into a different configuration of workplace relationships—one that transcends the pretenses of flash intimacy. The next chapter takes this reimagining of workplace relationships a step further, examining the case of the NYC ride-hail circuit. In this context, employers sought to cultivate flash intimacy through their rhetoric, but the structural configurations of the platform backfired in ways that disrupted workers' trust. Fueled by a sense of betrayal, workers interrogated displays of intimacy that lacked structural integrity. Rather than participate in a trust fall orchestrated by managers, workers stood upright, planting their feet and locking arms to advocate for a more stable foundation for workplace relationships.

7 Orchestrated Alliance

EXPOSING THE TRUST FALL IN THE NYC RIDE-HAIL CIRCUIT

The cold rain offered ideal money-making conditions. But on that particular morning in April 2017, hundreds of NYC ride-hail drivers passed up the chance to cash in on harried city dwellers' desire for a dry commute. Instead, an assortment of yellow cab, private luxury car, and platform-based drivers made their way to a nondescript glass building on Beaver Street in downtown Manhattan, home to the Taxi and Limousine Commission (TLC). They made the trek to attend the TLC's public hearing on the "disruption" of the ride-hail industry by digital platform companies such as Uber and Lyft.[1]

At the hearing, approximately eighty drivers from across the ride-hail sector volunteered to testify, seeking to add their voices to swirling debates about the platforms' impact on the local transportation infrastructure.[2] For their part, taxi drivers described how the unregulated influx of platform-based cars sharply undercut the value of taxi medallions—the coveted licenses needed to operate yellow cabs within the city. Previously reassured by the medallions' inflated value, many cab drivers were now forced to sell the licenses for a quarter of their previous worth.[3] "The consequences" of this so-called disruption, one cab driver testified, were "foreclosures, bankruptcy, marriages dissolved . . . [e]quities wiped out." "We feel betrayed," the man seethed.

Other drivers who had either transferred from yellow cab to platform driving or used platforms as a gateway into the industry argued they were "sold on a dream." Platform companies initially offered drivers a lucrative alternative to yellow cabs, but ongoing fare cuts and changes to commission structures now made it hard for platform drivers to even earn a living wage.[4] Moreover, platforms' practices of "algorithmic management" (e.g., incentive-based pay, blind passenger acceptance protocols) belied their claims of worker flexibility and autonomy. In practice, drivers were constantly tethered to their phones and enacted little control over trip decisions.[5] "The promise of good pay and flexibility has attracted many," one Uber driver testified, but "unfortunately, the fierce competition for market share between the app-based service providers has turned into a rapid race to the bottom." He urged the TLC to urgently take steps to rein in "service providers who do not seem to have a sense of morality."

Significant attention has been devoted to the exploitative working conditions within and adjacent to platform-based ride-hail work, with a 2023 *New York Times* headline even asking: "Has 'Gig Work' Become a Dirty Word?"[6] Such scrutiny, however, wasn't inevitable; rather, it was the product of drivers' on-the-ground advocacy efforts. In NYC, ride-hail drivers—most working via platforms forged a collective resistance to platform providers through alt-labor groups such as the New York Taxi Workers Alliance (NYTWA) and the Independent Drivers Guild (IDG).[7] Working together, they staged protests and strikes and lobbied the TLC to impose better work standards.[8]

These organizing campaigns are remarkable in a US context where union membership has been on the decline for decades and drivers' independent contractor status bars them from collective bargaining.[9] Equally astounding is the strong display of unity and collective action among a highly atomized and heterogeneous workforce. Ride-hail drivers spend the majority of their time alone in their cars, and over 90 percent of NYC drivers are born outside the US, originating from over one hundred different countries, creating a situation that would seemingly pose language and cultural barriers to relationship building.[10]

This chapter explores the processes through which NYC ride-hail drivers opted out of the trust fall in favor of adopting a *solidarity stance* focused more on collective well-being than on individual resilience. First

I examine how the institutionalization of trust in platform work reduced drivers' incentives toward trust-tuning in the face of disappointment. By *tuning out*, they fully confronted their sense of betrayal and found unity in their shared opposition to platform providers. Next I look at how competing crosscurrents within the circuit's visibility regime brought the economic dimensions of work to the fore, *bursting the bubble* that elsewhere severed notions of humanity from material well-being. As a result, drivers connected with others not through the hope of upward mobility but on the grounds of current needs. Finally, I review how drivers—caught between the dilapidated social contract of traditional work and the false promises of the future of work—eschew the morality of the fallen's glorification of suffering, coming together instead to pursue what I term *moral repair*. In sum, drivers pursued an *orchestrated alliance* rooted in solidarity rather than relying on the fleeting, paradoxical pleasures of flash intimacy sustained by trust.

TUNING OUT

In 2017 an exchange between Uber's then CEO, Travis Kalanick, and San Francisco driver Fawzi Kamel went viral.[11] In the dashcam video, Kamel—who'd just driven the CEO to his desired destination—confronted Kalanick over Uber's recent fare cuts. Kalanick responded to the driver with a market-based version of the "hands-tied" rationale that, as outlined in the last chapter, served to divert worker frustrations in other contexts. "We have to [cut fares]. We have competitors. Otherwise, we'd be out of a business," Kalanick explained. "We didn't go low-end because we wanted to. We went low-end because we had to." Kamel, however, firmly rejected this rationale, calling out the CEO's agency and power: "You had the business model in your hands. You could have the prices you want." Pivoting to a more blatant "just trust me" appeal, Kalanick teased Kamel with a forthcoming service rollout he expected would boost driver wages. "People are not trusting you anymore," Kamel clapped back. "I lost $97,000 because of you. I went bankrupt because of you."

Kalanick's approach in this interaction reflected his broader leadership style, which embodied the tenets—as outlined in chapter 4—of "maverick management": he spoke bluntly, took a careless approach to rules and even laws, and had a dearth of emotional intelligence that others simply shrugged off.[12] At The Jones, DTC, and Disruption, workers gave a wide berth to leaders like Kalanick, interpreting their missteps through a lens of personal trust that rendered them audacious and authentic. Within the ride-hail industry, that trust, while capable of being just as potent, proved more fragile.

"If there was more trust," one driver, Greg, explained, "we would stand by the company a lot more." He pointed to a politician who'd earned enough public trust to weather a viral controversy without losing support. With that kind of trust, Greg suggested, drivers might overlook Kalanick's errors, reasoning, "Hey, okay, they may have made a mistake, but here's all these positive things they've done. This is what else they can do." But as Kamel's words in the video made clear, drivers had lost all trust in Kalanick. Rather than reinterpreting the meanings of trust to address their disappointment, they rejected it outright, tuning out of interpersonal trust and embracing the pain and anger of betrayal. "This guy's pretty ruthless," Greg said of Kalanick. "He doesn't care who he had to step over."

The structure of labor relations within the ride-hail circuit is key to understanding why drivers were less inclined toward trust-tuning in their relationships with leaders like Kalanick. Ride-hail platforms lacked the abundant ritual and communal interchange between workers and leaders that fueled intimacy and maintained trust elsewhere. Drivers didn't experience platform providers or representatives as being "in the trenches" with them, nor were there frequent "between-the-lines" moments when they could interact with leaders outside of their formal company roles.[13]

Instead, as one driver, Diego, described, "everything is done through messages"—a communication mode that not only was cumbersome to enact behind the wheel but also stripped connections of nuance and context. Additionally, when performance issues arose, drivers faced the risk of "deactivation" from the platform rather than an opportunity for discussion or resolution, reinforcing the absence of personal relationships. Indeed, many drivers—feeling unheard by providers—tended to completely discount the human presence on the other end of these communications. One driver, Abe, spoke for many when he said, "There is no supervisor. There is no manager. It's just the app."

In response to driver frustrations and demands for more human engagement, platform providers initially attempted to bridge this gap by establishing phone banks and physical driver hubs. These touchpoints were staffed by "platform representatives" who were positioned similarly to middle managers in other work contexts. However, unlike those highlighted in chapter 5, these representatives failed to become a personal tie that "buffered" drivers from the harsh realities of the job. Despite communicating in real time with drivers, representatives lacked the necessary training and knowledge and ironically wound up replicating the automated presence they were intended to replace. "[Representatives] don't really hear what you're saying," one driver, Durene, said. "[They use] these form scripts." Driver hubs were even worse. Defined by long waits and overwhelmed staff, they were more reminiscent of the Department of Motor Vehicles than the workplaces described in previous chapters. If that wasn't bad enough, the aggressive surveillance by hawkish security guards made these spaces feel like fortified checkpoints.[14]

In the absence of social proximity, the trust that governed platform work was reduced to numbers.[15] Metrics like user ratings, driving statistics, and earnings were designed to act as standardized benchmarks—a shared evaluative framework that could travel across contexts.[16] Yet as sociologist Angèle Christin observes, metrics rarely function as universal or impartial truths; instead, they invite interpretation and negotiation within specific contexts.[17] For drivers, these numbers—rather than human connections—became the focal point of their interpretive efforts.

And rather than tuning toward trust, drivers tuned out—with earnings representing the clearest marker of their disillusionment with platform leaders. As rider fares went down over time, the costs of driving—licensing fees, car payments, insurance, fuel—remained steady or increased, leading to sharp declines in driver earnings.[18] "Usually after four years, you are going to see a raise in your salary," driver Fahad said. "But they go in reverse." Drivers like Fahad could have leaned into trust via their interpretations, attributing the decline to normal market fluctuations, regulatory decisions, or new drivers entering the industry, and some did. But many blamed leaders like Kalanick for slashing start-up incentives and fares.[19] "These people are doing business at the cost of drivers' sweat and blood," Fahad said bitterly, reflecting the profound sense of betrayal shared among many.[20]

Deprived of meaningful relationships with their supervisors, drivers turned to self-monitoring as a way to maintain their reputation and standing within the platform's impersonal ecosystem. Engaging in what I've elsewhere analyzed as "reputation auditing," they invested considerable time and effort in monitoring these metrics, challenging inaccuracies and reframing their meanings.[21] Driver Diego demonstrated the labor of reputation auditing while we sat chatting in his car.

Although he didn't personally put much stock in individual ratings, he knew a single bad score could drag down his average—and if his rating fell below a certain threshold, he risked deactivation.[22] He pulled up a recent negative rating, scrutinizing it alongside the driving data automatically collected by the app. "There were no wrong turns, nothing that I could say, 'Well, yeah, I did mess up,'" he explained, scanning through the metrics. "For that person to put 'safety' as an issue?" he said, shaking his head as he pointed to his performance data. "Braking, perfect. Acceleration, perfect. Speed, perfect. All that stuff is monitored!" If he faced deactivation, he planned to use these metrics in his defense, although conversations with other drivers revealed that this approach was often time-consuming and yielded only mixed results.

Paradoxically, the platform infrastructure that fostered social distance between drivers and leaders also created opportunities for drivers to connect with one another. As geographers Katie Wells, Kafui Attoh, and Declan Cullen have pointed out, platforms aim to deliver drivers to customers not only at just the right time but also "in exactly the right place."[23] Typically, these "just-in-place" labor practices disaggregate drivers—with an important exception. At metropolitan airports, rider demand tends to draw large pools of drivers to the same location, and to contend with airport regulations and congestion, platform companies employ technological innovations—such as digital "geo-fencing" and virtual queuing—to corral drivers into designated lots.

Stalled in place, sometimes for hours at a time, drivers talked with one another. "You're just sitting, waiting," Greg explained. "A lot of guys will walk up [to each other] and ask questions [. . .] and then, usually from there, a conversation starts up. [. . .] [D]rivers will exchange numbers." Airport lots, some outfitted with food trucks and porta-potties, served as a de facto "water cooler" where drivers compared notes and shared frustrations.

"Anytime you go to the airport," Abe told me, "you always hear new stuff" about what the platform companies are doing. Importantly, these conversations didn't occur in between-the-lines moments as described in chapter 3 but in outside-the-lines spaces free of managerial interference.[24] As a result, "venting" took on an angrier, more revolutionary tone.

Airport lots became a place where the airing of grievances weaved together the interests of an otherwise diverse and disaggregated group of drivers, uniting them in an oppositional identity.[25] Describing her engagement with other drivers at airport lots, Angel said, "It's about spreading the word, you know? Letting everybody know that we're not alone [. . .] to listen to the other stuff that's going on." The conversation even extended to online driver boards and WhatsApp groups. One driver, Gail, explained how they worked: "Some people will say their little things and they'll put their little news in there . . . and then I come in with my side of the news, and we all come together. So, it's like our little circle, our, I don't know, the Round Table as they call it." And like the Knights of the Round Table, the conversations primed drivers for a quest. "A lot of times, you've got to draw out that agitation," labor organizer Tim noted of his unionizing work in other sectors. "Here, they're already agitated," he continued. "They are already pissed!"

Tim's comment highlighted what trust-tuning had denied those at The Jones, DTC, and Disruption: the powerful resource of their own anger. As Audre Lorde once wrote, "When we turn from anger, we turn from insight, saying we will accept only the designs already known, those deadly and safely familiar."[26] Heeding Lorde's warning, drivers differ from their counterparts in other work settings, trading in the temporary salve of workplace trust for the clarity and transformative strength of betrayal and fury. In doing so, they illuminate an important but underutilized avenue—worker indignation—in the pursuit of equality, dignity, and justice in American work.

BURSTING THE BUBBLE

"They call us partners," Uber driver, Tsering Sherpa told the *New York Times* in 2016. "But they're treating us like slaves."[27] "[Partners] is just a term [they use] because they can't say that we're employees," Nicolo, another driver, explained to me. In a poignant nod to familial narratives of work, he added, "We're just the stepchild—the black sheep—that stays on the outside."

At DTC, The Jones, and Disruption, the language and rituals of trust marked and secured spaces of intimacy—humanity bubbles—where personal work relationships were seemingly isolated from the casual cruelties of capitalism. Within these trusted workplace communities, workers felt "seen" by their colleagues, and they looked to these relationships to carve out unique experiences of work that contrasted with a broader employment system that was indifferent to their well-being.[28] Ride-hail executive narratives tried to emulate these relational ideals, but the platform structure that governed the NYC ride-hail circuit failed to deliver on that experience, often leaving drivers feeling more "watched" than seen. As a result of these crosscurrents of visibility, drivers shifted their focus away from the interpersonal dynamics of work and toward confronting their material labor conditions, essentially bursting the bubble that sustained harmony and compliance elsewhere.[29]

Platform provider discourse, especially in the initial stages of the ride-hail circuit, closely mirrored that of more traditional workplace leaders. Similar to executives like Shane at Disruption, platforms sought to cultivate a "partner mindset," using slogans like "Uber needs partners like you," to recruit drivers.[30] They also promoted an ethic of care, positioning themselves as breaking down traditional employment barriers and creating accessible economic opportunities for marginalized communities.[31] Providers built a reputation for being "helpful" and "generous" through early-stage monetary incentives (e.g., $500 for completing one hundred trips) and discounts on things like car maintenance and smartphone contracts.[32] "They would help you," driver Abe recalled, "with anything, like, to get a car or anything you needed." Reflecting on the sense of recognition such initiatives provided drivers, Gabe, an early adopter, reflected, "[They] brought dignity [to the work] in the eyes of the general public—'It's okay to be a cab driver.'"

However, as feminist communications scholar Brooke Erin Duffy observes, the pursuit of recognition in work is often bound up in *aspirational labor*—a commitment of effort, time, and resources made in the hopes of being valued, even when that recognition remains persistently out of reach.[33] While Duffy's work focuses on digital content creators whose labor hinges on visibility to audiences, the dynamic she identifies—of working toward an imagined future where one's labor is validated—is relevant here. Platform providers prompted drivers' aspirational labor by offering early incentives and symbolic gestures of appreciation, cultivating the impression of partnership and upward mobility. But, as with other settings explored in chapter 5, this promise rarely materialized into lasting reward.[34]

Unfortunately for platform providers, NYC ride-hail drivers' motivations toward aspirational labor diminished over time due to two structural features in the organization of work. First, providers' interest in shielding themselves from employment obligations and regulations led them to largely obscure human management within the labor process, replacing it with algorithms that monitored, directed, and evaluated drivers' activities.[35] This shift enabled providers to position themselves as market curators rather than employers, reducing institutional costs and accountability.[36] However, it also severed the essential human connections that made workers feel seen and that made workers feel seen and that sustained flash intimacy elsewhere.

For example, when an inebriated group of passengers called driver Cal "all kinds of stuff—N-word, bozo, b-word," he had no one to turn to for support. Indeed, Lyft representatives failed to have his back when the passengers subsequently gave Cal a poor rating for not completing the trip amid the name-calling and refused to intervene by adjusting or removing the poor rating, leaving him vulnerable to the consequences of a declining average. Similarly, Durene, who maintained a high rating on the platforms, was automatically deactivated from Uber one afternoon when a customer accused her of stealing an item they'd left behind in her car. While the company eventually reinstated Durene, she was deeply offended by the abrupt and depersonalized protocol, particularly given her impeccable record and her history of going out of her way to return items riders accidentally left behind. Interactions like these left workers like Cal and Durene feeling devalued within the circuit's infrastructure.

Platform providers further eroded driver motivations by functionally erasing their labor.[37] Platforms like Lyft used taglines such as "Your

Friend with a Car" to make their services seem safer and more accessible to riders.[38] But these taglines tapped into gendered and racialized tropes that frame acts of community and care as selfless and natural, obscuring the skill and professionalism required and making the work seem more like a friendly favor than a paid service.[39] This familiarity often bred disrespect. As Durene observed, "Sometimes customers will come in, and they don't care that they're still stepping into a private car, even though it's licensed. And so they have little respect for it." Low ride prices only reinforced this attitude. "I find that people who get the lowest rate—like, the cheap rides—they don't really care," Durene continued. "They don't consider, 'hey, I'm getting this smooth ride for just a couple of dollars.'" Platforms like Uber took this a step further by downplaying payment altogether to create a "frictionless" experience. For years, Uber's founder, Travis Kalanick, resisted adding a tipping option, claiming it would disrupt the seamless experience for riders.[40] In this way, the platforms prioritized customer convenience at the expense of drivers' sense of respect and recognition.

That is not to say that ride-hail platforms made drivers invisible. Drivers submitted to background checks just to qualify for the job—a process that laid their personal histories bare to an unseen system. Once onboard, their work became subject to formalized scrutiny, requiring them to log every expense and record each dollar earned for institutions like the Internal Revenue Service.[41] "I file a 1099 every year," Diego explained. "It's all on the record," Gabe added, "all online. You have to record everything, stay on top of every little thing." "I didn't care as much before about a flat tire or putting my meals on a credit card. It didn't really matter that much. But now, I have to think about all those things." And the visibility didn't stop there. As alluded to earlier, drivers were constantly monitored through ratings, ride acceptance rates, driving hours—even their driving style.[42]

But this visibility didn't feel like recognition; it felt like surveillance. Drivers didn't feel "seen" in any meaningful way—they felt "watched," subjected to an impersonal, objectifying gaze that imposed control without respect.[43] Nicolo, for example, demonstrated the disciplinary effect of ratings in the advice he gave to fellow drivers. "If you're getting a lot of bad ratings," he counseled them, "it's because (a) your car smells dirty or (b) they don't feel safe when you're driving." Underlying his well-intentioned advice was a knowledge about the biases that often shape passenger feedback. Drivers, who were more likely than the general population to be foreign born and who had comparatively lower income levels, often found themselves decoding racialized and class-based biases.[44] As they did so, they were often compelled to adopt more normative aesthetics, neutralizing cultural differences and smoothing away stress or fatigue to maintain good ratings.[45] "If you're too quiet or you look like you're evil—not that you're evil, but you have an angry face because you're stressed," Nicolo explained, "the passenger will feel that energy and will not want to rate you well." In short, what was presented as a tool of trust for riders became a relentless, often biased gaze that demanded conformity but withheld genuine respect from drivers.

Amid these crosscurrents of visibility, drivers felt the contradictions between the language of intimacy and business practices more acutely than workers at The Jones, DTC, and Disruption. The platforms touted partnership and empowerment, yet drivers like Gabe saw through the facade. "These companies are treating us as employees," he protested, "but they don't give us the benefits of employees." Highlighting platform policies like blind ride acceptance, which prevented drivers from knowing a passenger's destination (i.e., the trip's length) before deciding whether or not to accept it, he added, "If you're forced to do the work, even if it's not to your advantage, you're not an independent contractor. You're an employee. You just don't have the benefits."[46] Amid these tensions, drivers began to push back, exposing the disparity between platforms' gestures of support and their exploitative practices.

Gloria, for example, pointed out the insufficiency of symbolic tokens of recognition. "I don't think it's fair for private contractors to get stars," she said. "The last time I got stars was in kindergarten, and really, if I want to go get stars, I think I'd go to the stationery store and get me some in all colors." Others added to the critique, pointing out how an emphasis on ratings decentered the role of tips. "Great. That goes a long way," Diego quipped, "let me pull out my stars to pay my gas." Similarly, Durene scoffed at a recent platform notification she received that read, "You've hit your 3,000 five-star ratings goal. Congratulations! Share with your friends and family." "Why? I mean, why do I want to do that?" she wondered aloud before suggesting that a $300 gift certificate would be a more appropriate way to celebrate the accomplishment.

While workers discussed in chapter 6 often accepted the implicit norms of business practices—such as maintaining secrecy around things like pay and scheduling decisions—drivers took a more sustained and critical look at the cryptocorporation. In the area of earnings, for example, they collected screenshots of both driver and rider trip receipts, pointing out discrepancies in quoted fare prices between the two and calling on platform providers to pay them based on what riders paid as opposed to miles and minutes driven.[47]

Scrutiny of pay stubs also led to the discovery that several platforms were illegally deducting New York State sales tax from driver pay as opposed to customer fares. One driver, George, put it bluntly: "They do take more money than they're supposed to." Drivers brought up the issue in TLC hearings and in class action lawsuits, leading to Uber issuing an apology for the "mistake."[48] Drivers refuted the company's characterization, with Durene telling me, "We are not fooled," and the NYTWA formally stating, "Uber hasn't just wrongly calculated its commission; it has been unlawfully taking the cost of sales tax and an injured-workers' surcharge right out of driver pay."[49] The labor advocacy organization filed a complaint with the New York Attorney General, resulting in a $328 million payout from Uber and Lyft in 2023.[50]

These efforts marked a decisive break from the patterns observed at The Jones, DTC, and Disruption. While workers in those settings often clung to speculative promises or sought fleeting recognition, ride-hail drivers grounded their resistance in shared material realities. They documented wage theft, exposed illegal deductions, and demanded accountability from platforms that exploited their labor. In doing so, they transformed their grievances into tangible victories—millions in settlements and new regulatory scrutiny.

This shift underscores the power of collective class consciousness. For too long, labor resistance in the United States has been stymied by a persistent illusion—what John Steinbeck famously articulated as the belief that "the poor see themselves not as an exploited proletariat but as temporarily embarrassed millionaires."[51] Ride-hail drivers burst this bubble of misrecognition, turning away from trust in the powerful and from the feeble promises of aspiration and choosing the deliberate work of building solidarity to confront difficult realities.

MORAL REPAIR

"I find the people who are struggling a lot are more interesting [than those in positions of privilege or power]," driver Gabe said, his voice steady but reflective. "They're more connected to the reality of what's really going on." For Gabe, staying in an exploitative industry rather than escaping to something "safer" wasn't about stubbornness; it was about refusing to settle for the status quo. "Even though things are tough," he continued, "just the idea that you have somebody that's willing to fight with you is a comforting thing." Describing his engagement with the labor organization, IDG, he said, "It gave me a sense of, okay, there is an organization that I can belong to that is actually trying to help." "Whenever I find those people in my life," he added, "it makes me feel good." He laughed self-consciously as if surprised by his own feelings. "I don't want to be emotional, but it makes me feel good."

At The Jones, DTC, and Disruption, people forged trust amid adversity, bonding through a shared embrace of vulnerability. Through the morality of the fallen, suffering—and the resilience it demanded—emerged as potent social currency, elevating individual reputations and marking the boundaries of belonging. Yet as shown in chapter 2, these bonds had a stabilizing effect on the workplace, legitimizing dysfunction as useful and perpetuating cycles of hardship (and even abuse) as a rite of passage.[52] In the NYC ride-hail circuit, drivers like Gabe reimagined suffering, treating it not as a means of fortification but as a catalyst for change.

Poor work conditions were not a cross drivers would bear. Instead, they interpreted those conditions as signs of erosion and decay in the infrastructure of work—problems that demanded maintenance, repair, and revision. Science and technology studies scholar Steven Jackson argues that a focus on repair transcends the binary of nostalgia versus novelty, rejecting the fetishization of both the past and the future. It foregrounds an ethic of care, seeking sustainability through a balance of preservation and transformation.[53] Drivers like Gabe embraced a similar approach—moral repair—by advocating and organizing to bring about meaningful change to their working conditions, reframing suffering as a collective call to action.[54]

Platform drivers occupied a unique vantage point that allowed them to see the shortcomings of both traditional and emerging forms of work and made them particularly attuned to the need for repair. Those who'd been driving for years knew the underbelly of the taxi industry: the exploitative fleet owners who squeezed every dollar from drivers and, more recently, the predatory lenders who dangled medallion ownership as a lifeline, only to drown drivers in debt.[55] Others came to the job from different fields, burned out by what traditional employment had become. Cal, for example, had grown "disgusted working a nine-to-five job" after repeatedly confronting discriminatory practices and managers. Angel, who previously worked in security, described how that job took over her life. "They would call me to work for everything," she said. "I was basically working seven days [a week]. I didn't have time for myself." For Durene, ride-hail driving was a last resort after being laid off from her clerical job. Despite decades of experience, she found herself excluded from the job market. "They're more focused on cutting costs, not the quality of life for employees," she said quietly.

Drivers like these had experienced the erosion of US work conditions firsthand. They saw the social contract unraveling—work demanded more but returned less—and were wary of platforms claiming to offer a way out. Companies like Uber and Lyft initially marketed themselves as saviors. "[They] used to advertise more time with your family, more money in your pocket," Greg recalled, while Gabe remembered hearing the promise of "being your own boss and being able to make your own schedule." For a while, platforms appeared to deliver on these promises. Their steady but flexible offer of work was a particularly welcomed lifeline in the aftermath of the Great Recession's devastation. Gabe could take his daughter to therapy on weekdays—something a traditional job never allowed—while pulling in a six-figure salary. Gloria, a single mom of four, managed to balance caregiving and work, a feat she hadn't thought possible.[56] But as the market matured and platforms slashed rider fares to remain competitive, those same drivers saw paychecks shrink and their flexibility erode. Gabe, for example, said his earnings had plummeted—from $130,000 in 2012 to less than $40,000 in 2016—even though his hours stayed the same.

Unwilling to return to traditional work and disillusioned by platform providers' promises about the "future of work," drivers began to organize. "[Drivers] have community with one another," Tim told me, "like a solidarity feeling." Solidarity, he explained, was not rooted in "emotional trust" but in something more concrete: the belief "that they're going to do something, right?" Indeed, drivers who began getting involved with IDG expressed a wariness about trust, revealing just how contaminated appeals to it had become. Angel, who was contemplating membership, admitted, "I don't trust nobody. Who knows if these major companies are the owners of IDG," while George asked skeptically, "I mean, who can you trust?"[57]

This skepticism was on full display when I met Fahad at a LaGuardia Airport lot, where he was recruiting drivers for IDG. As we approached a group of ten drivers perched on tailgates, killing time between rides, they started cracking jokes when they saw Fahad's IDG pin. "What makes IDG different?" one of them asked, while another questioned the point of even staying in the industry. Fahad leaned into their frustration. "Do you think drivers have a problem?" he asked, his voice calm but insistent. The drivers exchanged annoyed glances—of course there were problems. Fahad pressed on: "What are our problems?" His question opened a valve and the grievances poured out: low fares, platforms' high commissions, and the regulators' aggressive ticketing were among the many issues mentioned. Fahad listened carefully before asking, "Who will solve these problems?" When someone quipped, "IDG will," Fahad shook his head. "No. *We* have to solve them together."

While Fahad only signed up a handful of drivers that day, the IDG's efforts were beginning to resonate. Drivers like George could point to tangible wins. "They've done a lot," he said, ticking off accomplishments like campaigns that pressured platforms to add tipping features and destination filters to the apps. "They're trying to improve the ride-sharing business because, right now, it's not great." Gail echoed this sentiment, but her reasoning struck a deeper, moral chord. "I'm going through a lot of personal stuff," she explained, "but I decided, why am I going to keep going through my personal things where maybe if I fix whatever is going on around in the world [. . .] then I could at least get that fixed." Her words came haltingly, as if testing out a fragile logic. "It's not just you going through it, you know?" she continued, plugging her personal problems into a collective framework. For drivers like Gail, moral repair offered more than just a connection: it offered purpose and a meaningful path forward.

The ethos of moral repair was evident in the drivers' fight for an in-app tipping option, a feature Uber in particular had long resisted.[58] In coordination with the IDG, drivers launched a citywide public awareness campaign, drawing attention to their demands and building public pressure. In February 2017, IDG then formally petitioned the TLC to mandate the feature.[59] At hearings that spring and summer, scores of drivers testified, sharing stories of grueling hours and dwindling pay and demanding a system that reflected their worth.[60]

By the end of the year, the TLC passed the rule, making in-app tipping a requirement across all platforms.[61] "Today's victory is more proof that thousands of drivers coming together with one voice can make big changes," driver and IDG member Jose said on the day the TLC approved the petition.[62] But the battle wasn't over. Labor activist Tina recalled how Uber rushed to implement its own version of the tipping feature before the rule took effect.[63] "They tried to take the wind out of our sails," she said. Still, drivers weren't deterred, shifting their focus to bigger demands like pushing for 20, 25, and 30 percent tip options rather than the paltry $1, $3, and $5 options Uber was offering.

As evident in their tip option initiative, drivers didn't confine their calls for moral repair to one another; they broadcast them across the diverse participants in the ride-hail circuit. They testified in public hearings, blogged about their experiences, and shared their struggles with journalists and researchers—anyone willing to listen.[64] In a 2018 *Forbes* article, for example, Uber driver Henry declared, "People talk about sweatshops in other countries, but they don't realize there's a big sweatshop in every U.S. city. Drivers are working at least 10 to 15 hours a day every day, drivers are dying, and I think that's also a tragedy."[65] By making their grievances public, drivers forced others—providers, regulators, riders, and society at large—to bear witness to their suffering, imparting on them a moral obligation to enact change.[66]

As drivers made their grievances public, they challenged not only the platforms but also the complicity of those who benefited from their exploitation. Fahad addressed the issue directly, turning to me as a symbolic stand-in for all riders. "You want a cheap ride," he said, "but you're not thinking about what you are actually doing. You are feeding this big corporation who is depriving and taking—you know, violating all the rights from the drivers." He articulated a moral standard: "If one person is treated bad—could be African American, could be Hispanic, immigrant, or driver—that means we [in society] still have to do our work. That means we are not up to par." For Fahad and others who'd been burned by both traditional and emerging work forms, this was about more than one-off worker demands. It was about confronting the systemic injustices underpinning the US economy—a moral reckoning that was long overdue.

CONCLUSION

The dynamics portrayed in this chapter are not necessarily generalizable, even to the broader ride-hail industry. As one driver put it, "Uber in New York City is a totally different game." NYC drivers are more likely than in other places to drive full-time as their primary source of income, and the TLC represents a particularly potent local government regulator absent in other localities.[67] Nevertheless, the drivers' orchestrated alliance is revealing in its rejection of the flash intimacy observed at DTC, The Jones, and Disruption.

In one vein, these dynamics are the proverbial canary in the coal mine for other businesses. They demonstrate that an unintended consequence of contingent and fragmented labor relations—increasingly adopted by employers—is the weakening of trust between workers and managers. Without recourse to the rituals and logics of trust facilitated by social proximity and privileged relationships, other employers are likely to struggle like platform providers did in realizing worker consent and quelling dissent. A telling indication of the shifting cultural power at stake is the managerial anxiety about worker loyalty and commitment that arose amid layoffs and transitions to remote work during the COVID-19 pandemic.[68]

Yet this argument raises the question of whether a workplace without trust is a desirable alternative. Indeed, the loss of trust in institutions and one another more broadly seems to have increased dogmatism and intolerance and fueled violence (e.g., January 6, 2021). Wouldn't the loss of trust at work simply increase toxicity, paranoia, and micromanagement? Isn't platform labor—with the absence of (vertical) trust—still characterized by bad, even worse, labor conditions than elsewhere?

Platform working conditions are not good, but neither are working conditions elsewhere. What's different in this setting is that workers did not see their suffering as noble, and they refused to wallow in it while tuning their understandings of trust and intimacy to match their realities. They called out relations of trust at work for what they were: corrupted, contaminated, and unearned. Yet as they did so, they did not turn away from humanity and care—in fact they demanded it. Their stance echoes Dr. Martin Luther King Jr.'s guidance during the civil rights era: workers accepted the reality of their disappointment not as noble suffering, but as a clear-eyed foundation for acting in the hope of something better.[69]

This clear-eyed assessment of workplace trust leads to the broader question of what we should do with this knowledge. The conclusion delves into the utility of changing the culture and narratives around work as a first step. Beyond questioning whether or not we can or should trust at work, I argue that we should not have to rely on this trust to the degree that we currently do. Interpersonal trust at work can be a powerful resource, but as I explain, equal and just workplaces will require changes in workplace structure and employment policy. Otherwise, when the trust fall fails, we'll all come crashing down.

Conclusion

There's been a cultural doubling down on the "human" aspects of work in recent years. "Now more than ever the world needs to shift its focus to human-centricity," the CEO of a global staffing company declared at the World Economic Forum's 2023 Davos meeting.[1] Meanwhile, business and management articles proclaim "Leaders in the Digital Age Must Think, Act, and Be Human" and "When Your Technical Skills Are Eclipsed, Your Humanity Will Matter More Than Ever."[2] Against the backdrop of rising automation and the proliferation of artificial intelligence, this emphasis feels understandable. Our capacity for creative thinking, empathy, and connection offers a comforting antidote to fears of a depersonalized, robotic future of work. Focusing on the interpersonal also helps offset some of the harsher realities of work today, like wage gaps and job insecurity. More intuitively, who wouldn't gravitate toward decency and connection? After all, no one wants to labor within an emotionally barren—or worse, toxic—workplace.

But beneath the seductive appeal of these narratives lies something unsettling. While human ingenuity holds the promise of tomorrow's solutions, it's been equally instrumental in creating the crises of today. Capitalism and technology—often cast as humanity's foil—are not soulless forces but human-made systems, born of individual decisions, shaped by group priorities, and steeped in cultural values.[3] Compounding this tension is the way these portrayals idealize human relationships, glossing over well-documented dangers like manipulation, abuse, and exploitation that can emerge within interpersonal connections.[4] At the same time, values like dignity, respect, and kindness—when paraded as distinctive virtues—are not recognized as fundamental workplace rights but instead framed as discretionary perks, contingent on workplace culture or leadership style.

Human connection is not a panacea for all of work's ills. In fact, these connections are often a source of strain and tension. Bonds with colleagues and supervisors can be enriching and emotionally rewarding, but they require significant investments of time and energy. Moreover, the benefits of work relationships are neither guaranteed nor equally distributed. Close ties can tether people to jobs and organizations that don't meet their needs, and even trusted mentors and peers can be a source of disappointment and betrayal. The flexibility exercised through one relationship can deprive another through favoritism and bias. Nevertheless, any disruptions to workplace ties are a liability for the labor market, making it necessary to continually tend to them. In sum, workplace intimacies are far more ambivalent than mainstream narratives about humanity, teamwork, and goodwill suggest.

This book unravels that ambivalence, showing how people stretch and pull interpersonal trust to bridge the gap between the image of a romanticized "human" workplace and its more complicated reality. In doing so, *Trust Fall* invites readers to question the stories we tell about work and the silent bargains we make to navigate it. Readers will recognize their own experiences in the text: the ache of belonging that prompts participation in trials by fire and the mix of anxiety and satisfaction that percolates in the trenches. Some will nod in recognition, recalling the tired compulsion to show up for happy hours or the resigned smile at a manager's claim that their hands are tied. Others may cringe, thinking back on moments they confused social ease for the freedom to act without restraint. Managers might even second-guess long-held leadership strategies. For those knowingly burdened by the weight of trust, the book offers validation; for others, it names the quiet unease they've long felt but couldn't articulate. By interrogating these dynamics, *Trust Fall* offers not only a critique but a vocabulary—a way to articulate our experiences of work and to spark fresh, urgent conversations about its future.

EMPOWERING NEW CONVERSATIONS

Trust Fall moves the conversation beyond platitudes about workplace humanity, shifting the focus toward the political dimensions of power and its distribution.[5] The term *trust fall* itself brings attention to the individual vulnerabilities and burdens imposed by the erosion of traditional structures of work stability—such as internal career ladders and union protections—while revealing how these changes consolidate power in the hands of employers. Similarly, concepts like humanity bubbles offer a framework and language for naming and talking about the hard-to-specify and often convoluted processes through which workers are both lured and guilted into giving their all at work. When integrated with cryptocorporations, this concept can also help fuel discussions about how the interpersonal minutiae within humanity bubbles serve to distract from broader structural issues. Collectively, the book's vocabulary equips workers with the cultural tools to challenge and rewrite an unfair social contract that expects people to devote themselves to jobs and institutions that will never love them back.

It is also my hope that this vocabulary can help those critiquing the status quo to rebuff accusations of being self-centered, brattish, or naïve. Such labels seek to divide the workforce across age, occupation, and industry groups, undermining worker solidarity. Regardless of whether one is a Gen Zer or a baby boomer, toiling in restaurants or offices, occupying part-time entry-level roles or high-ranking managerial positions, workers of all stripes will likely find themselves entangled in the trust fall at some point in their working lives. While each group experiences the trust fall's consequences differently, their shared navigation of today's turbulent work landscape offers a potentially powerful basis for solidarity. By providing a language rich enough to encapsulate both difference and commonality, the book helps lay the groundwork for a broader sense of worker consciousness and a more robust labor movement.

To accommodate that goal, the concepts presented are intentionally "fuzzy"—much like trust itself—lacking both clear definitional boundaries and resisting binary categorizations such as good or bad, right or wrong. Take for example the term *flash intimacy*. The language invites readers to reflect on how quickly trust must be forged in the workplace while also highlighting how interpersonal trust is often at odds with and constrained by the broader conditions of work. The concept is thus both nascent and multilayered, ripe for productive debate and elaboration. It raises useful and lingering questions about the interconnectedness of these two ideas: How does the ostensibly harried pace of work shape the expectations we have of one another there, and vice versa? In a related vein, the concept of *morality of the fallen* focuses on the valorization of imperfection and dysfunction within the workplace, a phenomenon which in some contexts can be empowering but in others manufactures consent to bad work conditions. Each term is deliberately multitiered and porous, providing a rich cultural base for new sensemaking about work in the US.

This new vocabulary is timely. At the height of the 2020 coronavirus pandemic, employers drew on a reservoir of interpersonal trust when asking workers to risk their health and safety, take on extra responsibilities, and transform their homes into remote offices.[6] Workers' sacrifices were reciprocated shortly after with layoffs, resistance to wage increases, and demands to return to the office.[7] Decades of unreciprocated commitments between workers and employers were accentuated in that cultural moment. As a result, US workers have started to question their relationship to work. Taking advantage of a tight labor market during the Biden years, some workers walked away from bad job situations, while others stayed on but scaled back their efforts.[8] Labor activism also increased, with unionization campaigns mounted at prominent companies such as Starbucks, Amazon, and Google, and worker strikes organized from Hollywood to auto production lines.[9]

At this important inflection point, the introduction of concepts like *communions of crisis* becomes instrumental. This language can help employees discern and articulate subtle yet harmful social processes in their workplaces, where their dedication and earnestness are manipulated to their detriment. These concepts shift the narrative focus from worker reactions (e.g., the Great Resignation, quiet quitting) to the underlying situations that prompt those reactions. Readers can also draw inspiration from the stories within the book. They might start to protect "between-the-lines" spaces from managerial interference, fostering social environments in which oppositional ideas can emerge without immediate transformation into solutions or fear of reprisal. Beyond articulating specific tactics, the book provides fodder for a collective reckoning about what "trust" is doing in the workplace and whether its pursuit is worth the risks and sacrifices it requires.

The book's focus and themes are also relevant amid the long-term decline of trust in civic life. As the text demonstrates, workers go to great lengths to build and preserve trust at work. This begs the question: Could those efforts be better served elsewhere? While it can certainly be a fulfilling social hub, work has become the primary site of interaction and connection for many people, either because they enjoy what they do or because their material needs require it.[10] By reducing the pressure on workplace ties, individuals can divert time and energy into cultivating a broader social infrastructure that transcends their jobs. They can nurture bonds with friends, family members, and neighbors, and create new ties with strangers. These investments not only promise to facilitate individual flourishing, but the robust social infrastructure they bolster offers a sturdy foundation for democracy.

GROUNDING TRUST IN EQUITABLE RELATIONS

Employers (founders, owners, governing boards, and high-level executives) delving into this text are likely interested in learning how to do trust *right* within the workplace. They may be seeking trust-building strategies and formulas or content for managerial trainings focused on avoiding common pitfalls. My aim is to temper such interests, or perhaps more accurately redirect them. *Trust Fall* reveals that rather than serving as the gold standard indicator of a healthy workplace, interpersonal trust becomes somewhat nefarious when the stakes are vastly unequal across members of an organization. Indeed, it often smooths over the rifts between peaks of workplace privilege and power, sustaining inequality.

With trust demystified, employers can better identify and address the more fundamental issue of workplace inequality. Despite projecting an image of equality, inclusivity, and diversity, many workplaces remain deeply stratified, with contemporary work habits rooted in historical systems of inequality. For example, the use of performance metrics to increase productivity can be traced back to slave plantations.[11] Notions of the "ideal worker" harken back to a male breadwinner, female homemaker model, in which women's unpaid domestic labor bolstered men's single-minded devotion to paid work.[12] While our society has undoubtedly evolved, remnants of these unequal foundations endure, perhaps most notably within segregated jobs and highly disparate pay scales across the workforce.

US industries, occupations, and even tasks are often implicitly coded by gender and race, with the feminization of care work being a paradigmatic example.[13] This pervasive trend is sustained by a configuration of factors, including cultural stereotyping, the social identity of job incumbents, credentialing processes, and referral-based hiring.[14] Consequently, white men are disproportionately favored for high-paying professional and managerial roles, while women and people of color are often channeled into lower-status, lower-paid jobs in areas like personal and social services or agriculture.[15] These divisions shape the distribution of wealth and influence within the workforce, which in turn shape relational processes (such as opportunity hoarding and social closure) that reinforce workplace inequities.[16]

In these settings, even well-meaning interactions can become problematic. Take The Jones, for example, where a clear division existed between servers and bartenders (distinguishable by their white, button-down shirts) and bussers and food runners (clad in black, Jones-branded T-shirts).[17] The former group enjoyed greater visibility—actively engaging with restaurant guests and participating in pre-shift meetings—and they generally earned higher wages, establishing a hierarchical structure that positioned them at the core of the organization, with bussers and food runners relegated to the margins. Racial and ethnic differences between the two groups compounded the divide, with servers and bartenders being primarily native-born white workers, while bussers and food runners were predominantly immigrants and people of color. This mapping of racial-ethnic differences onto the workplace hierarchy insidiously blurred the lines between professional standing and personal worth, upholding an implicit sense of white supremacy that marred interactions between the two groups.

May, a white server, admitted, "I have a little bit of white guilt." She echoed many of her peers as she described trying not to come across as arrogant in her interactions with bussers and food runners: "I'm very conscious of sort of acting like a prima donna. I go out of my way to learn the support staff's names. I develop a rapport with them. So, when I ask them to do something, I'm not just barking orders at like a Brown person in a black shirt." Despite May's considerate and well-meaning approach, her need to actively remind herself of her colleagues' dignity and moral worth is indicative of the deep fractures of inequality that existed within the restaurant. Indeed, one might conclude that her concern does more to shore up her own status—ensuring the "correct" display of privilege—than to establish meaningful empathy and social connection.[18]

Pete, a Brazilian busser, spoke to the limits of kinship within this context. He described how the trust and care expressed by servers and bartenders often felt condescending and diminishing, more akin to pity than anything else. "I don't think they see me," he said, lamenting the dehumanizing vibe of the interactions, "as a *person* like them." To front-of-house staff, Pete continued, "You're 'cute.' I feel like some people, they have the sweet love for you, but not exactly, 'Oh, that's Pete. He's a guy from Brazil, a guy who's a professional with his art, a guy who's fucking bussing tables to do his living.' They don't see it that way." Instead of feeling like a person with multifaceted identities, Pete felt reduced to a "Brown guy in a black shirt," robbed of his complexity and relegated to a position of subordinance.

Similar manifestations of inequity can be seen in other well-intentioned workplace initiatives and interactions. For example, amid the nationwide racial reckoning that followed the brutal murder of George Floyd, many organizations sought to lift marginalized voices and recruit people of color onto committees tasked with improving racial equity. Yet many Black, Brown, and Indigenous workers disproportionately felt the burden, as they were asked to do emotionally exhausting and in many cases uncompensated labor, often with little organizational commitment behind them.[19]

Through these examples, I hope employers come to see that the central site for workplace change is not at the individual or interactional level, but at the level of structures. Individual "maverick managers," for instance, are neither heroes nor villains, and their displays of humility and vulnerability are not necessarily the problem. Gendered and racialized organizations (which defined both larger workplaces like The Jones and DTC and smaller ones like Disruption) are the issue. In this context, white men can afford the risks of maverick management—and are more likely to see its dividends—while members of other social groups embrace maverick management at great peril.

The primary target of reform, then, should be the gender and racial segregation of jobs. Work segregation is a long-standing problem, but it is not an intractable one. Overcoming entrenched divides, however, will require a willingness to think differently. As a first step in this direction, employers might consider conducting an audit of their organizational charts, identifying demographic clusters, examining coinciding disparities in authority and pay, and (potentially) reconfiguring current valuations of skill. Should bartenders earn more than line cooks? Should managers be paid more than individual contributors, and should they always have more authority?

Managerial positions, in particular, offer a generative space for workplace reimagining. These positions have traditionally served as an essential step in linear career progression, distinguished by their authority, status, and pay. Yet I would argue that managers offer *different*, not superior, value than many individual contributors. By focusing on management as a job type as opposed to an organizational stratum, employers could better link individual strengths with company needs. For one, a content-first approach prompts managerial specialization—of value, because tasks typically assigned to managers, like coaching (e.g., employee motivation, professional development, team dynamics) and operations (e.g., project management, cross-team communication, and work flow) often require distinct skill sets. Additionally, this approach acknowledges that not all individual contributors want to manage, nor do they all have the appropriate skills to do so. By decoupling career advancement from people management, employers can stop promoting ill-equipped or poorly motivated individuals into the role. Instead, they can create new pathways for employee growth (and higher pay) through technical expertise, advanced specialization, or lateral exploration. These changes offer an opportunity to reconfigure power within organizations while simultaneously enabling employers to better capitalize on workers' strengths.[20]

Notably absent from the managerial tasks outlined above are hiring and evaluation decisions (including promotions, layoffs, and firings). Such decisions serve as one of the most notable levers of power within the workplace, and yet they're often obscured within the cryptocorporation. As an alternative, employers might consider the creation of an organization-wide hiring and evaluation committee. While the details of this committee would vary across organizational context, an initial framework would focus on balancing continuity and change. For example, committee members could be nominated by company leaders, be elected by the internal workforce, and follow a staggered rotation system. To avoid stagnation, committee positions would be defined by clear term limits (e.g., one to three years), and they would be compensated through a salary bump to avoid exploitation. Moreover, the committee should be representative across gender and race and employ best practices (e.g., gender- and race-neutral job descriptions and targeted outreach to underrepresented populations) to promote a diverse workforce.[21] Through this structure, employers can increase transparency and reduce the immense personal weight they have long carried in owning these pivotal decisions.[22]

Employers might also consider greater limitations on their own tenure. While the pathways into executive roles would remain consistent (e.g., through founding, hiring, or promotion), term limits would restrict the duration of each individual's leadership and power. During their tenure, leaders would continue to be accountable to performance reviews, but they would also be responsible for thinking beyond year-to-year profits, developing a term-length plan, and investing time and energy in succession planning. Following their tenure, leaders could choose to transition into a nonexecutive role or leave the company. This approach could disrupt entrenched nodes of power and opportunity hoarding, reframing executive leadership as a unique but limited opportunity for change and growth as opposed to a final career destination. Term limits could also provide a necessary check on executive compensation, ensuring it aligns with position requirements and not one's influence.[23] Perhaps most pertinent for employers, this reform could help inject a regular influx of new ideas into the organizations, fostering a more dynamic, responsive, and innovative environment that can better survive the vagaries of the market.

This book demonstrates the challenges of trust amid widespread inequity and thus demands a profound rethinking of our work structures and attitudes. One-off trainings to improve communication and empathy are not enough to support a healthy climate of cooperation and teamwork. Given the widespread forecasting of workplace change over the next several decades, employers are at an important crossroads.[24] The time is right to challenge the status quo and pursue new ways of thinking about and organizing work. The discussion presented in this section does not offer paint-by-numbers solutions, and the purchase and implementation of these ideas will vary across organizational types and industries. Nevertheless, I hope it opens new doors and pathways for employers, giving them permission to think differently and offering a starting point for brainstorming and experimentation.

SUPPORTING A GENTLER LANDING

Trust is an essential fiber of the social tapestry, facilitating connection, providing psychological safety, enabling action amid uncertainty, and serving as a foundation for hope. In the US labor system, however, too much rides on interpersonal trust, with people looking to benevolent bosses, obliging social networks, and helpful coworkers to pick up the slack of a defunct infrastructure. Without adequate legal and institutional support, interpersonal trust quickly becomes a double-edged sword. While trust nurtures collaboration and acts as a conduit of information and opportunity, it can also be manipulated, breeding corruption and fostering biases. Power imbalances exacerbate these challenges, leaving workplace relationships vulnerable to exploitation and abuse.

As noted earlier, the pull of workplace trust may be weakening as workers start to question asymmetries in the social contract of work.[25] Surveys report growing labor dissatisfaction, with many frustrated employees pulling back their efforts, switching jobs, or exiting the workforce.[26] In a telling response to these trends, employers appear to be doubling down on trust, emphasizing the importance and value of face-to-face interactions and camaraderie. After announcing layoffs in 2023, for example, Meta CEO Mark Zuckerberg issued a return-to-office mandate, explaining, "[O]ur hypothesis is that it is still easier to build trust in person and that those relationships help us work more effectively."[27]

In truth, workers are often left with little choice *but* to trust managers and colleagues. Weak labor laws and unions mean workers have limited power to negotiate their terms of employment. In the absence of strong legal safeguards, workers who challenge company protocols or managerial decisions may fear retaliation, most notably in the form of job loss. While there is always the option to leave unfavorable job situations, the scarcity of government-sanctioned social benefits limits this approach to tight labor market periods and to those advantaged enough to muster the financial coverage. Thus, without durable supports, workers settle for less-than-ideal jobs and lean on trusted managers and colleagues to help make up the difference.

I hope policymakers reading *Trust Fall* are inspired to enact institutional support measures that can supplement interpersonal workplace trust and mitigate its coerced nature. One crucial step in doing so will be to develop a *stronger institutional framework for unions*. An important vehicle of collective worker voice, unions help workers secure higher wages, demand better working conditions, and even improve job stability.[28] Unfortunately, unionization is substantially lower in the US than in many other industrialized countries: only about 10 percent of wage and salary workers compared to 65 percent in Sweden, 32 percent in Italy, and 26 percent in Canada.[29] Even as union popularity rises, membership rates continue to decline.[30]

The disconnect between union support and union membership is not simply due to worker passivity, although right-to-work laws in twenty-six states enable workers to benefit from union representation without paying dues.[31] Approximately half of nonunion workers in the US say they would join a union if they could.[32] Unfortunately, the National Labor Relations Act (NLRA) excludes large swaths of the workforce, including agricultural and domestic workers and independent contractors—fields in which women and people of color tend to be overrepresented.[33] Moreover, many employers actively suppress unionization within their companies. Amazon, for example, spent over $4 million on "union-avoidance" consultants in 2021.[34] Some employers threaten workers who try to organize, holding the loss of jobs, pay, and benefits over their heads.[35]

To address the issue, policies to strengthen worker voice would necessarily need to expand labor rights to domestic and agricultural workers as well as independent contractors. In addition, employer penalties for intervening in unionization efforts should be significantly increased. In many cases, the consequence for violating the NLRA is equivalent to a hand slap, making the breach worth the union-busting outcomes for many companies.[36] Greater penalty fines and criminal charges, in particular, could help deter employers' anti-union tactics. Labor law should also expand workers' representation options beyond exclusive collective bargaining unions, which are sometimes out of reach. Other, less potent forms of representation might include elected workplace monitors (individuals who ensure employers' internal compliance with labor laws), work councils (nonsupervisory workers who confer with management about issues such as health and safety, scheduling, equity, and new technologies), and worker seats on corporate boards.[37]

While these policies would help to expand and broaden worker representation, additional reforms could extend unions' reach. Sectoral bargaining—industry-level bargaining systems like those popular in Europe—could help unions move beyond a firm-by-firm negotiating approach to support more workers.[38] Indeed, this model has been shown to be more effective at reducing income inequities than the enterprise model that currently dominates in the US.[39] Additionally, workplace topics beyond wages and working conditions, such as the environmental and community consequences of business decisions, should be available for union negotiation. Under current laws, these topics are off-limits, but they often have a strong influence on workers' lives (e.g., housing costs, consumer privacy).[40]

In addition to strengthening unions, *better employment protections and standards* could provide structural guardrails that would make interpersonal trust less consequential. Most notably, a transition from "at-will" employment to a "just-cause" dismissal standard would bolster job security, alleviating the intense uncertainty and insecurity that US workers feel in their jobs. Under the prevailing system, private-sector employers can fire workers for arbitrary reasons and without warning, and in the case of illegal firings, the burden of mounting a legal challenge is shouldered almost entirely by individual workers.[41] A just-cause system, in contrast, would require employers to provide workers with due process, notifying them of performance concerns prior to termination, offering them adequate—and legally protected—time to address the concerns, and specifying a reason for termination that meets an agreed upon and predefined standard.[42] In addition, mandatory severance pay—at least in some conditions of dismissal—and limits to noncompete agreements could further prevent terminations from fully upending workers' lives, easing existential anxiety.[43]

Wage and work-hour standards can also reduce workers' vulnerability to abuses of vertical trust by protecting their income and schedule from managerial whims. The purchasing power of the current federal minimum wage has dropped by 20 percent since it was last updated in 2009. It is time for a substantial increase, and future increases should be tied to inflation to ensure that wages keep pace with the cost of living.[44] Additionally, adjusting loopholes in pay protections—such as allowing employers to count worker tips toward minimum hourly wages and salary exemption thresholds for overtime pay—would further ensure that workers are paid adequately for their time.[45] In terms of work hours, paid sick days should be universal.[46] Additional schedule protections might include requirements for schedules to be posted at least two weeks in advance, protected "right to request" schedule arrangements (that protect workers from retaliation), and extra pay for on-call scheduling.[47]

Employment protections and standards are only as strong as their enforcement. The current system is insufficient and overwhelmed.[48] The dominant complaint-based approach to enforcement targets individual cases versus systemic issues.[49] "Fissured" workplaces (in which multiple companies manage labor terms and contracts) make it difficult to pinpoint compliance responsibility, and mandatory arbitration clauses and class action waivers reduce workers' legal recourse to violations.[50] Alternatively, a "strategic enforcement" approach would analyze broad noncompliance patterns within an industry to tackle systemic problems, and "joint employer" standards would hold all companies sharing control of workers' employment accountable.[51] In addition, mandatory arbitration clauses and class action waivers, which almost always benefit the employer, should be banned.[52]

Finally, a *more robust public safety net* can help reduce workers' dependence on employers. Unemployment insurance serves as an essential lifeline for workers who lose their jobs, providing them with cash benefits to stay afloat. Yet unemployment insurance coverage varies across states.[53] Establishing a federal minimum for the benefit duration period (e.g., twenty-six weeks) could help strengthen this crucial support.[54] In addition, policymakers might consider a needs-based approach to unemployment insurance's wage replacement, with, for example, low earners receiving 75 percent of their prior wages and higher earners receiving 50 percent (up to a maximum limit). An additional dependent allowance would provide further support to parents and caregivers.

Decoupling benefits such as health care and retirement plans from the labor market can further strengthen workers' position vis-à-vis employers. Yet publicly sponsored social insurance programs are under constant attack. The development of legal protections and funding structures that shield programs such as Medicaid, Medicare, and Social Security from short-term political trends and partisan agendas should therefore be a top priority. At the same time, other measures, such as mandatory employer retirement contributions (in addition to wages) and low-cost, portable benefits programs can also help reduce the grip employers have on workers' well-being.[55]

Moreover, building up the care infrastructure in the US can help workers manage family needs without one-on-one bargaining with employers. By implementing federally mandated paid family and medical leave, the US can join the ranks of peer nations to ensure that workers can care for health and family needs without the risk of financial ruin.[56] In addition, affordable childcare is essential, and while universal childcare is a long-term goal, income-based childcare subsidies can offer lower-income families support in the interim. In terms of eldercare, the expansion of home and community-based services can offer a middle-road solution that maximizes patients' independence while minimizing costs.

In a political climate where deregulation and anti-union sentiments dominate federal policy, the recommendations in this book (summarized in table 4) face an uphill battle. Yet these structural changes remain crucial for addressing systemic inequities in the workplace. Such reforms are not simply matters of policy but of collective responsibility, requiring advocacy, persistence, and a willingness to reimagine deeply entrenched norms. Without a concerted effort to counteract the erosion of workers'

Table 4. Summary of Recommendations for Employers and Policymakers

Employers	*Policymakers*
• **Conduct organizational audit:** identify demographic clusters and disparities. • **Evaluate and challenge skill valuations:** assess whether current pay structures align with roles. • **Redesign career progression models:** decouple career advancement from people management, creating opportunities for growth based more firmly on individual skill, expertise, and interest. • **Establish a rotating and representative hiring and evaluation committee:** foster more democratic decision-making and promote a more diverse workforce. • **Implement executive term limits:** disrupt entrenched power dynamics and encourage fresh strategic thinking.	*Union framework* • **Expand labor rights:** include domestic workers, agricultural workers, and independent contractors. • **Increase penalties for union busting:** deter employer interference. • **Broaden worker representation and bargaining rights:** introduce options like workplace monitors and work councils, enable sectoral bargaining, and expand the scope of union negotiations. *Employment protections/standards* • **Transition from at-will to just-cause system, ban noncompetes, and increase severance:** improve workers' job security. • **Strengthen wage and hour standards:** increase pay floors, ensure overtime and on-call pay, and mandate advanced scheduling and sick leave. • **Ban restrictive employment practices and enhance enforcement:** ensure worker power and improve employer accountability. *Public safety net* • **Transition to a more stable social benefits system:** reduce workers' dependence on employers. • **Strengthen the care infrastructure:** provide caregivers with paid leave to improve the cost and quality of caregiving.

rights and protections, the burden of trust will continue to fall unevenly across the workforce, exacerbating existing inequalities.

. . . . .

Trust is a precious resource in today's employment landscape, serving as a conduit of power and mobility, a mark of honor, and the key to belonging. Against the backdrop of widespread societal distrust, the concentration of trust within our work lives may seemingly offer moments of refuge—a sense of sanity—in an increasingly fragmented and chaotic world. Yet this concentration also magnifies the already outsized power of business owners and corporations, entities that in the US often enjoy greater rights and protections than the average citizen.[57] A monopoly on trust allows employers to more easily appropriate narratives of care and community and shape personal connections, channeling them toward organizational goals rather than individual and collective needs.[58] The result is a society in which work is elevated as a primary life force even as it perpetuates inequities that undermine social cohesion and stability.[59]

In the years since this research was conducted, the COVID-19 pandemic created a rare opportunity to confront long-standing assumptions about work. It brought attention to the undervalued labor of "essential" workers, challenged rigid notions of when and where professional work must occur, and exposed the untenable demands placed on individuals juggling care and work responsibilities.[60] Perhaps most disturbing, the pandemic revealed how readily economic interests were valued above human lives and well-being—an idea laid bare by Texas Lieutenant Governor Dan Patrick's call for people to sacrifice their well-being to reopen the economy, epitomized in his comment, "There are more important things than living."[61] Moments like these revealed not just the fragility but the duplicity of workplace trust.

As employers aggressively advocate for a "return to normal," the lessons emerging from this book urge caution in trusting them or normalcy. Echoes of the hierarchy of trustworthiness, for example, can be heard in employers' requests for professionals to return to the office. These pleas or mandates—often framed as efforts to restore interpersonal trust—coexist with surveillance tools and policies that betray a fundamental distrust in remote workers' discipline and productivity.[62] Meanwhile, hybrid work solutions are offered up as "gifts," even as these arrangements are configured to serve employers' interests by reducing costs while preserving the managerial benefits of interpersonal connection.[63] In hourly work, the hands-tied rationale remains alive and well. Employers lament labor shortages and claim an inability to raise wages as they redirect the burden of fair compensation onto customers. The introduction of "tip screens" into new service interactions and elevated benchmarks in tipping norms exemplify these shifts—practices that reframe living wages into an issue of individual generosity rather than employer responsibility.

Instead of perpetuating the fetishization of trust as the crux of employment, *Trust Fall* challenges us to imagine a different path forward—one on which trust and connection will be reclaimed from the workplace and reinvested in the broader fabric of society. It invites us to ask: What if the energy we expend trusting mediocre managers was rerouted toward building mutual support with our neighbors? What if we redirected the frustrations we vent through "proper" workplace channels into collective action demanding better working conditions? Instead of nurturing "workplace families," what if we prioritized care and solidarity within our broader communities? In so doing, we would take the first steps in restoring trust as a foundation for relationships and social contracts that foster true reciprocity, accountability, and equity.

Acknowledgments

I imagine writing a book is never easy. This one proved particularly challenging due to the many tumultuous events that unfolded during the process—from global and cross-country moves to car accidents, family health emergencies, and the devastating impacts of not one but two hurricanes. I want to begin, perhaps unconventionally, by expressing my gratitude to my family for their unwavering support. Noah, my partner in life, kept me grounded and nurtured throughout it all. My heartfelt thanks go to my parents, Liz and Lu, for their unshakeable belief in me and their eagerness to problem solve alongside me; to my brother, Daniel, for his dry humor and for housing me during key moments of my writing; to my in-laws, Sue, Lou, and Nicole, for their unconditional acceptance; and to Sam, our dog, whose spunk and attitude make life fun. I am deeply privileged to have such an exceptional family, and I am profoundly grateful for their love and support.

My wider network of family and friends has cheered on this project for years. Thank you to Mary Farren (in memoriam), Mary Molloy, Jill Kaner, Fred Howe, Gayle Shelden, Eleanor McMahan, Christina Fite, Karrie Gawron (who helped produce the figure for chapter 1), Carolina Gastley, Joris Gjata, Shanta Dey, Lisa Gulesserian, McCaye Nixon, Suneha Seetahul, Leah Brackett, and Jamie Patton. Special thanks to Joshua Brown for being the ideal writing accountability partner and for reminding me that "inching" is how books get done.

To the people at The Jones, DTC, Disruption, and the NYC ride-hail circuit, thank you for opening up a piece of your lives to me. Your good-faith engagement with this project transformed my understanding of workplace trust from black and white into a full technicolor experience. I hope you feel that same richness reflected back in the analysis. There are people I can't name individually to protect confidentiality; however, I do feel comfortable thanking Molly Buchholz, Juanina Kocher, and Jordan Snow for the inroads they helped me make in the field.

The National Science Foundation (Award No. 1738706) and the University of Virginia Bankard Fund for Political Economy provided crucial early-stage financial support, enabling this research to take off and freeing resources for me to later hire developmental editors. Joanna Pinto-Coelho offered invaluable feedback, helping me refine my ideas and clarify my writing. Olson Pook is an exceptional writing coach who often believed in my ideas more than I did and pushed me to fully embrace the vocabulary and framework I developed. Thanks also for early manuscript planning and advice from Audra Wolfe and Carolyn Bond.

This project took root at the University of Virginia, guided by the ever-inspiring Allison Pugh, whose intellectual energy gave it the spark it needed to grow. I am also grateful to Elizabeth Gorman, who saw me as a scholar of work long before I claimed the title for myself, and to Ira Bashkow, Simone Polillo, Andrea Press, and Josipa Roksa, whose mentorship shaped my intellectual trajectory. My graduate colleagues, especially Matthew Braswell, Michele Darling, Denise Deutschlander, Megan Jeulfs, Andrew Lynn, Candace Miller, Licheng Qian, and Catalina Vallejo, fostered a lively and thoughtful academic community at UVA. I am also thankful to Jaime Hartless, Fauzia Husain, and Gabriella Smith for sustaining our writing group many years after graduate school. And to the UVA alumni—particularly, Tristan Bridges, Jenifer Silva, Christina Simko, Benjamin Snyder, Julia Ticona, and Francesca Tripodi—who extended a hand to those coming through behind you, I am so grateful.

I've had the privilege of belonging to several other enriching academic communities. At the University of Georgia, I appreciate the productive dialogue I had with James Dowd, Diana Graizbord, Jeff Shelton, and Justine Tinkler, as well as the collective discussion following my colloquium presentation. While I was a postdoc at the University of Sydney School of Business, Marian Baird, Rae Cooper, Meraiah Foley, Elizabeth Hill, Elspeth Probyn, and Ariadne Vromen helped me become a more interdisciplinary and global thinker. The Work and Family Researchers Network's Early Career Fellowship Program and the American Sociological Association's Organizations, Occupations, and Work Section provided additional academic refuge, giving me safe spaces to fully expand my thinking. And beyond these institutions, thanks are also due to those who shared thoughts, reviewed materials, and provided exemplars from their own work, often after simply receiving a "cold" email from me. Thank you, especially, to Caitlyn Collins, Sarah Damaske, Katherine Maich, Ashley Mears, Megan Tobias Neely, Lindsey Trimble O'Connor, Patrick Reilly, Aliya Hamid Rao, and Jaclyn Wong.

Naomi Schneider's belief in this book from the initial proposal stage, along with her patience through several delays, meant the world to me. Thanks also to the entire UC Press team for shepherding this project to publication.

And to the many coffee shops where this book was written—especially Swallow Café in Brooklyn, Shenandoah Joe's in Charlottesville, The Bower in Manly, Field Day Coffee in San Luis Obispo, Jittery Joe's and Hendershot's in Athens, Urban Grounds in Tarpon Springs, and Harbor Coffee in Atlanta—thank you for providing the space and the fuel to bring this book to fruition.

APPENDIX Crafting Resonance, a Lyrical Approach

Trust Fall is in a strange position vis-à-vis trust. It delivers what I hope is a potent critique of interpersonal trust in the workplace. But at the same time, the book makes a bid for your trust as a reader, rooted in the rigor of its data, the integrity of its argument, and the perspective it brings. This is a different kind of trust: expert trust. Yet like all forms of trust, it's no less vulnerable to abuse.

There's been much hand-wringing lately about what makes for trustworthy social science.[1] Some argue trust in research relies on its replicability, while others call for fact-checking and unfiltered access to data as mechanisms for ensuring validity.[2] Yet realities—especially social realities—are rarely as static or simple as such measures presume. For example, two people may look at the same sky and agree it's blue, but this doesn't mean the sky is always blue or that their perceptions of blue are identical. Each gaze has its own lens, and realities are multiple and fluid.[3]

In an era of "alternative facts," it may seem risky—even irresponsible—to highlight the plurality and partiality of truth. Yet even so-called objective truths—when cherry-picked or misappropriated—become powerful kindling for disinformation and conspiracy theories, illustrating that objectivity alone is no safeguard against misuse.[4] Thus, rather than defensively stripping down complexity, social science should contribute its strongest assets to the conversation: its ability to illuminate the role of context, perspective, and power.

To this end, Allison Pugh and I make the case for *resonance* as a standard of value, particularly in regard to the production of qualitative research.[5] By resonance, we do not simply mean a text is relevant. Resonant ideas must do more than echo one's social world; they must produce a chord that honors that world's nuance, tension, richness, and diversity. Resonant social science connects what we know to what we don't, bridging cultural worlds distanced through congealed social practices, beliefs, and institutions. They are the studies that ignite "a-ha" moments, providing the tools—language, images, or framework—to help surface overlooked experiences or give shape to inchoate feelings, allowing us to see familiar realities in unexpected ways.[6] As English poet and cultural critic Matthew Arnold once put it, when resonant ideas "reach society, the touch of truth is the touch of life, and there is a stir and growth everywhere."[7]

Of course, resonance isn't a fixed trait but emerges within particular relationships.[8] That's to say, a cultural object or idea does not necessarily possess some essential resonance, nor does that resonance unfold as a uniform process. Instead, something becomes resonant in specific contexts, and its resonance evolves over time. A song, for example, may resonate painfully with one listener suffering from heartbreak, evoke giddiness in another falling in love, and later strike a chord of nostalgia for both. Each individual interaction, each new situation, adds layers of significance, giving resonance its dynamic quality.

With *Trust Fall*, my aim was not to offer universal explanations or prescriptive truths, but rather to cultivate resonance, to spark moments of recognition and inquiry that reveal the layered complexities of social realities. I sought to create a space in which readers could grapple with the tensions, contradictions, and power dynamics that shape workplace trust, igniting a dynamic and evolving conversation about our collective and individual relationships to work.

A LYRICAL APPROACH

The late Palestinian American literary critic and political activist Edward Said criticized the Western narrative form as, among other things, too linear and neat. The narrative, Said argued, condensed the multiplicity of Palestinian life into a singular entity and reduced its characters to mere stereotypes. Palestinian prose, he pointed out, was less ordered but more revealing, reflecting the complex textures of precarity, suffering, resilience, and diversity that defined the authors' lives. "Our characteristic mode, then, is not narrative," Said wrote, "but rather broken narratives, fragmentary compositions, and self-consciously staged testimonials, in which the narrative voice keeps stumbling over itself, its obligations, and its limitations."[9]

I was struck with a similar sentiment as I gathered and analyzed data for this book. US workers, I observed, were not free *or* oppressed, satisfied *or* dissatisfied, consenting *or* resisting, naïve *or* strategically sophisticated; they were all of the above, and sometimes all at once. Moreover, the organizations I studied were constantly shifting—growing, downsizing, even growing while downsizing—so much so that most of the people I spoke with are no longer in the same role, many are not at the same organization, and one company (Disruption) has ceased to exist altogether. Thus, the scenes I observed and the stories people told me felt splintered and partial, like pieces of broken reflective glass that would never quite be assembled into a functioning mirror.

To package the narrative of trust at work too neatly would do a disservice to the heterogeneity, complexity, and fluidity of the American work landscape; it would, in other words, impede the book's resonance. *Trust Fall's* structure, therefore, follows a more "lyrical" approach, as suggested by Andrew Abbott, prioritizing moment, emotion, and location.[10]

Rather than documenting and explaining social reality in a linear fashion, a focus on the *moment* brings reality, in all its dynamism, to life. In this spirit, *Trust Fall* organizes its empirical chapters around three distinct yet loosely connected moments, assembled under the umbrella of a broader theme or idea. The workplaces—DTC, The Jones, and Disruption—serve as unique canvases for exploring these moments, which capture recurring patterns of workplace trust while leaving room for nuance and variation.

Zooming in on moments allows the text to highlight the meaning and significance embedded in seemingly mundane work routines and interactions.[11] The drama of the moment is deconstructed, as the text provides background, describes the stakes, and interrogates power dynamics. This deep dive into the subtleties of the moment can, at times, make for choppy or disjointed copy. But within each dip and through each turn, understanding becomes more multidimensional, spreading its tentacles out beyond the text to connect to readers' personal and political landmarks in ways that invite reflective engagement.

Similarly, the book as a whole is structured around three motifs: humanity bubbles, morality of the fallen, and trust-tuning. These motifs are not links in a causal chain that unfold linearly to create flash intimacy. Rather, they are unique yet sometimes overlapping snippets of a social dynamic, each breathing detail and insight into what is happening with trust at work. Flash intimacy and its motifs do not reflect or extend one cohesive theoretical paradigm; instead, these concepts draw on multiple ideas from across disciplines and genres that help to flesh out individual moments. Said differently, the moments in this book are not arranged in service of Theory; instead, theories are used in service of the moments to provide context and perspective.

The flow of *emotion* across a social scene, much like the contrast dye used in medical imaging, can reveal its internal contours, identifying surges of energy and sites of friction and injury. Through an intentional blend of observations and interviews, *Trust Fall* invites readers to explore the space in which interiority meets sociality, probing the dissonances and harmonies that emerge when various meanings, relationships, and structures of work converge. The analysis mines muffled tears, sudden outbursts, snarky remarks, and small gestures (alongside individual accounts and observed interactions), using these elements as a barometer for charting the visceral dynamics of workplace climates. The goal is not for readers to merely feel for workers and managers but to feel *with* them, learning how they attach to certain beliefs and ideas, how their affects are labeled and embodied, and how these emotional undercurrents shape individual dispositions, team dynamics, and decision-making.

The book also pays close attention to emotions that remain unexpressed, using their absence or concealment as cues for decoding what Arlie Hochschild calls a setting's "feeling rules."[12] These, Hochschild explains, are the norms that guide not only what we feel but also what (and how) we think we *should* feel. Crucially, these feeling rules often align emotional expression with prevailing cultural beliefs about race, gender, and class.[13] They dictate who can or should feel what: for instance, that women should display care and empathy, while only white men can be angry or confrontational. These feeling rules thus underscore the role of emotions as a medium of power, illuminating how individuals strategically and sometimes forcefully use emotions in their self-presentation and interactions with others.[14]

Throughout the research, my own emotions often acted as compass and conduit, helping me tap into hard-to-access aspects of the workplace. For instance, a few days after I invited Adam, DTC's CEO, to participate in an interview, his close colleague Devon casually approached me, peppering me with questions about the study. My body tensed with anxiety as I worried whether my access to DTC may be on the line, and the encounter imprinted on me how personal ties among influential figures can be harnessed to safeguard power. Similarly, I felt a surge of shame when I didn't immediately see myself in others' descriptions of trustworthiness: an emotional jolt that ironically deepened my understanding of trust's moral dimensions. These emotional encounters were thus key to the analysis.[15]

Location is perhaps misleading nomenclature for the emphasis on perspective within lyrical sociology. Intellectual curiosity and rigor are not derived simply from inhabiting a particular location but from traveling across locations. *Trust Fall* takes on this nomadic stance, digging beneath the surface of a seeming consensus of workplace trust to map an internal cacophony of ambivalence, contingency, and contradiction. The journey cuts through different work settings, across organizational divisions and roles, and within crossroads of inequalities, identifying pockets of privilege and disadvantage that sometimes conflict and other times overlap. In traversing this variegated tangle of meaning and power, inconsistencies and peculiarities are not detours from the journey but are in fact integral points along the way.

Both the advantages and pitfalls of this nomadic stance are shaped, in part, by my own social position. My father and his family were born in Egypt, where our roots go back many generations but which we were forced to leave in the 1950s. As Sephardic Jews, we are both a minority in the Muslim-dominated Arab region and a minority among US Jews, who more commonly identify as Ashkenazi. The other half of my family is also relatively new to the US, with my maternal grandmother arriving in New York from Scotland as a widowed woman in her early thirties. My extended family is thus a diaspora scattered across cities and continents. These ancestral ties offered a stark contrast growing up in a small, rural, majority white, majority Baptist town in northeastern Georgia. Lacking a southern accent and sporting a headful of curly hair and an olive complexion growing up, neighbors, teachers, and friends struggled to place me, perennially probing "where I was from," whether I was "mixed," and—because neither of my parents was Protestant—if I wanted to be "saved." As a result, my sense of self has always felt simultaneously expansive and provisional, linked to many but fully belonging to none.

Consequently, I'm primed to read a room, adapt quickly, and move fluidly between groups, attributes I've found useful as a researcher and analyst. This perspective has helped me recognize the constructed and contextualized quality of social identity, the biases and power of normativity, and the resolute voices of the repressed. At the same time, my desire to fit in—coupled with the privilege of being able to "pass" as a member of various groups—hinders my view. Familiar as I am with the costs of personal erasure tied to assimilation, I'm less attuned to the experiences that emerge from standing out or actively resisting conformity. While I strive to let the voices of my research participants and scholars from different social positions guide me where I fall short, secondhand knowledge only partially fills the historical, material, and political gaps that exist.

By weaving together resonant moments, emotional attunement, and nomadic exploration, *Trust Fall* illuminates the textured landscape of workplace trust in ways that a more conventional narrative might miss. Like the workplace relationships it examines, the book's methodology acknowledges that truth emerges not from rigid frameworks but through careful attention to context, contradiction, and lived experience. The result is not one singular story but an ongoing dialogue that hopefully continues even after the reader closes the book.

Notes

INTRODUCTION

1. I use pseudonyms to protect the confidentiality of research participants, except for ride-hail companies like Uber and Lyft, as they neither participated in this research nor were formal employers of the drivers I interviewed. For more on the debates around using pseudonyms in social science research, refer to Jerolmack and Murphy, "Ethical Dilemmas and Social Scientific Trade-Offs"; and Pugh and Mosseri, "Trust-Building Versus 'Just Trust Me.'"

2. Big tech, finance, and consulting firms offer almost six-figure starting salaries, as noted by Borchers, "Behold, the New Starting Salary." In contrast, career websites like Indeed, Payscale, and Glassdoor put starting marketing and advertising salaries between $35,000 and $40,000. All four industries are known for their demanding work conditions and long hours.

3. I capitalize racial signifiers like Black and Brown in the text, but I do not capitalize white or its derivatives in order to reject the sentiments and practices of white supremacists. The cost of this choice is the risk of upholding socially constructed racial hierarchies by enabling whites to appear unraced—an "unmarked" category implicitly serving as a reference for other races.

4. Slack is a communications platform that's popular in many modern offices.

5. DiMaggio, *Twenty-First-Century Firm*; Kalleberg, *Good Jobs, Bad Jobs*; and Rosenfeld, *What Unions No Longer Do.*

6. For a helpful review of the robust literature on social networks in labor market outcomes, refer to Castilla, Lan, and Rissing, "Social Networks and Employment" (parts 1 and 2).

7. While social scientists lack a consensus regarding the definition of trust, "a willingness to make oneself vulnerable to another" is used as a baseline definition here, following others such as Mayer, Davis, and Schoorman, "Integrative Model of Organizational Trust"; Rousseau et al., "Not So Different After All"; and Schilke, Reimann, and Cook, "Trust in Social Relations."

8. For more on trust as glue, refer to Elster, *Cement of Society*. For more on trust as lubricant, refer to Arrow, *Limits of Organization*; and Fukuyama, *Trust*.

9. Simmel, for example, argues that trust is "one of the most synthetic forces within society," and without it, "society itself would disintegrate." *Sociology of Georg Simmel*, 318 and *Philosophy of Money*, 177. On institutional trust, refer to Bachmann and Inkpen, "Understanding Institutional-Based Trust Building"; and Zucker, "Production of Trust." On expert trust, refer to Giddens, *Consequences of Modernity*. On generalized trust, refer to Fukuyama, *Trust*; and Yamagishi, "Trust as Social Intelligence." On interpersonal trust, refer to Cook, "Networks, Norms, and Trust"; Lewis and Weigert, "Trust as a Social Reality"; and Weber and Carter, *Social Construction of Trust*.

10. Pew Research Center, *Public Trust in Government*.

11. Edelman, "2018 Edelman Trust Barometer"; Gallup, "Confidence in Institutions"; Davern et al., "General Social Survey"; Gottfried, Walker, and Mitchell, "Skepticism of News Media Healthy"; and AP-NORC Center and the GSS Staff. Confidence in Institutions.

12. Barbaro et al., "Public Health Officials Under Seige"; Natanson, "Trust in Teachers Is Plunging"; Van Green, "Few Are Confident in Tech Companies."

13. According to an independent analysis of Pew Research Center's "American Trends Panel Wave 40" data, slightly over half of white Americans report trust in the police and scientists, while less than 10 percent of Black Americans and less than 15 percent of Latinx Americans report trusting them. For more on the institutional dynamics that drive these trust discrepancies refer to Alexander, *New Jim Crow*; Nelson, *Body and Soul*; and Roberts, *Fatal Invention*.

14. These questions are part of the 2022 GSS Quality of WorkLife module (latest available).

15. Refer to the 2008 National Study of the Changing Workforce (latest available public use data); and *Edelman Trust Barometer* (multiple editions between 2018 and 2022). In an independent analysis of the 2018 data (year of study completion), I found that at least 80 percent of all race, gender, and class groups (divided into income quartiles) said they trusted their managers and separately could rely on coworkers (the one exception being just 79 percent of Black respondents saying they trusted their managers).

16. Putnam, *Bowling Alone*.

17. To be sure, workplace trust complicates the conventional typology. While it often takes the form of interpersonal trust, it operates within institutional settings.

18. Generalized trust (measured here and also sometimes referred to as "social trust") is admittedly also quite abstract, but it focuses more explicitly on (albeit imagined) interpersonal dynamics. In 2018, 32 percent of GSS respondents reported such trust, compared to 46 percent in 1972. In 2022 (last available wave), trust of others dropped even lower, to 25 percent.

19. While 64 percent of the top 20 percent of 2018 American earners ($75,000+) believed most people could be trusted, only 34 percent of the bottom 20 percent of earners (<$17,500) agreed (income distinctions based on the Current Population Survey (CPS) Annual Social and Economic (ASEC) Supplement). Meanwhile, studies of particularized trust or trust of people "like me" are helpfully reviewed in Smith, "Race and Trust."

20. Coleman, *Rules of Estrangement*; Cox, "State of American Friendship"; and Pillemer, *Fault Lines*.

21. Reilly, "Culture Wars Could Be Coming"; and Volpe, "Holiday Dread."

22. Dimock, "How Americans View Trust." The political scientists Nathan Kalmoe and Lilliana Mason further report that over 40 percent of partisan voters view the other side as "downright evil." *Radical American Partisanship.*

23. Pugh, *Tumbleweed Society.*

24. This contrasts with the "just-cause" framework of other rich democracies (and found in US public and unionized workplaces). Unlike at-will employment, in which individual workers must mount legal challenges and prove an illegal firing (narrowly defined), the just-cause framework requires *employers* to document and prove a valid reason for firing. Andrias and Hertel-Fernandez, *Ending At-Will Employment*; and ILO, "Valid and Prohibited Grounds". These challenges are further exacerbated by employers' use of mandatory individual arbitration agreements, which compel workers to waive access to federal courts and collective arbitration; refer to Colvin, "Growing Use of Mandatory Arbitration." C-level executives represent a notable exception to at-will employment in the United States, with their contracts typically specifying a need for a termination rationale and/or guaranteeing a severance payout; refer to Schwab and Thomas, "Empirical Analysis of Employment Contracts."

25. Cappelli, *New Deal at Work*; Davis, *Managed by the Markets*; and Ho, "Disciplining Investment Bankers."

26. Naidu and Carr, "If You Don't Like Your Job"; US Department of the Treasury, "State of Labor Market Competition." In April 2024 the Federal Trade Commission issued a rule banning noncompetes, but businesses are actively working to reverse the rule; refer to Moreno, "Business Groups Sue to Stop."

27. According to the US Bureau of Labor Statistics (BLS), "Union Members—2022," the US union membership rate was approximately 10 percent in

2022, about half what it was two decades earlier and much lower than in comparable countries. For more on the dynamics of business-labor conflict in the United States, refer to Drutman, "How Lobbyists Conquered American Democracy."

28. Kalleberg, *Good Jobs, Bad Jobs.*

29. DuGay, *Consumption and Identity at Work*; and Vallas and Cummins, "Personal Branding and Identity Norms."

30. BLS, "Number of Jobs." As the contingent workforce continues to grow—5.9 million people in 2017—work instability is likely to become an even more common feature of work life: BLS, "Contingent and Alternative Employment Arrangements."

31. For more on the negative experiences of those in relatively "good" jobs, refer to Kelly and Moen, *Overload*; Williams, *Gaslighted*; and Wynn, "Misery Has Company."

32. BLS, "Number of Jobs"; Williams, "Laid Off More, Hired Less." On inequality in hiring, refer to Gorman, "Gender Stereotypes"; Pager, Western, and Bonikowski, "Discrimination in Low-Wage Labor Market"; and Rivera, *Pedigree.* On inequality in downsizing, refer to Kalev, "How You Downsize"; and Williams, *Gaslighted.*

33. For more on gender and racial inequities that overlap with job polarization, refer to Glenn, "From Servitude to Service Work"; and Hatton, "Mechanisms of Invisibility." For more on the characteristics of bad jobs, refer to Duffy, "Doing the Dirty Work"; Guendelsberger, *On the Clock*; Henly, Shaefer, and Waxman, "Nonstandard Work Schedules"; and Lambert, "Passing the Buck."

34. On average, about 5 percent of workers hold multiple jobs at once. BLS, "Jobholders by Selected Characteristics."

35. This is the legacy of welfare capitalism, in which corporations provided economic and social benefits to quell union activity and negative public sentiment. See: Jacoby, *Modern Manors*; and Tone, *Business of Benevolence.*

36. For example, Collins, *Making Motherhood Work*; Cooper, *Cut Adrift*; Damaske, *Tolls of Uncertainty*; Hays, *Flat Broke with Children*; Morduch and Schneider, *Financial Diaries*; and Sherman, *Those Who Work.*

37. Megan Tobias Neely calls this the "portfolio ideal worker"; "Portfolio Ideal Worker," 279. Refer also to Lane, *Company of One*; Smith, *Crossing the Great Divide*; and Vallas and Christin, "Work and Identity."

38. Indeed, many prominent accounts of trust in the economic sphere assume a long-term relationship history, which is no longer an empirical reality for many (e.g., Granovetter, "Economic Action and Social Structure").

39. Barbalet, "Characterization of Trust"; and Giddens, *Consequences of Modernity.*

40. Beckert, "Trust and Performative Construction of Markets"; Giddens, *Modernity and Self-Identity*; and Möllering, *Trust.*

41. Luhmann, "Familiarity, Confidence, Trust"; and Seligman, *Problem of Trust.*

42. Jaffe, *Work Won't Love You Back.*

43. Petersen, "How Leaders Can Build a Culture of Trust"; and Brower, Lester, and Korsgaard, "Want Your Employees to Trust You?"

44. At least at the time of this book's publication.

45. Mayo, *Human Problems of Industrial Civilization.*

46. Illouz, *Saving the Modern Soul*, 91. For more on the importance of trust at work, particularly within management, refer to Jackall, *Moral Mazes*; Kunda, *Engineering Culture*; and Pearce, "Employability as Trustworthiness."

47. Sennet, *Corrosion of Character.*

48. Adler, "Market, Hierarchy, and Trust"; Graham, *On the Line at Subaru-Isuzu*; and Turco, *Conversational Firm.*

49. Wingfield, *Gray Areas.*

50. For example, McPherson, Smith-Lovin, and Cook, "Birds of a Feather."

51. Swidler, "Culture in Action."

52. For more on how language shapes our understandings, refer to cognitive scientist Lera Boroditsky's book *7,000 Universes.*

53. Dirks and de Jong, "Trust Within the Workplace."

54. "Great Place To Work® Trust Index©."

55. Cottom, "Citizens No More."

56. Blair-Loy, *Competing Devotions*; Gregg, *Work's Intimacy*; Lamont, *Dignity of Working Men*; and Rumens, "Researching Workplace Friendships."

57. Schawbel, "Work Friendships Are Critical"; and Williams, "Life Support." Concerns linking remote work and loneliness can be found in Brooks, "Hidden Toll of Remote Work" and in the discussion with Charlie Warzel and Anne Helen Petersen on the *Ezra Klein Show* podcast episode "The Office Is Dying."

58. For more on the ties between employer provision of social benefits and labor participation, refer to Albiston and Fisk, "Precarious Work and Precarious Welfare"; and Quadagno, "Welfare Capitalism." For examples of company perks, refer to Luckerson, "10 Most Lavish Job Perks"; and Satran, "Intimate Look at 'Family Meal.'"

59. Hacker, *Great Risk Shift*; Ho, *Liquidated*; Sennett, *Culture of New Capitalism*; and Standing, *Precariat.*

60. Granovetter, *Getting a Job.*

61. McGuire, "Gender, Race, and Shadow Structure"; Pedulla and Pager, "Race and Networks"; and Royster, *Race and Invisible Hand.*

62. Sociologist Melissa Gregg argues in *Work's Intimacy* that networking is not just about getting a job but also about demonstrating employability. For more on the importance of social networks in the contemporary labor market, refer to Gershon, *Down and Out*; Neely, "Fit to Be a King"; and Williams, Muller, and Kilanski, "Gendered Organizations in New Economy."

63. Botsman, *Who Can You Trust?*; Hearn, "Structuring Feeling"; and Sharone, "Social Capital Activation." Existing social inequities are often reproduced

and amplified through these digital technologies. Sharone, "LinkedIn or Linked-Out?"; and Ticona and Mateescu, "Trusted Strangers."

64. Lewicki and Brinsfield, "Building Social Capital"; and Smith, *Lone Pursuit.*

65. Neely, *Hedged Out.*

66. Levine, *Ain't No Trust*; and Smith, *Lone Pursuit.*

67. Smith, "Don't Put My Name on It."

68. For example, Uzzi, "Embeddedness in Financial Capital."

69. Gershon, *Down and Out in New Economy.*

70. For example, Dirks and Ferrin, "Trust in Leadership"; and Fiske, Cuddy, and Glick, "Universal Dimensions of Social Cognition."

71. Cottom, "Citizens No More."

72. On how contradictions within managerial logics create space for worker agency, refer to Leidner *Fast Food, Fast Talk*; Sallaz, "House Rules"; Vallas, "Adventures of Managerial Hegemony"; and Vallas, "Empowerment Redux." For more on trans-organizational power and control, refer to Vallas and Hill's "Rethinking Power in Organizations, Institutions, and Markets," which applies aspects of Foucault's theory of governmentality to the workplace.

73. Sinek, "Make You Feel Safe."

74. Arlie Hochschild's foundational and groundbreaking theory of emotional labor, presented in *The Managed Heart*, remains extremely salient, yet it has suffered from conceptual bleed, often being applied broadly in ways that do not align with its theoretical arguments: Beck, "Concept Creep of 'Emotional Labor.'"

75. Tweedy, "Laboring Lesbians."

76. For example, Paules, *Dishing It Out.*

77. As, for example, an isolated state or rational calculus.

78. Recently, Gil Eyal and Cristian Capotescu have called for a new scholarly approach to trust as a verb, not a noun, in "Trust Is a Verb," which is aligned with my approach.

79. Giddens, *Consequences of Modernity*; and Luhmann, *Trust and Power.*

80. Lewis and Weigert, "Trust as Social Reality"; and Möllering, *Trust.*

81. People tend to trust those with power and credentials, and research demonstrates that both gender and race can sometimes act as a credential. Ray, "Theory of Racialized Organizations"; Rivera, *Pedigree*; and Smith and Overbeck, "The Leaders' Rosy Halo."

82. Ho, *Liquidated*; and Neely, *Hedged Out.*

83. Gorman, "Gender Stereotypes"; and Travis, Thorpe-Moscon, and McCluney, *Emotional Tax.*

84. For more on the stratifying influence of cultural and relational processes, refer to Lamont, Beljean, and Clair, "What Is Missing?"; Tilly, *Durable Inequality*; and Tomaskovic-Devey and Avent-Holt, *Relational Inequalities.*

85. As the famous Thomas theorem argues, "If men define situations as real, they are real in their consequences."

86. Szerszynski, "Risk and Trust."

87. Mizrachi, Drori, and Anspach, "Repertoires of Trust."

88. Relational sociologists have long argued that meanings emerge within social relationships and are fluid. Abbott, "Things of Boundaries"; Emirbayer, "Manifesto for Relational Sociology"; Tilly, *Why?*; and Zelizer, "I Became a Relational Economic Sociologist."

89. In *Cruel Optimism*, Lauren Berlant defines the term as a state of being in which "something you desire is actually an obstacle to your own flourishing."

90. For example, Colquitt, Scott, and Lepine, "Trust, Trustworthiness, Trust Propensity"; Misztal, *Trust in Modern Societies*; and Sheppard and Sherman, "Grammars of Trust."

91. Kanter, *Men and Women of Corporation*; Levine, *Ain't No Trust*; Smith, *Lone Pursuit*; and Neely, *Hedged Out*.

92. In *Slouching Towards Bethlehem*, Joan Didion suggests her advantage as a reporter was being "physically small, so temperamentally unobtrusive, and so neurotically inarticulate that people tend to forget that my presence runs counter to their best interests" (xiv). Similarly, my small stature, social awkwardness, and outsider status during fieldwork seemed to encourage people to open up—seeing me as a student to teach, a peer to befriend, or an outsider to confide in. Like Didion, I recognized the benefits of rapport for my study while grappling with the power and ambivalence of observing and writing about others' lives.

93. Jerolmack and Khan, "Talk Is Cheap"; Lizardo, "Improving Cultural Analysis"; and Rinaldo and Guhin, "How and Why Interviews Work."

94. DTC followed a core periphery model of organization, in which more stable jobs with benefits make up the core and contingent jobs make up the periphery. Doeringer and Piore, *Internal Labor Markets*; Osterman, *Employment Futures*; and Smith, "New Forms of Work Organization."

95. Indeed, 87 percent of my interview participants at The Jones were front-of-house employees or managers, and 88 percent of my DTC participants were full-time, in-office employees.

96. Lauren Alfrey analyzes the semantic maneuvers workplace actors in primarily white organizations make in order to defend their workplaces as diverse. "Diversity, Disrupted."

97. Refer also to Wilson, *Front of the House* and Ribas, *On the Line* for more on racial segmentation in restaurants and elsewhere.

98. According to data from the US Equal Employment Opportunity Commission in 2020, white men make up 31 percent of the workforce but hold 57 percent of senior executive and managerial positions. "Charge Statistics." For more on gendered and racialized logics and structures within organizations, refer to

Acker, "Hierarchies, Jobs, and Bodies"; Jones, "Cisgendered Workspaces"; and Ray, "Theory of Racialized Organizations."

99. Prior to each interview, people were informed about the risks of participation and signed consent forms. All interview participants completed a short demographic paper survey prior to or directly after our conversation.

100. Pugh, "What Good Are Interviews?" I also found Robinson and Schulz's "iterated questioning approach" particularly useful in probing meaningfully and deeply into participants' narratives. "Eliciting Frontstage and Backstage Talk."

101. Pugh and Mosseri, "Trust-Building vs. 'Just Trust Me'"; and Rinaldo and Guhin, "How and Why Interviews Work."

102. I emailed around forty start-ups with my pitch, but only a few responded, and Disruption was the only one to participate. After initial contact with company leaders, I presented my pitch to the full team, who all consented to my involvement.

103. For more on circuits, refer to Mears, *Pricing Beauty*; Mosseri, "Being Watched and Being Seen"; and Zelizer, *Social Meaning of Money*.

104. Levin, "Uber's Scandals and PR Disaster."

105. Lawrence, "Uber Paid Six-Figure Sums".

106. Intersectional scholars have stressed the importance of such "process-centered" and "intercategorical" approaches for studying overlapping, relational inequalities. Choo and Ferree, "Practicing Intersectionality"; Collins, *Black Feminist Thought*; Glenn, "Social Construction and Institutionalization"; and McCall, "Complexity of Intersectionality."

107. Keister and Moller, "Wealth Inequality in United States"; Oliver and Shapiro, *Black Wealth/White Wealth*; and Pfeffer and Killewald, "Generations of Advantage."

108. O'Brien, "Depleting Capital"; Portes, "Social Capital"; and Stack, *All Our Kin*.

109. Wingfield, "Where Work Has Been."

110. Refer to Chen, *Cut Loose*; Pugh, *Tumbleweed Society*; and Sharone, *Flawed System/Flawed Self*.

CHAPTER 1. FLASH INTIMACY

1. For example, Covey, *Speed of Trust*; Feltman, *Thin Book of Trust*; Robbins, *We're All in This Together*; and Stickel, *Building Trust*.

2. In this way, my work follows the path set by scholars studying the cultural, relational, and emotional dimensions of work, which are gendered, raced, and classed. For example, Fletcher, *Disappearing Acts*; Hochschild, *Managed Heart*; Pugh, *Last Human Job*; and Wingfield, "Are Some Emotions 'Whites Only?'"

3. In her study of gendered occupations in Pakistan, Fauzia Husain describes in *The Stigma Matrix* how women in male-dominated settings often lack "relational agency," or the ability to enlist others to forward their goals.

4. Stehle and Weber, *Precarious Intimacies.*

5. While most accounts of trust presume intimacy, I take a more active view of the relationship between trust and intimacy, drawing on sociological processes of boundary and relational work to understand how people erect boundaries (e.g., between intimacy and business) and establish particular meanings, norms, and practices associated with different sides of that boundary. Refer to Bandelj, "Relational Work and Economic Sociology"; Pachucki, Pendergrass, and Lamont, "Boundary Processes"; Zelizer, "How I Became a Relational Economic Sociologist."

6. Zelizer, *Purchase of Intimacy*, 14.

7. The phrase "haven in a heartless world" can be traced to Lasch, *Haven in a Heartless World.* Feminist scholars have observed how this ideology exists to reinforce gender inequities. For example, Hays, *Cultural Contradictions of Motherhood*; and Williams, *Unbending Gender.*

8. Refer to Zelizer, *Purchase of Intimacy.*

9. In a previous article, for example, I argue that working mothers—especially those from disadvantaged backgrounds—sometimes reconfigure gendered notions of care to include financial provision. Mosseri, "Finding Middle Ground." This is similar to how men traditionally viewed their provisions of care in financial terms. Coltrane, *Family Man.*

10. For example, Heimer, "Doing Your Job"; and Rath, *Vital Friends.*

11. Jones, Woods, and Guillaume, "Effectiveness of Workplace Coaching"; and Krzywdzinski and Greb, "Teamwork."

12. While care work scholars have illuminated the often invisible labor of this work (e.g., Crain, Poster, and Cherry, *Invisible Labor*; Daniels, "Invisible Work"; Folbre, *Invisible Heart*; and Glenn, "Creating a Caring Society," scholars studying the informal economy have demonstrated how money and bureaucracy can enable and/or regulate intimacy (e.g., Bernstein, *Temporarily Yours*; Hoang, *Dealing in Desire*; and Parreñas, *Illicit Flirtations*).

13. Sherman, *Uneasy Street.*

14. Yet as Neely's *Hedged Out* shows, gift-giving and favors often directly impact financial deals. Zelizer's concept of "relational work" is particularly useful in describing how people match meanings and media of exchange to uphold false boundaries between intimacy and the market. "How I Became a Relational Economic Sociologist."

15. Lainer-Vos, "Practical Organization of Moral Transactions"; Mears, "Working for Free in VIP"; and Wood, "Powerful Times."

16. At DTC, for example, many employees were ineligible for performance-based bonuses, and even eligible nonmanagers received a mere 4.5 percent bonus compared to the 10 percent plus bonus offered to those above the director level.

17. Hochschild, *Second Shift.*

18. For example, Chen, *Cut Loose*; Hatton, *Coerced*; Kantor and Twohey, *She Said*; and Piketty, *Capital in Twenty-First Century*. Cech, *Trouble with Passion*; Gregg, *Work's Intimacy*; McGuire, "Intimate Work"; Rao and Neely, "What's Love Got to Do"; Reid and Ramarajan, "Seeking Purity, Avoiding Pollution"; and Weeks, "Down with Love."

19. Ellipses within quotes indicate a pause in speech. Bracketed ellipses signify omitted material.

20. Sociologists have traced a *therapeutic narrative*—which stresses the idea of drawing strength from suffering—within self-help texts, public media, social institutions, and everyday talk. Bellah et al., *Habits of the Heart*; Illouz, *Oprah Winfrey and Glamour of Misery*; Silva, *Coming Up Short*; and Simko, "Oprah and Politics of Consolation."

21. Along similar lines as my critique, psychologists have started to question the validity of "post-traumatic growth." Engelhard, Lommen, and Sijbrandij, "Changing for Better or Worse?"; and Infurna and Jayawickreme, *Redesigning Research on Post-Traumatic Growth.*

22. Grazian, *Blue Chicago;* MacCannell, *Tourist*; Marwick, *Status Update*; Ocejo, *Masters of Craft*; and Serazio, *Authenticity Industries.*

23. Garofalo, "Doppelgangers in Digital World."

24. Grazian, "Demystifying Authenticity"; and Peterson, "In Search of Authenticity."

25. Duffy, "Manufacturing Authenticity"; Fine, "Crafting Authenticity"; Peterson, *Creating Country Music*; and Wherry, "Social Sources of Authenticity."

26. Digital content producers, for example, claim authenticity by highlighting their amateur status, affordable style, and unconventional beauty to differentiate themselves from high-fashion and mainstream media personas, while politicians position themselves as outsiders to the establishment by using plain language and popular rhetoric to embody an authentic persona. Duffy, *(Not) Getting Paid*; Lacatus and Meibauwe, "Saying It Like It Is"; Salisbury and Pooley, "#nofilter Self"; and Shane, "Semiotics of Authenticity."

27. Bell, "Being Your Best Self."

28. Duffy, Miltner, and Wahlstedt, "Policing 'Fake' Femininity"; Garratt, "Authenticity and Racism"; and Schwarz, "Symbolic Economy of Authenticity."

29. Acker, "Hierarchies, Jobs, and Bodies"; Ray, "Theory of Racialized Organizations"; and Wingfield and Alston, "Maintaining Hierarchies in White Organizations."

30. Heilman, "Description and Prescription"; Pager and Karafin, "Bayesian Bigot?"; Ridgeway and Correll, "Unpacking the Gender System"; and Wingfield and Chavez, "Getting in, Getting Hired."

31. Alinor and Tinkler, "Take Off Your Hoodie"; and Ferguson, *Bad Boys.*

32. Benard and Correll, "Normative Discrimination and Motherhood Penalty"; and Williams, Blair-Loy, and Berdahl, "Cultural Schemas, Social Class."

33. Organizational scholars theorize that rule-breaking is both a part of everyday organizational life but also not universally allowed. Martin et al., "Against the Rules"; and Ray, "Theory of Racialized Organizations." Michela Musto's study of middle-school students demonstrates how stratified tolerance of rule-breaking in the classroom informs gendered perceptions of exceptionalism that benefit boys. "Brilliant or Bad."

34. The intense hate that actress Anne Hathaway received on the internet in 2013—referred to as "Hathahate"—reflects how too much enthusiasm and effort can trigger distrust and contempt, especially among women. Petersen, "What Is Anne Hathaway Trying to Tell Us?"

35. There is a long history of framing women's thoughts, emotions, and behaviors as pathological (e.g., female hysteria in the eighteenth and nineteenth centuries).

36. As Shamus Khan has argued in *Privilege,* ease is often the embodiment of social privilege.

37. While *trauma bonding* typically refers to the attachment that develops between an abuser and abusee, I use it here to refer also to the connections that develop among people collectively experiencing a negative situation.

38. While the absence of outright expressions of distrust and betrayal may be attributed to interviewer bias, with people not wanting to gossip or "be negative" about colleagues when talking to an outside researcher, I don't think such bias fully accounts for my findings. Indeed, people *did* gossip about coworkers with me, even within the interviews, and they often shared personal stories in which they had confronted upsetting behavior from others at work. They were, however, careful with how they framed these stories.

39. This argument is aligned with Terence McDonnell and colleagues' theory that resonant cultural objects—whether they be language, symbols, or artifacts—help people solve problems and connect the unknown to the known. McDonnell, Bail, and Tavory, "Theory of Resonance."

40. Adler, "Market, Hierarchy, and Trust"; Colquitt, Scott, and LePine, "Trust, Trustworthiness, and Trust Propensity"; Mayer, Davis, and Schoorman, "Integrative Model of Organizational Trust"; and McAllister, "Affect- and Cognition-Based Trust."

41. Gershon, *Down and Out in New Economy*; Kay and Wallace, "Mentors as Social Capital"; and Neely, *Hedged Out.*

42. Anteby, Chan, and DiBenigno, "Three Lenses on Occupations"; Castilla, "Gender, Race, and Network Advantage"; and Rivera, *Pedigree.*

43. Farrugia et al., "Hospitality Work and Affective Labor"; Hodson, "Group Relations at Work"; and Kanter, *Men and Women of Corporation.*

44. Fine, "Friendships in the Work Place"; Roy, "'Banana Time'"; and Rumens, "Firm Friends."

45. Gregg, *Work's Intimacy*; Hochschild, *Time Bind*; and Pedersen and Lewis, "Flexible Friends?"

46. For more on intimate partner violence, see Armstrong, Gleckman-Krut, and Johnson, "Silence, Power, and Inequality"; Stark, *Coercive Control*; and Sweet, *Politics of Surviving*. For more on the exploitations of (women's) social reproductive labor, see Calarco, *Holding It Together;* Dalla Costa and James, *Power of Women*; and Federici, *Wages Against Housework*.

47. On sexual harassment at work, see Berdahl and Moore, "Workplace Harassment"; Chamberlain et al., "Sexual Harassment in Organizational Context"; Mueller, De Coster, and Estes, "Sexual Harassment in Workplace"; and Saguy and Rees, "Gender, Power, and Harassment." On normative and relational control at work, see Barker, "Tightening the Iron Cage"; Burawoy, *Manufacturing Consent*; Edwards, *Contested Terrain*; Kunda, *Engineering Culture*; and Wood, *Despotism in Demand*.

48. Smelser, "Rational and Ambivalent in Social Sciences."

49. Geschiere, *Witchcraft, Intimacy, and Trust*. Mark Granovetter also notably discusses the risk of malfeasance in trusted social relationships in his treatise on embeddedness ("Economic Action and Social Structure"), while the same idea is central to Guido Möllering's notion of trust as "suspension" in *Trust*.

50. Carroll, *Through the Looking-Glass*, 124.

51. It also helps workers achieve the "façade of controlled ambiguity," which labor scholar Gideon Kunda argues in *Engineering Culture* is "characteristic of the successful self" in normative workplace cultures (204).

52. Aviv, *Strangers to Ourselves*, 24.

53. Chen, *Cut Loose*; Pugh, *Tumbleweed Society*; and Sharone, *Flawed System/Flawed Self*.

CHAPTER 2. COMMUNIONS OF CRISIS

1. At the time of the study (2016), NYC restaurants were required to pay tipped workers $9.00 per hour, but they could draw $1.50 per hour from the worker's tips to cover that obligation.

2. Lyng, "Edgework"; and Lyng, "Sociology at the Edge." As noted in the introduction, trust becomes salient amid uncertainty and risk because it enables people to take provisional actions. Giddens, *Modernity and Self-Identity*; and Möllering, *Trust*.

3. Best, "Security, Economy, Population"; and Snyder, *Disrupted Workplace*.

4. Klein, *Shock Doctrine*; Rahm Emanuel, Obama's one-time chief of staff, famously expressed this sentiment amid the 2008 financial crisis during remarks at the Wall Street Journal CEO Council, but similar notions have periodically been attributed to world leaders.

5. In *The Elementary Forms of Religious Life*, sociologist Emile Durkheim refers to this as "collective effervescence."

6. In *Social Systems*, theorist Niklas Luhmann sketches out how autopoiesis can be applied to the social world.

7. Granter, McCann, and Boyle, "Extreme Work/Normal Work."

8. Building on Durkheim and Goffman, Randall Collins, in *Interaction Ritual Chains*, defines rituals as "a mechanism of mutually focused emotion and attention producing a momentarily shared reality, which thereby generates solidarity and symbols of group membership" (7). For more on rituals, refer to Turner, *Ritual Process*; and Xygalatas, *Ritual*.

9. The pattern outlined here broadly follows the three-stages of rites of passage identified by van Gennep in *The Rites of Passage*.

10. While crossing the threshold at The Jones was defined by the rush, the stress and unpredictability of client meetings, presentations, and live promotional events constituted this phase at DTC and Disruption.

11. Notably, servers who asked hosts to avoid seating them back to back were not praised for their self-awareness and dedication to quality service; rather, they were demeaned for their inability to keep up. And cooks who were speedy but aggressive were preferred over those who were slower but nicer.

12. Rehashing war stories often occurred over drinks at DTC and Disruption as well, although they also had more formal "postmortem" meetings, during which they crafted stories.

13. Brown, "Society and the Supernatural," 137.

14. For example, Smith, *Wealth of Nations*. For a recent critique of capitalist values and systems, refer to Piketty, *Capital in the Twenty-First Century*.

15. Brown, "Society and the Supernatural," 142.

16. Brown, "Society and the Supernatural."

17. As discussed in the introduction, DTC was also a gendered and racialized organization led primarily by white men. Disruption was gendered and racialized, yet as the three-person operations team included one white woman and two biracial men, it was less starkly so compared to the other two. For more on gendered and racialized organizations, refer to Acker, "Hierarchies, Jobs, and Bodies"; and Ray, "Theory of Racialized Organizations."

18. To protect DTC's confidentiality, none of these examples represent projects actually executed by the agency.

19. Becker's "Notes on the Concept of Commitment" and England, Folbre, and Leanna's "Motivating Care" offer valuable foundational insight into these motivations. For novel empirical examinations, refer to Adler, "Choosing Bad Jobs"; Duffy, "Romance of Work"; and Showers, "Moving Onward and Upward."

20. For example, Acker, "Hierarchies, Jobs, and Bodies."

21. At The Jones, people referred to those who failed to participate fully in communions of crisis—slacking on setup/closing duties, seeking to be cut early, avoiding business shifts—as unwilling to get in the trenches. At Disruption,

people who opted for less challenging or urgent client projects were often said to be eschewing the trenches.

22. Adam's statement reflects a "burn and churn" managerial approach, which leads to toxic workplace cultures; refer to Kantor and Streitfeld, "Inside Amazon"; and Zaleski, "We Are All 'Amabots' Now."

23. Similarly, managers jumped in to help workers run food, put in orders, and bus tables during the rush at The Jones, and operations team members at Disruption contributed to printing out materials, preparing codes, and the like when joining in the trenches.

24. Berdahl et al., "Work as a Masculinity Contest"; Munsch, "Strength, Stamina, and Structural Violence"; and Reid, O'Neill, and Blair-Loy, "Masculinity in Male-Dominated Occupations." This research also builds on earlier work by Ely and Meyerson on the role of heroism in men's career strategies. "Advancing Gender Equity in Organizations."

25. For more on tokenism and how it plays out in different workplace environments, refer to Kanter, *Men and Women of the Corporation*; Turco, "Cultural Foundations of Tokenism"; Williams, "Glass Escalator"; and Wingfield, "Racializing the Glass Escalator."

26. In research conducted by Erin Kelly and colleagues, a white-collar professional woman shrewdly refers to such individuals as "arsonist firefighters." "Gendered Challenge, Gendered Response."

27. Cook and Glass, "Glass Cliffs and Organizational Saviors"; and Ryan and Haslam, "Glass Cliff." The glass cliff becomes even steeper and more dangerous for women of color, who are facing both racial and gendered biases; refer to Payton, "Black Women and the Glass Cliff."

28. McAdams, *Redemptive Self*, xiv.

29. In "The Social Psychology of the World Religions," Weber argues that redemption is key to theodicies of suffering, helping people make sense amid the irrationality of fate. He notes, however, that the content and mechanics of this redemption depended upon one's particular "image of the world" (280).

30. While DTC and The Jones didn't have the same master narrative for describing their company's evolution, the adversity experienced within local crises (e.g., a big pitch, a busy shift) was always described in terms that suggested the challenge served a broader purpose (e.g., providing clarity for the team, making the team stronger).

31. In *Making Good*, Maruna describes the promotion of such black-and-white dichotomies within many redemption stories.

32. Others have also pointed to the tendency to scapegoat amid crises; refer to Hart, "Symbols, Rituals, and Power." For empirical examples refer to Daniels et al., "Has Pandemic Threat Stoked Xenophobia?"; and O'Flynn, Monaghan, and Power, "Scapegoating During a Time of Crisis."

33. Maruna, *Making Good*, 145. Prior to and during the crisis, for example, the team failed to agree on a clear brand message that could help them communicate

their services to clients and attract new business. In fact, Logan laughed knowingly when I admitted to not understanding what it was that Disruption actually did. "The reason I'm laughing," she explained, "is because we've really changed our messaging quite a bit." "And [we] will be again," she added tentatively.

34. While federal paid leave was nonexistent at the time, major paid parental measures were passed in New York State and New York City in 2016. However, these measures had not yet been implemented, and the length of paid leave and eligibility requirements varied; refer to New York City Health Department, "Paid Family Leave"; and Editorial Board, "States Lead on Paid Family Leave."

35. McAdams argues that redemption is *the* normative narrative in American culture; refer to *Redemptive Self.*

36. Tedeschi and Calhoun, "Posttraumatic Growth." Refer to Sheryl Sandberg and Adam Grant, *Option B*, for a popular take on this idea, particularly within the workplace.

37. More broadly, communions of crises—including trials by fire, getting in the trenches, and redemption narratives—operate similarly to hazing rituals, which have been shown to create negative impacts such as sexual exploitation and mental distress: Nuwer, *Hazing.*

38. McAdams, *Redemptive Self,* 235.

39. James Young, for example, makes this point convincingly in his essay on Holocaust commemorations; refer to "Against Redemption."

40. Morrison, "Grendel and His Mother," 261. In her essay, Morrison decenters the white, male, able-bodied hero's gaze in *Beowulf,* bringing to life the marginalized—and as she argues, racialized—characters of Grendel and His Mother.

41. While restaurant servers have the opportunity to earn more tips during a rush, this pay is far from guaranteed, as it is contingent on consumer preferences and behaviors. In an unpublished manuscript, I report on interviews I conducted with fifty-five professionals working in finance, technology, management consulting, and media to demonstrate how workplace cultures, in an attempt to eschew blame for employee burnout, frame long hours as an individual problem of inefficiency as opposed to a broader workplace issue. As a result, displays of overwork can be a double-edged sword, with some workers criticized for working "harder, not smarter." Mosseri, "Managed Absence." For more on overtime pay restrictions for exempt workers, refer to Shierholz and Schmitt, "Court Decision Based on Flawed Logic."

42. Morrison, "Grendel and His Mother," 262.

CHAPTER 3. BETWEEN THE LINES

1. Sociologist Joseph Gusfield similarly highlights how drinking is a transitional space. "Passage to Play."

2. Turner, *Dramas, Fields, and Metaphors*, 274.

3. Turner, "Liminality and Communitas."

4. Turner, for example, refers to liminality as "anti-structure," while Bakhtin, writing on the carnival, describes such spaces as being where "the world is destroyed so that it may be regenerated and renewed." *Rabelais and His World*, 48. Howard-Grenville et al., in "Liminality as Process for Cultural Change," bridge these theoretical ideas with cultural sociologist Ann Swidler's theory of culture in action during "unsettled times" in "Culture in Action."

5. See introduction.

6. Similarly, Turner discusses how the disorder and danger of liminal moments serve as a profound reminder of one's humanity, thereby fostering social connection. "Liminality and Communitas."

7. Tavory and Fine argue that trust leads people to more readily interpret misalignment in interactions with benevolence, even when no such goodwill is intended. "Disruption and Theory of Interaction Order," 378.

8. For a racial analysis of grey areas broadly defined, refer to Wingfield's *Gray Areas*.

9. Kantor and Twohey, *She Said*; Billingsley, "Racialized and Classed Contexts"; Bemiller and Schneider, "It's Not Just a Joke"; and Pérez, *Souls of White Jokes*.

10. Collins, "Stratification, Emotional Energy"; Summers-Effler, "Micro Potential for Social Change"; and Tavory and Fine, "Disruption and Theory of Interaction Order."

11. Oldenburg, *Great Good Place*, 52. Oldenburg refers specifically to the bar as a third space, and I expand on this notion to include in-office bars and other workplace drinking sites. Other third spaces include churches, parks, beauty parlors, coffee shops, gyms, and social media sites.

12. While the psychoactive properties of alcohol help drive inhibition, cultural associations and social contexts also play an important role. Bancroft, *Drugs, Intoxication, and Society*; and Douglas, *Constructive Drinking*.

13. For more on the revolutionary potential of between-the-lines moments, refer to Goffman, "Go to More Parties?"; and Summers-Effler, "Micro Potential for Social Change."

14. Oldenburg, *Great Good Place*; Sismondo, *America Walks into a Bar*; and Slingerland, *Drunk*. Gay bars, for example, served as a central battleground in an important period of the LGBTQIA movement, providing respite from oppressive heteronormativity, emboldening queer expression, and galvanizing political engagement. Armstrong, *Forging Gay Identities*; and Ghaziani, *There Goes the Gayborhood?*

15. Hersey, *Rest Is Resistance*, 141.

16. McCluney et al., "Costs of Code-Switching."

17. On the production of "cool" workplace environments, refer to Frenette and Ocejo, "Sustaining Enchantment."

18. Reid's identity as a biracial, gay man came with its own complications. However, his ability to "pass" more easily as white influenced how he navigated drinking sessions compared to Hai, whose skin tone was notably darker.

19. On the appropriation of cool, refer to Lott, *Love & Theft*; *and* Tate, *Everything But the Burden*.

20. For more on whiteness as a credential, refer to Ray's "Theory of Racialized Organizations." For more on gender as a credential, refer to Ridgeway and Correll, "Unpacking the Gender System."

21. Anderson, "White Space."

22. Hai acknowledged positive stereotypes as well but said those never seemed to emerge.

23. For more on how drinking provides a setting for interpersonal oppression, refer to May, *Urban Nightlife*; Nixon and Crewe, "Pleasure at Work?"; and Tinkler, Becker, and Clayton, "Kind of Natural, Kind of Wrong."

24. Other researchers have noted the obligatory nature of work-focused drinking networks; for example, Gregg, "On Friday Night Drinks"; and Keane, "Join Us for Drinks." In a cross-cultural example, Gately reports on the "water trade" (mandatory after-hours drinking sessions) among Japanese businessmen in the latter half of the twentieth century. *Drink*.

25. For example, DTC's CEO Adam wanted to fire another executive because, in his words, "He never goes out for a beer with me."

26. For more on inequities of informal networking-type events, refer to Mickey, "Organization of Networking and Gender Inequality"; Ortlieb and Sieben, "Balls, Barbecues, and Boxing"; and Williams, Muller, and Kilanski, "Gendered Organizations in New Economy."

27. Notably, women's drinking tends to be policed more strictly than men's. Brown and Gregg, "Pedagogy of Regret"; Day, Gough, and McFadden, "Warning!"

28. Quoted in profile published by Project For Public Spaces.

29. Hartless, "Questionably Queer"; and Rushbrook, "Cities, Queer Space, and Cosmopolitan Tourist."

30. In *Exit, Voice, and Loyalty*, Hirschman focused primarily on consumer behaviors, but his framework has since been widely adopted by employment and workplace researchers.

31. For more on workplace voice, refer to Dundon et al., "Meanings and Purpose of Employee Voice"; and Barry, Dundon, and Wilkinson, "Employee Voice."

32. Freeman and Medoff, *What Do Unions Do?*

33. Dundon and Gollan, "Re-Conceptualizing Voice in the Non-Union Workplace"; and Kochan et al., "Worker Voice in America."

34. As discussed in more detail later, venting and complaining can lead to stigmatization. On the other hand, internalized frustration risks resentment and organizational inaction, and leaving comes with financial and career uncertainties.

35. Their statements reflect what Allison Pugh terms "meta-feelings," which culturally situate emotions, shaping how safe, free, or proud someone feels in expressing them. "What Good Are Interviews?"

36. Ahmed, *Complaint!*, 6.

37. Paige Sweet argues for a *sociological* understanding of gaslighting that can reveal "how macro-level social inequalities are transformed into micro-level strategies of abuse." "Sociology of Gaslighting," 852.

38. In "Our Silicon Valley, Ourselves," Tamara Kneese advocates for public venting through personal essays, emphasizing the political value of worker voices.

39. Unfortunately, many of her colleagues were afraid to do so based on the risks outlined later in this section, leaving this potential unrealized.

40. I observed this in firsthand managerial trainings I attended, but such tactics are also documented by Eva Illouz in *Saving the Modern Soul.*

41. For more about contrasting perspectives on worker voice, refer to Wilkinson and Barry, "Voices from Across the Divide."

42. Dobbin and Kalev show, for example, that workplace diversity programs tend to ostensibly address representation issues while leaving structures of workplace inequality intact. "Civil Rights Revolution at Work."

43. Organizational scholar Amy Edmonson has documented the value of "psychological safety"—a belief that they will not be punished or ridiculed for speaking up—within organizations. For positive outcomes associated with psychological safety, refer to *The Fearless Organization.*

44. Refer to Cooper et al., "Gender Matters," for the gendered dynamics of this process.

45. In many cases, this cultural mandate demanded free labor from lower-ranked workers. Hirshfield and Joseph, "We Need a Woman"; Lerma, Hamilton, and Nielsen, "Racialized Equity Labor." Venting differs from gossip, which involves spreading information or rumors about others, often with malicious intent, in its focus on expressing one's own emotions. Although Lanie and her managers dismissed gossip as trivial, research shows it can enhance workplace transparency. Sobering, "Watercooler Democracy."

46. For more on the prevalence of this ethos in modern workplaces, refer to Cabanas and Illouz, "Making of a 'Happy Worker'"; DePalma, "Passion Paradigm"; and Rao and Neely, "What's Love Got to Do with It?"

47. E.g., Walker and Hamilton, "Employee–Employer Grievances."

48. Theories of tokenism suggest that low numerical rarity and low societal status increase the likelihood of stereotyping. Kanter, *Men and Women of the Corporation*; Roth, "Social Psychology of Tokenism"; Williams, "Glass Escalator"; and Wingfield, "Racializing the Glass Escalator." For more on gender and race stereotypes at work, refer to Heilman, "Description and Prescription"; and Wingfield, "Modern Mammy and Angry Black Man."

49. Sociologists have highlighted the pain produced by a lack of "recognition." Lamont, "Addressing Recognition Gaps"; and Pugh, "Connective Labor as Emotional Vocabulary."

50. Ahmed, *Complaint!*

51. Kellogg, *Challenging Operations.*

52. Stated in a 2015 interview. Barney, "'Daily Show with Trevor Noah.'"

53. As Fine and de Soucey highlight "Joking Cultures," one is considered a true member of the group when they demonstrate they can easily take a joke. Yet as Quinn notes, the interplay within humor also reflects the distribution and patterns of power. "Paradox of Complaining."

54. Fine, "One of the Boys"; Miller, "Not Just Weapons of the Weak"; and Quinn, "Paradox of Complaining."

55. There is a history of using humor as a shield for pain within the Black community (e.g., "playing the dozens"). Gordon, "Humor in African American Discourse." At the same time, self-deprecating humor also runs the risk of reinforcing racial stereotypes and hierarchies. Pérez, *Souls of White Jokes.*

56. DuBois, *Souls of Black Folk.*

57. In *The Art of Creation*, Arthur Koestler calls this process of bringing together two separate worlds of meanings as "bisociation." For more on the productive tension of jokes, refer to Tavory, "Situations of Culture."

58. On colorblind ideology, refer to Bonilla-Silva, *Racism Without Racists.* In the "Trump era," explicit racist language has prompted a new progressive racial narrative, "woke whiteness," which Gabriella Smith in "Woke" describes as virtue signaling and a bid for racial redemption. Shawn's use of "woke" critiques both colorblind ideology and the performative aspects of woke whiteness.

59. Lyman, "Fraternal Bond as Joking Relationship."

60. Fine, "One of the Boys"; and Pérez, *Souls of White Jokes.*

61. For similar observations of resistance in service work, refer to Paules, *Dishing It Out*; and Sherman, *Class Acts.*

62. Guzman, "Talking Shit, Egos, and Tough Skin"; and Murphy, "Humor Orgies as Ritual Insult."

63. For more on this double bind for both women and people of color, see Ahmed, *Feminist Killjoy*; and Weaver, *Rhetoric of Racist Humor.*

64. Quinn, "Paradox of Complaining."

65. On the managerial uses of humor at work, refer to Romero and Cruthirds, "Use of Humor in Workplace."

66. Michael Flaherty calls this tinkering with social reality through humor "reality play." *Formal Approach to Study of Amusement.*

67. Researching racial discourse among stand-up comedians, Pérez calls this taken-for-granted rule about not engaging in discourse "about a group you don't represent" a *racial common sense* strategy. "Learning to Make Racism Funny."

68. South Asian Americans navigate identities shaped by cultural stereotypes that polarize their occupational status (e.g., cab driver versus engineer) and by immigration discourse that often compares them to whites. Thakore, "Must-See TV"; and Koshy, "South Asians and Complex Interstices of Whiteness."

69. Interpersonal harassment can be one way in which both junior and senior men attempt to reclaim power over women in authority positions. McLaughlin, Uggen, and Blackstone, "Sexual Harassment, Workplace Authority."

70. Quoted from her *New York Times* op-ed. Gay, "Jada Pinkett Smith Shouldn't Have."

71. Kalev, "How You Downsize."

72. Research demonstrates how informal workplace interactions are often a site of discrimination and disrespect for marginalized workers; see, for example, Bell and Nkomo, *Our Separate Ways*; Turco, "Cultural Foundations of Tokenism"; and Wingfield, *Flatlining*.

73. In this vein, my research joins a broader debate on the role of informal workspaces and communities. Fleming and Sewell, "Looking for the Good Soldier"; Hodson, "Worker Resistance"; and Korczynski, "Communities of Coping."

74. Boltanski and Chiapello, *New Spirit of Capitalism*, 27.

CHAPTER 4. MAVERICK MANAGEMENT

1. In *Economy and Society*, Weber famously contrasted charismatic legitimacy with both traditional and legal-rational legitimacy.

2. In *Don't Take It Personally*, Zerubavel also focuses on atypical presentations as a key to establishing charismatic legitimacy, while Wagner-Pacifici and Tavory highlight the importance of rupture in "Politics as a Vacation." For more on the performative element of this strategy, see Reed, "Charismatic Performance."

3. Feagin and Ducey, *Elite White Men Ruling*.

4. This dominance contributed to the gendering and racialization of the organizations as managerial dictates and evaluation criteria were built around their particular experiences and interests. Acker, "Hierarchies, Jobs, and Bodies"; Ray, "Theory of Racialized Organizations"; and Wingfield and Alston, "Maintaining Hierarchies in White Organizations."

5. In *Don't Take It Personally*, Zerubavel notes how charismatic leaders' projection of eccentricity helps them attract personal devotion based on their individual idiosyncrasies. For a similar example in the context of politics, refer to Luebke, "Political Authenticity."

6. As Kanter famously highlighted in *Men and Women of the Corporation*, tokenism attracts a bright light of visibility. See Zerubavel for a helpful summary distinction between specific (who) personhood and generic (what) personhood. *Don't Take It Personally*.

7. As the sociologist Cecilia Ridgeway explains in *Framed by Gender*, people use stereotypes, or widely shared cultural beliefs about a social identity group, as a starting point for figuring people out. Regardless of whether someone personally endorses such beliefs, stereotypes remain consequential because they are entrenched in social institutions and are assumed to represent what "most people" think. For more on prominent stereotypes observed in empirical research, see Goff et al., "Ain't I a Woman"; Fiske, "Interpersonal Stratification"; and Heilman, "Gender Stereotypes and Workplace Bias."

8. Research participants didn't specifically use the term *maverick management*; rather, I employ it as an analytical concept to summarize the behaviors observed. For more on the history of the term see Strong, "Texan Origins of the Word 'Maverick.'"

9. Weber, *Economy and Society*.

10. Referring to infamous charismatic leaders such as Stalin and Hitler, Hannah Arendt notes, "[They] can remain in power only so long as they keep moving and set everything around them in motion." *Origins of Totalitarianism*, 306.

11. Reed, "Charismatic Performance."

12. Brown, *Gifts of Imperfection*, 51.

13. For more on how bureaucracy is cast as emasculating, see Neely, *Hedged Out*.

14. Junior account professional Jerry told me, for example, "[Leadership is] able to no problem go in check out all my emails and stuff like that," while creative director Calvin said, "I mean, it's a workplace. . . . You're paying me to work for you. Like what privacy should I have in that situation, you know?" Refer to Kantor and Sundaram's reporting in "Rise of the Worker Productivity Score" for more on expanding workplace surveillance.

15. Orwell, *1984*. For scholarly takes on the inequities of privacy and surveillance, refer to Browne, *Dark Matters*; Gilliom, *Overseers of the Poor*; and Roth, "Right to Privacy Is Political."

16. Connell, *Masculinities*; Brekhus, "Sociology of the Unmarked"; and Frankenberg, *White Women, Race Matters*.

17. Kanter, *Men and Women of the Corporation*; and Wingfield and Wingfield, "When Visibility Hurts and Helps."

18. Hochschild, *Managed Heart*; and Wingfield, "Are Some Emotions Marked 'Whites Only'?"

19. Bell and Nkomo, *Our Separate Ways*. Catalyst researchers refer to this need to armor up as an "emotional tax." Thorp-Moscon, Pollack, and Olu-lafe, *Empowering Workplaces Combat Emotional Tax*.

20. Wade, "Michelle Obama Tells Colbert.'"

21. Weber, *Economy and Society*.

22. For critical perspectives on "truth," refer to Collins, *Black Feminist Thought*; Gilligan, *In a Different Voice*; Harding, *Science Question in Feminism*; and Mills, *Racial Contract*.

23. In the language of organizational scholars Glenn Carroll and Dennis Ray Wheaton, marginalized groups had to build "moral authenticity," a belief in the sincerity of one's motives and actions, alongside "type authenticity," a belief that one is generally what they claim to be (e.g., a leader). For white men, the latter was often taken for granted, making it easier to focus solely on the former. "Organizational Construction of Authenticity."

24. This aligns with sociologist Allison Pugh's concept of "connective labor," in which the emotional work of making others feel seen and valued is central to workplace relationships. *Last Human Job.*

25. For more on the role of fallibility in performing authenticity and humanness, refer to Luebke, "Political Authenticity"; and Pugh, *Last Human Job.*

26. Castilla, "Gender, Race, and Meritocracy"; Correll et al., "Inside the Black Box"; and Puwar, *Space Invaders.*

27. McGoey, *The Unknowers.* Social researcher Arthur McLuhan and colleagues have also expanded some of these ideas to focus on incompetence more broadly, in "The Cloak of Incompetence."

28. Typically, researchers have focused on feigned incompetence as a resistance strategy among disgruntled workers, yet my research demonstrates it can also be a strategy of power adopted by managers. Hodson, "Worker Resistance"; Roscigno and Hodson, "Organizational and Social Foundations."

29. For example, Carlson and Hans, "Maximizing Benefits and Minimizing Impacts"; and Hochschild, *Second Shift.*

30. The Chinese have a phrase for this: "nande hutu." In *Ignorance Is Bliss,* Mieke Matthyssen provides a detailed history of this philosophy and practice in Chinese culture, and Louise Sandararajan offers an interesting analysis of its role in the context of high-trust societies in the book's postscript.

31. Stone and Colvin, "Arbitration Epidemic."

32. Notably, none of the managers at Disruption identified solely as white men. CEO Shane and vice president of talent Reid both identified as biracial men, while Logan, the VP of marketing, identified as a white woman. Despite his biracial identity, Shane successfully accomplished maverick management at Disruption, while Reid and Logan did not. This difference may be a result of Shane's higher degree of workplace authority. In addition, he might have benefited from positive racial stereotyping as a Japanese American (e.g., "model minority" tropes) that portrayed him as particularly well-suited to a high-status career in science, technology, engineering, and mathematics and which helped offset negative racial biases (e.g., assumptions of poor social skills and "yellow peril" narratives that depict Asian people as a threat). Shane also "passed" as white, enabling him to often bypass the oppression of identifying with a marked, racialized group and to enjoy the benefits of unmarked whiteness—a practice not equally available to all biracial groups or individuals. For more on the practices, patterns, and privileges of racial/ethnic passing, refer to Sasson-Levy and

Shoshana, "'Passing' as (Non)Ethnic"; Shiao, "Meaning of Honorary Whiteness"; and Waters, *Ethnic Options*; but also see Chow, "Privileged but Not in Power," for a nuanced account of Asian American experiences in US workspaces.

33. Gouldner, *Patterns of Industrial Democracy.* Gouldner also noted how this "mock" approach typically drove team cohesion, whereas other approaches to rule enforcement promoted internal conflict.

34. Refer also to Sallaz's *The Labor of Luck* for more on how rule-breaking is often tolerated when the ends are believed to justify the means.

35. Weber famously referred to the process through which rationality curtails individual freedom as the "iron cage": *Protestant Ethic and the Spirit of Capitalism.*

36. Martin et al., "Against the Rules"; and Ray, "Theory of Racialized Organizations."

37. The Compassionate Care Act, which legalized medical marijuana in New York, was signed into law in 2014. In 2021, several years after the study's completion, the adult recreational use of marijuana was legalized in New York, but it remains illegal at the federal level.

38. Alexander, *New Jim Crow.*

39. Ridgeway, Korn, and Williams, "Documenting Devalued Difference." While focusing specifically on the experiences of women, Tsedale Melaku also discusses the invisible labor associated with being one of a very small number of Black people in white spaces. "Black Women in White Institutional Spaces."

40. For other empirical examples of the raced and gendered dimensions of rule-breaking, refer to Ferguson, *Bad Boys*; and Musto, "Brilliant or Bad."

41. Refer to Fletcher's *Disappearing Acts* for more on the undervalued nature of this kind of labor.

42. Wade noted that he actually referred to the *idea* as stupid, but deliberately wanted the inference that the person was stupid to hang in the air.

43. For more on the decoupling of formal policy from informal organizational life, refer to Meyer and Rowan, "Institutionalized Organizations." Indeed, this is true even in organizations where people try to follow the rules in good faith but are hindered by complexity. Perrow, *Normal Accidents.*

44. Vaughan, Challenger *Launch Decision.*

45. Diaz, *Trust*, 266.

46. Hodson et al., "Ascension of Kafkaesque Bureaucracy."

47. Neely, "Fit to Be King."

CHAPTER 5. HEAVY TIES

1. This distinction is based on the theoretical foundation set by Granovetter in "Strength of Weak Ties" and *Getting a Job.*

2. Matthew Desmond faced a similar predicament in his discovery of fleeting yet intense and highly reciprocal relationships among the urban poor. "Disposable Ties and the Urban Poor." Like Desmond's disposable ties, heavy ties are high stakes. While the former are shaped by contexts infused with immediacy and desperation, the latter unfold more gradually, shaped by the need to navigate longer-term considerations and power dynamics.

3. Notably, the paradox in the "strength of weak ties" is that both strong and weak ties *can* be heavy ties, suggesting that perhaps a different means of classification may provide new theoretical purchase.

4. The inclusion of reciprocity and emotional intensity within the strong/weak ties framework speaks to relational stakes, but the theory—and much subsequent research—aggregates the five strength factors, making the role of each difficult to parse. The framework also assumes relational symmetry, ignoring how power differences between parties shape relational stakes. Media scholar Nancy Baym calls the work of maintaining heavy workplace ties "relational labor." Baym focuses on media workers' relationship with audiences, while I apply the term to workers' on-the-job relationships with peers, managers, and clients. Baym, "Connect with Your Audience!"

5. While bridging and buffering looked fairly similar across sites, bartering was slightly different at Disruption and DTC than at The Jones. In these settings, workers didn't trade shifts but swapped favors, engaging in what Strauss calls "articulation work" with one another to meet deadlines, push task requests through the pipeline, and provide cover amid absences. "Work and Division of Labor."

6. Portes discusses "negative social capital," which can lead to exclusion, excess claims, freedom constraints, and downward leveling. "Social Capital," 18. See also O'Brien, "Depleting Capital?"

7. For more on negative and/or depleting ties, refer to Offer, "Negative Social Ties"; Stack, *All Our Kin*; and Wallerstein, "Risky Ties and Taxing Ties."

8. For example, Portes and Sensenbrenner, "Embeddedness and Immigration"; and Wherry, Seefeldt, and Alvarez, "To Lend or Not to Lend."

9. Interestingly, Cook, Hardin, and Levi argue that these measures undermine the need for trust at work. *Cooperation Without Trust.*

10. This reflects a broader trend toward the individualization of risk in the contemporary economy. Hacker, *Great Risk Shift.*

11. Refer to Lambert's "Passing the Buck" and Van Oort's *Worn Out* for more on employer demands for open availability among hourly workers.

12. The former tended to be slightly older, with small children or other significant family care responsibilities, including caring for parents, grandparents, or a terminally ill spouse. The latter tended to be younger, some in relationships and others not.

13. Refer to Wynn and Rao, "Failures of Flexibility" for more on how perceived control can sometimes undermine worker power and flexibility.

14. Michelle was, notably, one of the few workers with family financial support.

15. This is part of Sharma's larger criticism of an oversimplified, polarized understanding of "speed-up" and "slow-down" discourse, which ignores the complexity and politics of time. *In the Meantime.* Dan Clawson and Naomi Gerstel make a similar point in *Unequal Time.*

16. HotSchedules® (The Jones's scheduling program) uses data on "POS sales, year-on-year trends, weather, local events" to drive schedule forecasting; see https://www.fourth.com/product/hotschedules. For more regarding on-demand scheduling, refer to Lambert, "Passing the Buck"; and Schneider and Harknett, "Hard Times."

17. Clocking in required a fingerprint scan to prevent workers from doing it for each other. Late clock-ins were tracked, capturing both true tardiness and forgetfulness. The system also blocked early clock-ins, even if staff started early. Only managers could adjust times retroactively.

18. Clawson and Gerstel use *web of time* in *Unequal Time* to refer to the interconnectedness of workplace schedules. Contemporary work arrangements frequently prioritize employer flexibility over worker flexibility; see, for example, Chun "Flexible Despotism"; and Smith, "New Forms of Work Organization."

19. For more on the moral dimensions of reciprocity, see Gouldner, "Norm of Reciprocity"; and Mauss, *Gift.*

20. Wood, "Powerful Times," 1074. See also Mears, "Working for Free in VIP"; Wood, *Despotism on Demand.*

21. Bartering within Indigenous communities and communal relations during the Great Depression offer two telling examples.

22. For example, Faulkner and Anderson, "Short-Term Projects and Emergent Careers"; Neff, "Changing Place of Cultural Production"; and Sharone, "LinkedIn or LinkedOut?"

23. Putnam famously distinguished between bridging and bonding social capital, with the latter representing ties within a tight-knit group. *Bowling Alone.*

24. For helpful reviews of this literature, refer to Castilla, Lan, and Rissing, "Social Networks and Employment"; and Trimble and Kmec, "Role of Social Networks."

25. Digital labor scholars have been particularly prescient in highlighting this previously invisible work; see Abidin, "Visibility Labor"; Baym, "Connect with Your Audience!"; Duffy, *(Not) Getting Paid*; and Ticona, *Left to Our Devices.*

26. The consequences of negative social capital are arguably more intensified in the "reputation economy." Gandini, *Reputation Economy*; and Hearn, "Structuring Feeling."

27. Gershon, *Down and Out in New Economy.*

28. Baumeister et al., "Bad Is Stronger Than Good."

29. Molm, Takahashi, and Peterson, "Risk and Trust in Social Exchange."

30. For example, McDonald, "What's in 'Old Boys' Network"; Pedulla and Pager, "Race and Networks in Job Search"; Alegria, "Escalator or Step Stool"; Ghosh and Barber, "Gender of Multiculturalism"; Kanter, *Men and Women of Corporation*; and Wingfield, "Racializing the Glass Escalator."

31. For more on the ideal worker norm that guides workplace structures, practices, and interactions, refer to Acker, "Hierarchies, Jobs, and Bodies"; and Wooten and Couloute, "Production of Racial Inequality."

32. Jones, "Cisgendered Workspaces"; and Yavorksy, "Cisgendered Organizations."

33. A robust literature exists on the gendered biases and stereotypes that exist in the workplace. Refer to Gorman and Mosseri, "Organizational Characteristics Shape Gender Difference," and Heilman, Caleo, and Manzi, "Women at Work," for two recent helpful reviews.

34. Yavorksy, "Cisgendered Organizations."

35. This "hustle"—and its perception by others—is gendered, racialized, and classed. For example, Hill, *Hustle Ethic*; and Williams, Blair-Loy, and Berdahl, "Cultural Schemas, Social Class."

36. Professionalism—specifically norms of appropriate workplace attire—tends to be coded white and cismasculine. See, for example, Alinor and Tinkler, "Take Off Your Hoodie"; and Waring and Waring, "Looking the Part."

37. For more on the value of workplace mentors, refer to Kay and Wallace, "Mentors as Social Capital." Research suggests the benefits of mentoring are not the same across gender and race. See, for example, Ibarra, Carter, and Silva, "Why Men Still Get More Promotions."

38. In general, networking requires people to mask their instrumental motives. Pultz and Sharone, "Intimate Dance of Networking."

39. For example, Starr, Prescott and Bishara, "Noncompetes in U.S. Labor Force."

40. Rushin, "Bridge Poem," 52.

41. In many cases, this is by design; Kalev and Dobbin, "Middle Managers into Diversity Leaders."

42. Most cases of workplace discrimination and harassment go unreported. Berrey, Nelson, and Nielsen, *Rights on Trial*; Cortina and Berdahl, "Sexual Harassment in Organizations"; and McCann, Tomaskovic-Devey, and Badgett, "Employers' Responses to Sexual Harassment."

43. See the introduction for a description of these built-in inequities.

44. For similar research findings, refer to Hirshfield and Joseph, "We Need a Woman"; Melaku," Black Women in White Spaces"; Lerma, Hamilton, and Nielsen, "Racialized Equity Labor."

45. When performed by women, feminized tasks such as mentoring or sponsoring tend to be overlooked. Fletcher, *Disappearing Acts*; and Heilman and Chen, "Same Behavior, Different Consequences." Refer to Correll et al.'s "Black Box of Organizational Life" for an in-depth view of gendered performance evaluations.

46. According to NYC's Paid Sick Leave Law in 2016, employers cannot require documentation from a licensed health-care provider until the employee uses more than three consecutive workdays as sick leave (which Matilda did not).

47. Research consistently demonstrates a motherhood penalty for women's labor market outcomes. For example, Budig and England, "Wage Penalty for Motherhood"; and Williams and Segal, "Beyond the Maternal Wall."

48. Hartless analyzes how such divides—which were often generational—played out among democratic supporters in the 2016 presidential election. "#ImWithHer or #FeelTheBern."

49. Refer to Romero's "Crossing Immigration and Race Border" for a useful critique of assimilation theories.

50. Jackman, *Velvet Glove.* While Jackman describes this process as largely instrumental, I noted paternalistic behavioral patterns emerging in both rational and irrational ways.

51. Macomber, "Men as Allies"; and Messner, Greenberg, and Penetz, *Some Men.*

52. Research studies find that such trainings are often unsuccessful at changing behaviors. Devine and Ash, "Diversity Training Goals, Limitations."

53. While the confidentiality of HR conversations is often implied, it is rarely guaranteed. RaQuel Hopkins, "Real Deal Around HR Confidentiality"; and SHRM, "Why HR Confidentiality Is Essential."

54. Berrey, Nelson, and Nielsen, *Rights on Trial*; and Dobbin, *Inventing Equal Opportunity.*

55. Bolton and Muzio, "Paradoxical Processes of Feminization"; and Flanagan, "Problem with HR."

56. Over half of private-sector charges filed with the Equal Employment Opportunity Commission in 2019 included an allegation of retaliation. US Equal Employment Opportunity Commission, "Charge Statistics FY 1997 Through FY 2019." See also McCann, Tomaskovic-Devey, and Badgett, "Employers' Responses to Sexual Harassment."

57. The biased design and implementation of formal systems and tools has been well-established across sociological disciplines. For example, Kalev, "How You Downsize"; and Noble, *Algorithms of Oppression.*

58. Refer to Mosseri et al.'s "Between Frustration and Invigoration" and Van Oort's *Worn Out* for useful empirical examples of how surveillance doesn't protect workers.

59. North and Hatch, *Circus Kings*, 12.

CHAPTER 6. CRYPTOCORPORATION

1. Economic sociologists have previously analyzed how economic exchanges are sometimes reframed in personal terms to increase legitimacy. For example, Haylett, "One Woman Helping Another"; and Zelizer, *Social Meaning of Money.*

2. The cryptocorporation is not to be confused with the digital currency cryptocurrency. Like cryptocurrencies, cryptocorporations boast democratic operations, but their functioning remains obscure to many.

3. This normative emphasis—particularly in the white-collar workplace—has been well-documented in, for example, Gregg's *Work's Intimacy* and Kunda's *Engineering Culture.*

4. In *Nice Is Not Enough*, Pascoe details how students and teachers focus on forging personal connections and building inclusive cultures but draw clear lines against discussing "politics," defined broadly as "inequalities and the ideologies that justify or challenge inequalities" (43).

5. The phrase "thought-terminating cliché" was coined in the 1960s by psychologist Robert Lifton in *Thought Reform and the Psychology of Totalism.* More recently, linguist Amanda Montell analyzed thought-terminating clichés in both radical and mainstream settings in *Cultish.*

6. For more on the fractured economy and fissured workplace, refer to Bartley, Soener, and Gershenson, "Power at a Distance"; Davis, *Vanishing American Corporation*; and Weil, *Fissured Workplace.*

7. Rossman, "Obfuscatory Relational Work," 54. Rossman actually outlines three forms of such labor: bundling, gift exchange, and brokerage. The latter, by which actors find a third party to accept responsibility for the exchange, is most prominent in the findings presented here.

8. In *Ghost Work*, researchers Mary Gray and Siddharth Suri argue that outsourced workers' labor is often made invisible, particularly in tech environments. Here, however, I find that even though outsourced workers were often invisible in terms of material recognition, they were highly visible in the context of accountability.

9. Kanter, *Men and Women of Corporation.*

10. For more on the inequities of the shadow structure, refer to McGuire, "Gender, Race, and Shadow Structure."

11. In *Moral Mazes*, Robert Jackall shows how, because managerial success is often a function of their expediency, managers are prone to engage in cognitive gymnastics to avoid confronting ethical dilemmas while progressing their careers.

12. Technology scholars highlight how designers and powerful economic actors often promote a false human-technology binary to achieve their own ends. For example, MacKenzie and Wajcman, *Social Shaping of Technology*; and Suchman, *Human-Machine Reconfigurations.*

13. See Leidner's *Fast Food, Fast Talk* and Sherman's *Class Acts* for more on the possibilities and limitations of worker-client alliances.

14. The term *partner* was not explicitly used across sites, but managers across the three companies sought to foster a sense of ownership among workers. For example, The Jones CEO, Stuart, told folks attending a new-employee orientation,

"We want everyone to participate, have ownership, feel empowered to create an experience." Such utterances were common.

15. For evidence of entrepreneurial ethos, refer to Neely, "Portfolio Ideal Worker." For communal ethos, refer to Sennett, *Culture of the New Capitalism*.

16. Gregg, *Counterproductive*, 117.

17. There is a noteworthy parallel in norms of secrecy around worker pay.

18. Freud, "Uncanny." Heidegger offers a complementary account of the uncanny that, for some, may feel more aligned with sociological analysis, given its focus on one's connection with the social, cultural, and historical world. *Introduction to Metaphysics*.

19. My analysis is deeply indebted to Marx's foundational theory of alienated labor and to Hochschild's subsequent analysis of alienation through emotional labor. Marx and Engels, *Economic and Philosophic Manuscripts*; and Hochschild, *Managed Heart*. One key point of difference that I see between Hochschild's analysis and my own is that while she focuses on alienation from one's self, I focus on workers' alienation from their needs.

20. Alegria, "Broadening Participation"; and US Equal Employment Opportunity Commission, "Diversity in High Tech."

21. For more on the burdens of representing diversity in homogenous workplaces, refer to Hirschfield and Joseph, "We Need a Woman"; Miller and Roksa, "Balancing Research and Service"; and Plater, "Symbolic Aesthetic Labor."

22. The use of trust as a means of mitigating intimate dangers is also discussed in Peter Geschiere's *Witchcraft, Intimacy, and Trust*.

23. To be sure, Shane and Reid were biracial/white. Nevertheless, white men *also* make up a majority of leaders in the broader tech industry. US Equal Employment Opportunity Commission, "Diversity in High Tech."

24. Refer to Meyers's *Working Democracies* and Sobering's *The People's Hotel* for rich, detailed accounts of such organizations.

25. Refer to Benjamin's *The Bonds of Love* for an insightful psychoanalytic account of the importance of mutual recognition.

26. Refer to Hochschild's *The Time Bind* for more on how workplace perks—like meals, on-site laundry, and fitness equipment—create a homelike atmosphere.

27. At the time of the study (2016), NYC restaurants were required to pay tipped workers $9.00 per hour, but they could draw $1.50 per hour from the workers' tips to cover that obligation, which The Jones did. The MIT Living Wage Calculator finds that to support themselves and/or their family in 2016, a full-time worker had to earn $21.32 hourly—which most Jones's staff did not.

28. This practice was particularly impactful in NYC, where many restaurant guests were international and visiting from countries that lacked a tipping culture.

29. Laemmli also provides an empirical account of restaurant managers outsourcing responsibility for work conditions to customers. "Workers and Their Foes."

30. All legal actions in NYC at the time.

31. This incident was previously analyzed in Pugh and Mosseri, "Trust-building vs. 'Just Trust Me.'"

32. And, in the case of bartender guests, return the favor when the team went to their workplace.

33. Zelizer, *Purchase of Intimacy.*

34. Zelizer, "How I Became a Relational Economic Sociologist."

35. Zelizer calls the four elements of economic interactions—relationship, transaction, media, and meanings—"relational packages."

36. For example, recall from chapter 1 how manager Ashley expressed underlying concerns that workers would take advantage of their intimacy in ways that undermined her authority or hurt the business.

37. Bey raps this in the song, "APESHIT" on The Carters' album, *Everything Is Love.*

38. Workers' response is a tangible illustration of Lapavitsas's argument of how money is associated with power, highlighting perhaps unexpected opportunities for bounded agency. "Relations of Power and Trust." Refer to Mosseri, "Finding Middle Ground," for more on the concept of "bounded agency."

39. Adler, "Choosing Bad Jobs."

40. Adler, "Choosing Bad Jobs."

41. In many cases, passion-driven jobs are also not lucrative or secure, with workers often making significant sacrifices in turn for "fulfilling" work. Cech, *Trouble with Passion.*

42. Hochschild, *Commercialization of Intimate Life*, 3.

43. Weeks, *Problem with Work*; and Zelizer, *Purchase of Intimacy.*

CHAPTER 7. ORCHESTRATED ALLIANCE

1. Uber entered the NYC market in 2011, followed by Lyft in 2014. Other companies in this space include Gett, Juno, Hailo, and TaxiMagic.

2. TLC Chair Meera Joshi summarized the main tenets of the debate in opening remarks at the April 2017 hearing. The full transcript of the hearing can be accessed on the TLC's Commission Meetings page: https://www.nyc.gov/site/tlc/about/commission-meetings.page.

3. Rosenthal, "Taxi Drivers Trapped in Loans."

4. Parrott and Reich, *Earnings Standard for App-Based Drivers.*

5. Rosenblat and Stark, "Algorithmic Labor and Information Asymmetries."

6. In the article, Kellen Browning argues, "the term 'gig work,' in the minds of many, has become a stand-in for low-paid or exploitative work—in part because of how people perceive companies like Uber." "'Gig Work' a Dirty Word?" For other media coverage of platforms' negative impact, see, for example, Goncharova,

"Ride-Hailing Drivers Slaves to the Surge"; Tolentino, "Working Yourself to Death." The issue has also been the topic of state and national congressional hearings; for example, in 2019 the New York State Senate held a hearing, *Examination of the Gig Economy,* and the US House Transportation and Infrastructure committee held a hearing, *Examining the Future of Transportation Network Companies.*

7. The NYTWA represents nonstandard workers (specifically drivers) and is an affiliate of the American Federation of Labor-Congress of Industrial Organizations. The IDG is an affiliate of the International Association of Machinists and Aerospace Workers (IAM). The IDG formed in 2016 through a voluntary recognition agreement between IAM and Uber. It provides drivers with access to Uber management, the ability to appeal deactivation decisions via an independent panel, and discounted legal services. Neither group, however, had the right to collective bargaining at the time of the study.

8. Conger, Xu, and Wichter, "Uber Drivers' Day of Strikes'"; and Santora and Surico, "Uber Drivers Protest Fare Cuts."

9. This decline remains despite greater support for unions and widely covered union activity in recent years. McCarthy, "Approval of Labor Unions at Highest Point"; and Rosalsky, "You May Have Heard." Scheiber, "Uber Drivers Are Contractors."

10. Parrott and Reich, *Earnings Standard for App-Based Drivers*; Price, "NYCC Transportation Committee Public Comment"; and Taxi and Limousine Commission, "2018 Factbook."

11. Newcomer, "Uber CEO Argues Over Falling Fares."

12. Near the end of the video, Kalanick exemplified his "plain talk" style, going off on Kamel by saying, "Some people don't like to take responsibility for their own shit. They blame everything in their life on somebody else." Examples of his "endearing incompetence" and "discretionary rule-bending" can be seen in articles such as Foroohar's "TIME Person of the Year 2015 Runner-Up" (see Eric Schmidt quote) and Yglesias's "Uber's Toxic Culture of Rule Breaking."

13. In a rare mention of driving *for* Uber on *The Late Show with Stephen Colbert,* Kalanick aligned more with supplemental income drivers versus full-time drivers, saying, "For me, it's just fun." "5-Year Anniversary Remarks." In *Super Pumped,* journalist Mike Isaac describes an extreme party culture at Uber headquarters, detailing the particularly lavish X to the X party in 2015. Drivers were not among the attendees.

14. In one of Uber's "Greenlight" hubs, a security guard who noticed my loitering accused me of being a "spy" and told me to leave.

15. Refer to Espeland and Steven's "Commensuration as a Social Process" and Porter's *Trust in Numbers* for more on this as a broader societal trend.

16. Chan, "Rating Game."

17. Christin, *Metrics at Work.*

18. In *Hustle and Gig*, Alexandrea Ravenelle outlines UberX's reduction in its base fares from $6.00 to $2.55 and in its minimum fare from $12.00 to $7.00 between June 2014 and January 2016. Over this same time period, the per mile rate went from $3.00 to $1.75, and the per minute rate went from $0.70 to $0.35 (75). In addition to the cost of purchasing or leasing a car and maintaining it, NYC drivers must pay for the license and registration, automobile inspections, commercial insurance, and other miscellaneous required costs.

19. Santora and Surico, "Uber Drivers Protest Fare Cuts."

20. Eighty percent of the NYC drivers I interviewed expressed growing distrust of platform companies and their leaders. These drivers, with experience ranging from months to years, often worked for multiple platforms simultaneously.

21. Mosseri, "Being Watched and Being Seen." See also Flyverbom et al., "Visibilities in the Digital Age."

22. Alex Rosenblat reported in *Uberland* this threshold was typically anything under 4.6 (out of 5).

23. Wells, Attoh, and Cullen, "'Just-in-Place' Labor," 320.

24. Kellogg, *Challenging Operations*.

25. See also Chen, "Uber Labor Movement Born"; Wells, Attoh, and Cullen, *Disrupting D.C.*

26. Lorde, "Uses of Anger," 283.

27. Santora and Surico, "Uber Drivers Protest Fare Cuts."

28. Refer to Michèle Lamont's *Seeing Others* and Allison Pugh's *The Last Human Job* for more on the power of interpersonal recognition.

29. Mateescu and Ticona refer to these as "visibility regimes." "Invisible Work, Visible Workers."

30. As personally observed on advertisements and as reported in Rosenblat's *Uberland*.

31. Economic empowerment was one of several social goods promoted by company leaders. Kalanick "5-Year Anniversary Remarks"; and Zimmer, "Third Transportation Revolution."

32. For example, Huet, "Uber Continues to Finance Its Drivers"; and Uber, "Drive When You Want."

33. Duffy, *(Not) Getting Paid*. See also Gregg, "Hack for Good"; and Mackenzie and McKinlay, "Psychic Life of Cultural Work."

34. For example, Abidin, "Visibility Labour"; Bucher, "Want to Be on the Top?"; and Cotter, "Playing the Visibility Game."

35. Rosenblat and Stark, "Algorithmic Labor and Information Asymmetries."

36. Rosenblat, for example, notes that "Uber maintains it is not a taxi company—it's a technology company that uses neutral algorithms to merely facilitate connections between consumers and drivers." *Uberland*, 58. By classifying drivers as "independent contractors," platform companies seek to avoid mandates for minimum wage and overtime and disability pay and liability

for workplace discrimination. Kaltner, "Employment Status of Uber and Lyft Drivers"; and Tomassetti, "Does Uber Redefine the Firm?"

37. Refer to Gray and Suri, *Ghost Work*, Irani, "Difference and Dependence Among Digital Workers," and Mateescu and Elish, *AI in Context* for more on how low-paid labor is intentionally made less visible in the tech industry.

38. Cockayne, "Sharing and Neoliberal Discourse"; and Singer, "Make 'Sharing' Apps Seem Selfless."

39. For example, Crain, Poster, and Cherry, *Invisible Labor*; Daniels, "Invisible Work"; and Hatton, "Mechanisms of Invisibility."

40. Fitzsimmons, "Require Uber to Provide Tipping Option."

41. Refer to Brayne, "Surveillance and System Avoidance," and Ticona and Mateescu, "Trusted Strangers," for more on institutionalized visibility.

42. Chan, "Rating Game"; and Rosenblat, *Uberland.*

43. Mosseri, "Being Watched and Being Seen."

44. Comparing data from Parrott and Reich's previously cited analysis with 2016 American Community Survey data of the NYC population, I found that while over 90 percent of drivers were foreign born, only 38 percent of NYC residents were. Similarly, only 17 percent of drivers reported a BA or higher, while 39 percent of NYC residents did.

45. Williams and Connell discuss the need for service workers to appeal to certain aesthetics in "'Looking Good and Sounding Right.'" In the context of ride-hail platform work, specifically, Alex Rosenblat and colleagues highlight how ratings can become biased. "Discriminating Tastes."

46. Some platforms have since added "long trip notifications" to reduce uncertainty for drivers; see, for examples, Uber's "180 Days of Change" campaign. Researchers make a similar point. Mishel and McNicholas, "Uber Drivers Are Not Entrepreneurs"; and Rosenblat and Stark, "Algorithmic Labor and Information Asymmetries."

47. Griswold, "Uber Drivers Make Sure Company Doesn't Underpay Them."

48. Scheiber, "Uber to Repay Millions to Drivers."

49. Wong, "Uber Admits Underpaying Drivers."

50. New York State Attorney General's Office, "Attorney General James Joins Uber and Lyft Drivers"; and New York Taxi Workers Alliance, "$328 Million Uber/Lyft Settlement."

51. Wright, *Short History of Progress*, 124.

52. As is likely clear by now, the morality of the fallen parallels Nietzsche's "slave morality" in elevating suffering as meaningful but operates instead as a mechanism of connection rather than envy or resentment. *On the Genealogy of Morality.*

53. Jackson, "Rethinking Repair."

54. Feminist scholar Margaret Urban Walker defines moral repair as restoring trust after harm, while I align with Jackson's focus on the ongoing work of maintaining and transforming social systems. *Moral Repair.*

55. Hodges, *Taxi!*; and Mitra, "Driving Taxis in New York City."

56. For more on the benefits and constraints of flexibility in the gig economy, refer to Gulesserian, Veen, and Baird, "'Gig' Work and Fatherhood," and James, "Platform Work-Lives in Gig Economy."

57. There were valid reasons for their reticence given the IDG's formal ties to Uber at the time. Scheiber, "Uber Has a Union of Sorts."

58. Drivers frequently commented on Uber's discouragement of tipping; Diego, for example, told me, "They've invested more money into telling the customers no tipping. Right? You saw the video. 'No tipping.'"

59. IDG, "On Tipping."

60. Full hearing transcripts are available on the TLC's Commission Meeting page.

61. TLC, "Promulgation of Rules for Tipping."

62. IDG, "Independent Drivers Guild Celebrates Tipping Victory."

63. Hawkins, "Uber Finally Caves."

64. At times, these precarious alliances backfired. Wells and colleagues, for example, describe how a journalist outed drivers who were tricking the platform apps by turning their phones off and on in unison to manipulate dynamic pricing systems. "'Just-in-Place' Labor." Similarly, media outlets reported in 2022 that Uber paid academic researchers to feed favorable research to the media. For example, Lawrence, "Uber Paid Academics Six-Figure Sums." In my own interactions with drivers, many expressed an initial wariness, explaining they'd been burned by undercover platform providers, cops, and even journalists in the past.

65. Burns, "Drivers Urge Lawmakers to End 'Exploitative Ways.'"

66. Mosseri, "Being Watched and Being Seen."

67. Over 60 percent of NYC drivers log an average of more than thirty hours a week on the apps and report ride-hail wages as being the primary source of income for their households. Parrott and Reich, *Earnings Standard for App-Based Drivers*. Racabi, "Effects of City–State Relations."

68. Richardson, "You Want Your Employees to Return"; and Thompson, "Three Myths of Great Resignation."

69. King, "New Sense of Direction."

CONCLUSION

1. Adecco Group, "4 Takeaways for Future of Work."

2. Gelmi, "Leaders in the Digital Age"; and Raman and Flynn, "When Your Technical Skills Are Eclipsed."

3. For example, Fraser and Jaeggi, *Capitalism*; and Suchman, *Human-Machine Reconfigurations*.

4. For example, Stark, *Coercive Control*; and Calarco, *Holding It Together*.

5. See also Pascoe, *Nice Is Not Enough*; and Weeks, *Problem with Work*, epilogue.

6. For example, Burke, "Big Transition"; Domonoske, "Grocery Workers Keep America Fed"; and Newton, "Facebook Will Shift Jobs to Remote Work."

7. Barnett and Li, "Tech Layoffs Are Happening Faster"; Chapman, "Elon Musk Demands Tesla Workers Return"; and Olson, "There's No Labor Shortage."

8. Tapper, "Quiet Quitting"; and Gittleman, "'Great Resignation' in Perspective."

9. Tarasov, "Unions Are Forming."

10. Indeed, the concentration of trust in the workplace should give us pause. History shows that monopolizing trust is a dangerous game. As outlined in Gambetta, *Sicilian Mafia*; Tikhomirov, "Regime of Forced Trust"; and Zuckerman, *Mistrust*, such patterns consolidate dependence in ways that can lead to oppressive and exploitative systems—not unlike the shadowy paternalism of the Italian mafia or the authoritarian grip of Stalin's Russia. These examples may seem extreme, but they underscore the risks of centralizing trust in a single locus, leaving individuals vulnerable to coercion cloaked as care.

11. Desmond, "American Capitalism Is Brutal."

12. Acker, "Hierarchies, Jobs, and Bodies"; and Williams, *Unbending Gender*.

13. Acker, "Hierarchies, Jobs, and Bodies"; Glenn, "From Servitude to Service Work"; Ray, "Theory of Racialized Organizations"; and Wingfield and Alston, "Maintaining Hierarchies in White Organizations."

14. Fernandez and Galperin, "Causal Status of Social Capital"; Gorman, "Gender Stereotypes, Same-Gender Preferences"; Pager and Karafin, "Bayesian Bigot?"; and Rivera, *Pedigree*.

15. Bonacich, "Theory of Ethnic Antagonism"; Charles and Grusky, *Occupational Ghettos*; Reskin and Roos, *Job Queues, Gender Queues*; and Weeden, "Occupational Segregation."

16. Tomaskovic-Devey and Avent-Hold, *Relational Inequalities*.

17. While The Jones was also characterized by a clear front-of-house/back-of-house divide, servers, bartenders, bussers, and food runners were all considered front-of-house workers.

18. For a similar argument, see Sherman, *Uneasy Street*.

19. Carpenter, "Diverse Employees Often Working Twice as Hard"; and Nance-Nash, "Diversity Initiatives Trap Workers of Colour."

20. Indeed, Charles Tilly argued that categories like "worker" and "manager" contribute to "durable inequalities." *Durable Inequality*.

21. For more on promoting diverse and equitable workplaces, see Sobering, "Relational Production of Workplace Equality"; and Wilcox and Koontz, "Workplace Well-Being."

22. For example, Goldberg, "When Your Boss Is Crying."

23. Baker, Bivens, and Schieder, "Reining in CEO Compensation."

24. For example, Brynjolfsson and McAfee, *Second Machine Age*; and Frey and Osborne, "Future of Employment."

25. McClain and Pendell, "Why Trust in Leaders Is Faltering"; and Palmer, "Amazon Workers Walk Out."

26. Collins, "Job Unhappiness at All-Time High"; and Parker and Horowitz, "Majority of Workers Who Quit."

27. Zuckerberg, "Update on Meta's Year of Efficiency."

28. Banerjee et al., "Unions Are Not Only Good for Workers"; and US Department of the Treasury, "Labor Unions and the Middle Class."

29. Organisation for Economic Co-operation and Development, Statistics, "Trade Union Density."

30. Rosalsky, "You May Have Heard of the 'Union Boom'"; and US Bureau of Labor Statistics, "Union Members—2022."

31. National Conference of State Legislatures, "Right-to-Work Resources."

32. Shierholz, Poydock, and McNicholas, "Unionization Increased by 200,000 in 2022."

33. US Congress, National Labor Relations Act.

34. McNicholas et al., "Employers Spend More Than $400 Million."

35. Lafer and Loustaunau, "Fear at Work."

36. McNicholas et al., "Unlawful."

37. See also Block and Sachs, "Clean Slate for Worker Power," for similar recommendations.

38. European Trade Union Institution, "What's Happening to Collective Bargaining in Europe?" Block and Sachs, "Clean Slate for Worker Power." Sectoral bargaining does reintroduce the "free-rider" problem of right-to-work laws, but it reduces perceptions of union versus nonunion competitive advantages at the company level, and it is ultimately more inclusive than other forms of bargaining.

39. Madland and Rowell, "Combating Pay Gaps."

40. Block and Sachs, "Clean Slate for Worker Power."

41. National Conference of State Legislatures, "At-Will Employment—Overview."

42. Andrias and Hertel-Fernandez, *Ending At-Will Employment*; and Tung, Odessky, and Sonn, "Just Cause Job Protections."

43. Currently severance pay is not mandated by federal law.

44. Baker, "What Minimum Wage Would Be."

45. Currently, the overtime salary threshold is approximately $35,000, but a proposed rule change would raise it to about $55,000. US Department of Labor, "Department of Labor Announces Proposal."

46. There are currently no federal legal requirements for paid sick leave.

47. See, for example, recommendations from the Economic Policy Institute. Golden, "Irregular Work Scheduling and Its Consequences."

48. Dobbin and Kalev, "Civil Rights Revolution at Work"; US Department of Labor, "FY 2020 Congressional Budget Justification."

49. Piore and Schrank, *Root Cause Regulation.*

50. Colvin, "Growing Use of Mandatory Arbitration"; and Weil, *Fissured Workplace.*

51. Fine et al., "Strategic Enforcement of U.S. Labor Standards"; and McNicholas and von Wilpert, "Joint Employer Standard."

52. Colvin, "Growing Use of Mandatory Arbitration."

53. US Department of Labor, "Comparison of State Unemployment Laws 2022."

54. Alternatively, Denmark's Flexicurity system may offer a potential model for policymakers. The system maintains at-will employment but couples it with employee-invested insurance funds and robust education and retraining programs, along with a comprehensive welfare system. As a result, employers enjoy flexibility, while workers maintain security.

55. The superannuation system in Australia may provide one template for brainstorming. Hultin, Jacquinot and Petrini, "Do Workers Need Portable Benefits?"

56. The average length of paid leave among countries that offer it is twenty-nine weeks. Miller: "World 'Has Found a Way to Do This.'"

57. Pollman, "Supreme Court and Pro-Business Paradox."

58. Tikhomirov, "Regime of Forced Trust."

59. Piketty, *Capital*; and Stiglitz, *Price of Inequality.*

60. Cooper and Mosseri, "Pandemic Has Impacted Women Most Significantly"; and Vasel, "Pandemic Forced Massive Remote-Work Experiment."

61. Madani, "Dan Patrick on Coronavirus."

62. Kantor and Sundaram, "Rise of Worker Productivity Score."

63. Kelly, "Google, Amazon and Others Continue to Lay Off Employees."

APPENDIX

1. Dominus, "When the Revolution Came for Amy Cuddy"; Lewis-Kraus, "They Studied Dishonesty"; and Lubet, "Ethnography on Trial."

2. Freese and Peterson, "Replication in Social Science"; Murphy, Jerolmack, and Smith, "Ethnography, Data Transparency"; and Open Science Collaboration, "Reproducibility of Psychological Science."

3. This is a dominant view among sociologists, as articulated in key texts across the discipline.

4. Klein, *Doppelganger*; *and* Tripodi, *Propogandists' Playbook.*

5. Pugh and Mosseri, "Trust-Building vs. 'Just Trust Me.'"

6. This work builds on other theories of resonance; see, for example, McDonnell, Bail, and Tavory, "Theory of Resonance"; and Messeri, "Resonant Worlds."

7. Arnold, *Essays in Criticism*, 106.

8. McDonnell, Bail, and Tavory, "Theory of Resonance."

9. Said, *After the Last Sky*, 38.

10. Abbott, “Against Narrative.”

11. Arlie Hochschild refers to these as “magnified moments.” “Commercial Spirit of Intimate Life.”

12. Hochschild, *Managed Heart*.

13. For example, Paap, *Working Construction*; Pierce, *Gender Trials*; and Wingfield, “Are Some Emotions ‘Whites Only.’”

14. Heaney, “Emotion as Power.”

15. Ellis, “Sociological Introspection.”

Bibliography

Abbott, Andrew. "Against Narrative: A Preface to Lyrical Sociology." *Sociological Theory* 25, no. 1 (March 1, 2007): 67–99.

———. "Things of Boundaries." *Social Research* 62, no. 4 (1996): 857–82.

Abidin, Crystal. "Visibility Labour: Engaging with Influencers' Fashion Brands and #OOTD Advertorial Campaigns on Instagram." *Media International Australia* 161, no. 1 (August 29, 2016): 86–100.

Acker, Joan. "Hierarchies, Jobs, and Bodies: A Theory of Gendered Organizations." *Gender & Society* 4, no. 2 (1990): 139–58.

Adecco Group. "4 Takeaways for the Future of Work from Davos 2023." January 26, 2023. https://www.adeccogroup.com/future-of-work/latest-insights/4-takeaways-for-the-future-of-works-from-davos-2023.

Adler, Laura. "Choosing Bad Jobs: The Use of Nonstandard Work as a Commitment Device." *Work and Occupations* 48, no. 2 (May 1, 2021): 207–42.

Adler, Paul. "Market, Hierarchy, and Trust: The Knowledge Economy and the Future of Capitalism." *Organization Science* 12, no. 2 (April 1, 2001): 215–34.

Ahmed, Sara. *Complaint!* Duke University Press, 2021.

———. *The Feminist Killjoy Handbook: The Radical Potential of Getting in the Way.* Basic Books, 2023.

Albiston, Catherine, and Catherine Fisk. "Precarious Work and Precarious Welfare: How the Pandemic Reveals Fundamental Flaws of the U.S. Social Safety Net." *Berkeley Journal of Employment & Labor Law* 42, no. 2 (June 2021): 257–320.

Alegria, Sharla. "Escalator or Step Stool? Gendered Labor and Token Processes in Tech Work." *Gender & Society* 33, no. 5 (October 2019): 722–45.

———. "What Do We Mean by Broadening Participation? Race, Inequality, and Diversity in Tech Work." *Sociology Compass* 14, no. 6 (2020): e12793.

Alexander, Michelle. *The New Jim Crow: Mass Incarceration in the Age of Colorblindness*. The New Press, 2010.

Alfrey, Lauren. "Diversity, Disrupted: A Critique of Neoliberal Difference in Tech Organizations." *Sociological Perspectives* 65, no. 6 (December 1, 2022): 1081–98.

Alinor, Malissa, and Justine Tinkler. "Take Off Your Hoodie: Assessing How Professional Attire Influences the Perception of Black Men as Threatening." *Du Bois Review: Social Science Research on Race* 18, no. 1 (March 2021): 97–117.

Anderson, Elijah. "'The White Space.'" *Sociology of Race and Ethnicity* 1, no. 1 (January 1, 2015): 10–21.

Andrias, Kate, and Alexander Hertel-Fernandez. *Ending At-Will Employment: A Guide for Just Cause Reform*. Roosevelt Institute, 2021.

Anteby, Michel, Curtis Chan, and Julia DiBenigno. "Three Lenses on Occupations and Professions in Organizations: Becoming, Doing, and Relating." *Academy of Management Annals* 10, no. 1 (January 2016): 183–244.

AP-NORC Center and the GSS Staff. *Confidence in Institutions: Trends in Americans' Attitudes Toward Government, Media, and Business*. March 11, 2015. https://apnorc.org/wp-content/uploads/2020/02/ConfidenceInstitutions-to-DTP-FORMATTED.pdf.

Arendt, Hannah. *The Origins of Totalitarianism*. Harcourt, Brace, Jovanovich, 1951.

Armstrong, Elizabeth. *Forging Gay Identities: Organizing Sexuality in San Francisco, 1950–1994*. University of Chicago Press, 2002.

Armstrong, Elizabeth, Miriam Gleckman-Krut, and Lanora Johnson. "Silence, Power, and Inequality: An Intersectional Approach to Sexual Violence." *Annual Review of Sociology* 44 (July 30, 2018): 99–122.

Arnold, Matthew. *Essays in Criticism*. Read Books Design, 2010.

Arrow, Kenneth. *The Limits of Organization*. W. W. Norton, 1974.

Aviv, Rachel. *Strangers to Ourselves: Unsettled Minds and the Stories That Make Us*. Farrar, Straus and Giroux, 2022.

Bachmann, Reinhard, and Andrew Inkpen. "Understanding Institutional-Based Trust Building Processes in Inter-Organizational Relationships." *Organization Studies* 32, no. 2 (February 1, 2011): 281–301.

Baker, Dean. "This Is What Minimum Wage Would Be If It Kept Pace with Productivity." Center for Economic and Policy Research, January 21, 2020. https://cepr.net/publications/correction-this-is-what-minimum-wage-would-be-if-it-kept-pace-with-productivity/.

Baker, Dean, Josh Bivens, and Jessica Schieder. "Reining in CEO Compensation and Curbing the Rise of Inequality." Economic Policy Institute, 2019. https://www.epi.org/publication/reining-in-ceo-compensation-and-curbing-the-rise-of-inequality/.

Bakhtin, Mikhail. *Rabelais and His World.* Indiana University Press, 1965.

Bancroft, Angus. *Drugs, Intoxication and Society.* Polity, 2009.

Bandelj, Nina. "Relational Work and Economic Sociology." *Politics & Society* 40, no. 2 (2012): 175-201.

Banerjee, Asha, Margaret Poydock, Celine McNicholas, Ihna Mangundayao, and Ali Sait. "Unions Are Not Only Good for Workers, They're Good for Communities and for Democracy." Economic Policy Institute, 2021. https://www.epi.org/publication/unions-and-well-being/.

Barbalet, Jack. "A Characterization of Trust, and Its Consequences." *Theory and Society* 38, no. 4 (April 24, 2009): 367–82.

Barbaro, Michael, Sydney Harper, Stella Tan, Rachel Quester, Davis Lin, Patricia Willens, Marion Lozano, and Chris Wood. "Public Health Officials Under Siege." *New York Times,* November 11, 2021.

Barker, James. "Tightening the Iron Cage: Concertive Control in Self-Managing Teams." *Administrative Science Quarterly* 38, no. 3 (September 1, 1993): 408–37.

Barnett, Andrew, and Ming Li. "Tech Layoffs Are Happening Faster Than at Any Time During the Pandemic." *Wall Street Journal,* January 3, 2023.

Barney, Chuck. "'The Daily Show with Trevor Noah': Get to Know the New Host." *Mercury News,* September 23, 2015.

Barry, Michael, Tony Dundon, and Adrian Wilkinson. "Employee Voice: Conceptualisations, Meanings, Limitations and Possible Integration." In *The Routledge Companion to Employment Relations.* Routledge, 2018.

Bartley, Tim, Matthew Soener, and Carl Gershenson. "Power at a Distance: Organizational Power Across Boundaries." *Sociology Compass* 13, no. 10 (2019): e12737.

Baumeister, Roy, Ellen Bratslavsky, Catrin Finkenauer, and Kathleen Vohs. "Bad Is Stronger Than Good." *Review of General Psychology* 5, no. 4 (December 1, 2001): 323–70.

Baym, Nancy. "Connect with Your Audience! The Relational Labor of Connection." *Communication Review* 18, no. 1 (January 2, 2015): 14–22.

Beck, Julie. "The Concept Creep of 'Emotional Labor.'" *Atlantic,* November 26, 2018.

Becker, Howard S. "Notes on the Concept of Commitment." *American Journal of Sociology* 66, no. 1 (1960): 32–40.

Beckert, Jens. "Trust and the Performative Construction of Markets." SSRN Scholarly Paper. Social Science Research Network, July 15, 2005.

Bell, Ella Edmondson, and Stella M. Nkomo. *Our Separate Ways: Black and White Women and the Struggle for Professional Identity.* Harvard Business Press, 2001.

Bell, Rowan. "Being Your Best Self: Authenticity, Morality, and Gender Norms." *Hypatia* 39, no. 1 (February 2024): 1–20.

Bellah, Robert N., Richard Madsen, William M. Sullivan, Ann Swidler, and Steven M. Tipton. *Habits of the Heart: Individualism and Commitment in American Life*. University of California Press, 1985.

Bemiller, Michelle, and Rachel Zimmer Schneider. "It's Not Just a Joke." *Sociological Spectrum* 30, no. 4 (June 2, 2010): 459–79.

Benard, Stephen, and Shelley Correll. "Normative Discrimination and the Motherhood Penalty." *Gender & Society* 24, no. 5 (October 1, 2010): 616–46.

Benjamin, Jessica. *The Bonds of Love: Psychoanalysis, Feminism, & the Problem of Domination*. Pantheon, 1988.

Berdahl, Jennifer, Marianne Cooper, Peter Glick, Robert Livingston, and Joan Williams. "Work as a Masculinity Contest." *Journal of Social Issues* 74, no. 3 (2018): 422–48.

Berdahl, Jennifer, and Celia Moore. "Workplace Harassment: Double Jeopardy for Minority Women." *Journal of Applied Psychology* 91, no. 2 (2006): 426–36.

Berlant, Lauren. *Cruel Optimism*. Duke University Press, 2020.

Bernstein, Elizabeth. *Temporarily Yours: Intimacy, Authenticity, and the Commerce of Sex*. University of Chicago Press, 2007.

Berrey, Ellen, Robert Nelson, and Laura Beth Nielsen. *Rights on Trial: How Workplace Discrimination Law Perpetuates Inequality*. University of Chicago Press, 2017.

Best, Jacqueline. "Security, Economy, Population: The Political Economic Logic of Liberal Exceptionalism." *Security & Dialogue* 48, no. 5 (2017): 375–92.

Billingsley, Brianna. "Racialized and Classed Contexts: Shifting Audiences and Changes in Emotional Labor Among Restaurant Servers." *Sociological Inquiry* 86, no. 4 (2016): 641–57.

Blair-Loy, Mary. *Competing Devotions: Career and Family Among Women Executives*. Harvard University Press, 2003.

Block, Sharon, and Benjamin Sachs. "Clean Slate for Worker Power: Building a Just Economy and Democracy." Labor and Worklife Program, Harvard Law School, 2020.

Boltanski, Luc, and Eve Chiapello. *The New Spirit of Capitalism*. Translated by Gregory Elliott. Verso, 2005.

Bolton, Sharon, and Daniel Muzio. "The Paradoxical Processes of Feminization in the Professions: The Case of Established, Aspiring and Semi-Professions." *Work, Employment and Society* 22, no. 2 (June 1, 2008): 281–99.

Bonacich, Edna. "A Theory of Ethnic Antagonism: The Split Labor Market." *American Sociological Review* 37, no. 5 (October 1, 1972): 547–59.

Bonilla-Silva, Eduardo. *Racism Without Racists: Color-Blind Racism and the Persistence of Racial Inequality in the United States*. Rowman & Littlefield, 2010.

Borchers, Callum. "Behold, the New Starting Salary for Some Graduates Is $100,000." *Wall Street Journal*, March 10, 2022.

Boroditsky, Lera. *7,000 Universes: How the Language We Speak Shapes the Way We Think*. Knopf Doubleday Publishing Group, 2018.

Botsman, Rachel. *Who Can You Trust? How Technology Brought Us Together and Why It Might Drive Us Apart*. Public Affairs, 2017.

Brayne, Sarah. "Surveillance and System Avoidance: Criminal Justice Contact and Institutional Attachment." *American Sociological Review* 79, no. 3 (June 1, 2014): 367–91.

Brekhus, Wayne. "A Sociology of the Unmarked: Redirecting Our Focus." *Sociological Theory* 16, no. 1 (1998): 34–51.

Brooks, Arthur. "The Hidden Toll of Remote Work." *Atlantic*, April 1, 2021.

Brower, Holly Henderson, Scott Wayne Lester, and Audrey Korsgaard. "Want Your Employees to Trust You? Show You Trust Them." *Harvard Business Review*, July 5, 2017.

Brown, Brené. *The Gifts of Imperfection: Let Go of Who You Think You're Supposed to Be and Embrace Who You Are*. Hazelden Publishing, 2010.

Brown, Peter. "Society and the Supernatural: A Medieval Change." *Daedalus* 104, no. 2 (1975): 133–51.

Brown, Rebecca, and Melissa Gregg. "The Pedagogy of Regret: Facebook, Binge Drinking and Young Women." *Continuum* 26, no. 3 (June 1, 2012): 357–69.

Browne, Simone. *Dark Matters: On the Surveillance of Blackness*. Duke University Press, 2015.

Browning, Kellen. "Has 'Gig Work' Become a Dirty Word?" *New York Times*, May 27, 2023.

Brynjolfsson, Erik, and Andrew McAfee. *The Second Machine Age: Work, Progress, and Prosperity in a Time of Brilliant Technologies*. W. W. Norton, 2014.

Bucher, Taina. "Want to Be on the Top? Algorithmic Power and the Threat of Invisibility on Facebook." *New Media & Society* 14, no. 7 (2012): 1164–80.

Budig, Michelle, and Paula England. "The Wage Penalty for Motherhood." *American Sociological Review* 66, no. 2 (April 2001): 204.

Burawoy, Michael. *Manufacturing Consent: Changes in the Labor Process Under Monopoly Capitalism*. University of Chicago Press, 1979.

Burke, Lilah. "The Big Transition." Inside Higher Ed, March 30, 2020. https://www.insidehighered.com/news/2020/03/31/faculty-discuss-their-quick-transition-online-instruction.

Burns, Janet. "Amid NYC Suicides, Drivers Urge Lawmakers to End Uber's Exploitative Ways." *Forbes*, March 20, 2018.

Cabanas, Edgar, and Eva Illouz. "The Making of a 'Happy Worker': Positive Psychology in Neoliberal Organizations." In *Beyond the Cubicle: Job Insecurity, Intimacy, and the Flexible Self*, edited by Allison Pugh. Oxford University Press, 2017.

Calarco, Jessica. *Holding It Together: How Women Became America's Safety Net.* Portfolio, 2024.

Cappelli, Peter. *The New Deal at Work: Managing the Market-Driven Workforce.* Harvard Business Press, 1999.

Carlson, Matthew, and Jason Hans. "Maximizing Benefits and Minimizing Impacts: Dual-Earner Couples' Perceived Division of Household Labor Decision-Making Process." *Journal of Family Studies* 26, no. 2 (April 2, 2020): 208–25.

Carpenter, Julia. "Diverse Employees Are Often Working Twice as Hard." *CNN Business*, February 30, 2018. https://www.cnn.com/2018/11/28/success/diversity-work-burden.

Carroll, Glenn, and Dennis Ray Wheaton. "The Organizational Construction of Authenticity: An Examination of Contemporary Food and Dining in the U.S." *Research in Organizational Behavior* 29 (January 1, 2009): 255–82.

Carroll, Lewis. *Through the Looking-Glass: And What Alice Found There.* Macmillan Children's Books, 1871.

Castilla, Emilio. "Gender, Race, and Meritocracy in Organizational Careers." *AJS: American Journal of Sociology* 113, no. 6 (May 2008): 1479–1526.

———. "Gender, Race, and Network Advantage in Organizations." *Organization Science* 33, no. 6 (November 2022): 2364–2403.

Castilla, Emilio, George Lan, and Ben Rissing. "Social Networks and Employment: Mechanisms (Part 1)." *Sociology Compass* 7, no. 12 (2013): 999–1012.

———. "Social Networks and Employment: Outcomes (Part 2)." *Sociology Compass* 7, no. 12 (2013): 1013–26.

Cech, Erin. *The Trouble with Passion: How Searching for Fulfillment at Work Fosters Inequality.* University of California Press, 2021.

Chamberlain, Lindsey Joyce, Martha Crowley, Daniel Tope, and Randy Hodson. "Sexual Harassment in Organizational Context." *Work and Occupations* 35, no. 3 (May 2, 2008): 262–95.

Chan, Ngai Keung. "The Rating Game: The Discipline of Uber's User-Generated Ratings." *Surveillance & Society* 17, no. 1/2 (March 31, 2019): 183–90.

Chapman, Wilson. "Elon Musk Demands Tesla Employees Return to Office." *Variety*, June 1, 2022.

Charles, Maria, and David Grusky. *Occupational Ghettos: The Worldwide Segregation of Women and Men.* Stanford University Press, 2004.

Chen, Adrian. "An Uber Labor Movement Born in a LaGuardia Parking Lot." *New Yorker*, February 8, 2016.

Chen, Victor Tan. *Cut Loose: Jobless and Hopeless in an Unfair Economy.* University of California Press, 2015.

Choo, Hae Yeon, and Myra Marx Ferree. "Practicing Intersectionality in Sociological Research: A Critical Analysis of Inclusions, Interactions, and Institutions in the Study of Inequalities." *Sociological Theory* 28, no. 2 (2010): 129–49.

Chow, Tiffany. "Privileged but Not in Power: How Asian American Tech Workers Use Racial Strategies to Deflect and Confront Race and Racism." *Qualitative Sociology* 46, no. 1 (March 1, 2023): 129–52.

Christin, Angele. *Metrics at Work: Journalism and the Contested Meaning of Algorithms*. Princeton University Press, 2020.

Chun, Jennifer. "Flexible Despotism: The Intensification of Insecurity and Uncertainty in the Lives of Silicon Valley's High-Tech Assembly Workers." In *The Critical Study of Work: Labor, Technology and Global Production*, edited by Rick Baldoz, Chuck Koeber, and Phil Kraft. Temple University Press, 2001.

Clawson, Dan, and Naomi Gerstel. *Unequal Time: Gender, Class, and Family in Employment Schedules*. Russell Sage Foundation, 2014.

Cockayne, Daniel. "Sharing and Neoliberal Discourse: The Economic Function of Sharing in the Digital on-Demand Economy." *Geoforum* 77 (December 1, 2016): 73–82.

Coleman, Joshua. *Rules of Estrangement: Why Adult Children Cut Ties and How to Heal the Conflict*. Harmony/Rodale, 2021.

Colbert, Stephen. "Travis Kalanick Interview." *The Late Show with Stephen Colbert*, September 9, 2015.

Collins, Caitlyn. *Making Motherhood Work: How Women Manage Careers and Caregiving*. Princeton University Press, 2019.

Collins, Leah. "Job Unhappiness Is at a Staggering All-Time High, According to Gallup." *CNBC*, August 12, 2022. https://www.cnbc.com/2022/08/12/job-unhappiness-is-at-a-staggering-all-time-high-according-to-gallup.html.

Collins, Patricia Hill. *Black Feminist Thought: Knowledge, Consciousness, and the Politics of Empowerment*. Routledge Chapman & Hall, 1990.

Collins, Randall. *Interaction Ritual Chains*. Princeton University Press, 2004.

———. "Stratification, Emotional Energy, and the Transient Emotions." In *Research Agendas in the Sociology of Emotions*. SUNY Series in the Sociology of Emotions. State University of New York Press, 1990.

Colquitt, Jason, Brent Scott, and Jeffery LePine. "Trust, Trustworthiness, and Trust Propensity: A Meta-Analytic Test of Their Unique Relationships with Risk Taking and Job Performance." *Journal of Applied Psychology* 92, no. 4 (July 2007): 909–27.

Coltrane, Scott. *Family Man: Fatherhood, Housework, and Gender Equity*. Oxford University Press, 1996.

Colvin, Alexander. "The Growing Use of Mandatory Arbitration." Economic Policy Institute, 2017. https://www.epi.org/publication/the-growing-use-of-mandatory-arbitration/.

Conger, Kate, Vicky Xiuzhong Xu, and Zach Wichter. "Uber Drivers' Day of Strikes Circles the Globe Before the Company's I.P.O." *New York Times*, May 8, 2019.

Connell, Raewyn. *Masculinities.* University of California Press, 1995.

Cook, Alison, and Christy Glass. "Glass Cliffs and Organizational Saviors: Barriers to Minority Leadership in Work Organizations?" *Social Problems* 60, no. 2 (May 1, 2013): 168–87.

Cook, Karen. "Networks, Norms, and Trust: The Social Psychology of Social Capital." *Social Psychology Quarterly* 68, no. 1 (March 1, 2005): 4–14.

Cook, Karen, Russell Hardin, and Margaret Levi. *Cooperation Without Trust?* Russell Sage Foundation, 2007.

Cooper, Marianne. *Cut Adrift: Families in Insecure Times.* University of California Press, 2014.

Cooper, Rae, and Sarah Mosseri. "Pandemic Has Impacted on Women Most Significantly." *Sydney Morning Herald*, June 4, 2020.

Cooper, Rae, Sarah Mosseri, Ariadne Vromen, Marian Baird, Elizabeth Hill, and Elspeth Probyn. "Gender Matters: A Multilevel Analysis of Gender and Voice at Work." *British Journal of Management* 32, no. 3 (2021): 725–43.

Correll, Shelley, Katherine Weisshaar, Alison Wynn, and JoAnne Delfino Wehner. "Inside the Black Box of Organizational Life: The Gendered Language of Performance Assessment." *American Sociological Review* 85, no. 6 (December 1, 2020): 1022–50.

Cortina, Lilia, and Jennifer Berdahl. "Sexual Harassment in Organizations: A Decade of Research in Review." In *The SAGE Handbook of Organizational Behavior*. Vol. 1, *Micro Approaches*, edited by Julian Barling and Cary Cooper. Sage Publications, 2008.

Cotter, Kelley. "Playing the Visibility Game: How Digital Influencers and Algorithms Negotiate Influence on Instagram." *New Media & Society* 21, no. 4 (December 14, 2018): 895–913.

Cottom, Tressie McMillan. "Citizens No More." *New York Times*, June 28, 2022.

Covey, Stephen. *The Speed of Trust: The One Thing That Changes Everything.* Free Press, 2006.

Cox, Daniel. "The State of American Friendship: Change, Challenges, and Loss." The Survey Center on American Life, June 8, 2021. https://www.americansurveycenter.org/research/the-state-of-american-friendship-change-challenges-and-loss/.

Crain, Marion, Winifred Poster, and Miriam Cherry. *Invisible Labor: Hidden Work in the Contemporary World.* University of California Press, 2016.

Current Population Survey. *Annual Social and Economic (ASEC) Supplement.* 2019. https://www.census.gov/data/tables/time-series/demo/income-poverty/cps-pinc/pinc-10.2018.html#list-tab-46897943.

Dalla Costa, Mariarosa and Selma James. *The Power of Women and the Subversion of the Community.* Falling Wall Press Limited, 1975.

Damaske, Sarah. *The Tolls of Uncertainty: How Privilege and the Guilt Gap Shape Unemployment in America.* Princeton University Press, 2021.

Daniels, Arlene Kaplan. "Invisible Work." *Social Problems* 34, no. 5 (December 1, 1987): 403–15.

Daniels, Chelsea, Paul DiMaggio, Cristina Mora, and Hana Shepherd. "Has Pandemic Threat Stoked Xenophobia? How COVID-19 Influences California Voters' Attitudes Toward Diversity and Immigration." *Sociological Forum* 36, no. 4 (September 1, 2021): 889.

Davern, Michael, Rene Bautista, Jeremy Freese, Pamela Herd, and Stephen Morgan. "General Social Survey 1972–2022." Sponsored by National Science Foundation. NORC at the University of Chicago, 2023.

Davis, Gerald. *Managed by the Markets: How Finance Re-Shaped America*. Oxford University Press, 2009.

———. *The Vanishing American Corporation: Navigating the Hazards of a New Economy*. National Geographic Books, 2016.

Day, Katy, Brendan Gough, and Majella McFadden. "'Warning! Alcohol Can Seriously Damage Your Feminine Health.'" *Feminist Media Studies* 4, no. 2 (July 1, 2004): 165–83.

DePalma, Lindsay. "The Passion Paradigm: Professional Adherence to and Consequences of the Ideology of 'Do What You Love.'" *Sociological Forum* 36, no. 1 (2021): 134–58.

Desmond, Matthew. "American Capitalism Is Brutal: You Can Trace That to the Plantation." *New York Times*, August 14, 2019.

———. "Disposable Ties and the Urban Poor." *American Journal of Sociology* 117, no. 5 (March 1, 2012): 1295–1335.

Devine, Patricia, and Tory Ash. "Diversity Training Goals, Limitations, and Promise: A Review of the Multidisciplinary Literature." *Annual Review of Psychology* 73 (January 4, 2022): 403–29.

Diaz, Hernan. *Trust*. Penguin, 2022.

Didion, Joan. *Slouching Towards Bethlehem: Essays*. Open Road Media, 2017.

DiMaggio, Paul. *The Twenty-First-Century Firm: Changing Economic Organization in International Perspective*. Princeton University Press, 2001.

Dimock, Michael. "How Americans View Trust, Facts, and Democracy Today." Pew Research Center, 2020. https://www.pew.org/en/trust/archive/winter-2020/how-americans-view-trust-facts-and-democracy-today.

Dirks, Kurt, and Bart de Jong. "Trust Within the Workplace: A Review of Two Waves of Research and a Glimpse of the Third." *Annual Review of Organizational Psychology and Organizational Behavior* 9, no. 1 (2022): 247–76.

Dirks, Kurt, and Donald Ferrin. "Trust in Leadership: Meta-Analytic Findings and Implications for Research and Practice." *Journal of Applied Psychology* 87, no. 4 (2002): 611–28.

Dobbin, Frank. *Inventing Equal Opportunity*. Princeton University Press, 2009.

Dobbin, Frank, and Alexandra Kalev. "The Civil Rights Revolution at Work: What Went Wrong." *Annual Review of Sociology* 47, no. 1 (2021): 281–303.

Doeringer, Peter, and Michael Piore. *Internal Labor Markets and Manpower Analysis*. M. E. Sharpe, 1971.
Dominus, Susan. “When the Revolution Came for Amy Cuddy.” *New York Times*, October 18, 2017.
Domonoske, Camila. “Grocery Workers Keep America Fed, While Fearing for Their Own Safety.” *NPR*, April 2, 2020. https://www.npr.org/2020/04/02/825376458/grocery-workers-keep-america-fed-while-fearing-for-their-own-safety.
Douglas, Mary. *Constructive Drinking: Perspectives on Drink from Anthropology*. Psychology Press, 2003.
Drutman, Lee. “How Corporate Lobbyists Conquered American Democracy.” *Atlantic*, April 20, 2015.
DuBois, W. E. B. *The Souls of Black Folk*. A. C. McClurg, 1903.
DuGay, Paul. *Consumption and Identity at Work*. Sage Publications, 1996.
Duffy, Brooke Erin. “Manufacturing Authenticity: The Rhetoric of ‘Real’ in Women’s Magazines.” *The Communication Review* 16, no. 3 (July 1, 2013): 132–54.
———. *(Not) Getting Paid to Do What You Love: Gender, Social Media, and Aspirational Work*. Yale University Press, 2017.
———. “The Romance of Work: Gender and Aspirational Labour in the Digital Culture Industries.” *International Journal of Cultural Studies* 19, no. 4 (July 1, 2016): 441–57.
Duffy, Brooke Erin, Kate Miltner, and Amanda Wahlstedt. “Policing ‘Fake’ Femininity: Authenticity, Accountability, and Influencer Antifandom.” *New Media & Society* 24, no. 7 (July 1, 2022): 1657–76.
Duffy, Mignon. “Doing the Dirty Work: Gender, Race, and Reproductive Labor in Historical Perspective.” *Gender & Society* 21, no. 3 (June 1, 2007): 313–36.
Dundon, Tony, and Paul Gollan. “Re-Conceptualizing Voice in the Non-Union Workplace.” *International Journal of Human Resource Management* 18, no. 7 (July 1, 2007): 1182–98.
Dundon, Tony, Adrian Wilkinson, Mick Marchington, and Peter Ackers. “The Meanings and Purpose of Employee Voice.” *International Journal of Human Resource Management* 15, no. 6 (2004): 1149–70.
Durkheim, Emile. *The Elementary Forms of Religious Life*. Translated by Karen E. Fields. Free Press, 1912.
Edelman. *2018 Edelman Trust Barometer: Global Results*. http://cms.edelman.com/sites/default/files/2018_02/2018_Edelman_Trust_Barometer_Global_Report_FEB.pdf.
Editorial Board. “States Lead the Way on Paid Family Leave.” *New York Times*, April 20, 2016.
Edmondson, Amy. *The Fearless Organization: Creating Psychological Safety in the Workplace for Learning, Innovation, and Growth*. John Wiley & Sons, 2018.

Edwards, Richard. *Contested Terrain: The Transformation of the Workplace in the Twentieth Century*. Basic Books, 1979.

Ellis, Carolyn. "Sociological Introspection and Emotional Experience." *Symbolic Interaction* 14, no. 1 (1991): 23–50.

Elster, Jon. *The Cement of Society: A Survey of Social Order*. Cambridge University Press, 1989.

Ely, Robin, and Debra Meyerson. "Advancing Gender Equity in Organizations: The Challenge and Importance of Maintaining a Gender Narrative." *Organization* 7, no. 4 (November 1, 2000): 589–608.

Emirbayer, Mustafa. "Manifesto for a Relational Sociology." *American Journal of Sociology* 103, no. 2 (September 1, 1997): 281–317.

Engelhard, Iris, Miriam Lommen, and Marit Sijbrandij. "Changing for Better or Worse? Posttraumatic Growth Reported by Soldiers Deployed to Iraq." *Clinical Psychological Science* 3, no. 5 (September 1, 2015): 789–96.

England, Paula. "Emerging Theories of Care Work." *Annual Review of Sociology* 31 (August 11, 2005): 381–99.

England, Paula, Nancy Folbre, and Carrie Leanna. "Motivating Care." In *For Love and Money: Care Provision in the United States*, edited by Nancy Folbre. Russell Sage Foundation, 2012.

Espeland, Wendy Nelson, and Mitchell L. Stevens. "Commensuration as a Social Process." *Annual Review of Sociology* 24 (1998): 313–43.

European Trade Union Institute. "What's Happening to Collective Bargaining in Europe?," 2019. https://www.etui.org/services/facts-figures/benchmarks/what-s-happening-to-collective-bargaining-in-europe#:~:text=However%2C%20the%20fact%20that%20collective,to%20ensure%20extensive%20bargaining%20coverage.

The Ezra Klein Show. "The Office Is Dying: It's Time to Rethink How We Work." Accessed November 4, 2023. https://www.nytimes.com/2022/08/16/opinion/ezra-klein-podcast-anne-helen-petersen-charlie-warzel.html.

Eyal, Gil, Larry Au, and Cristian Capotescu. "Trust Is a Verb!: A Critical Reconstruction of the Sociological Theory of Trust." *Sociologica* 18, no. 2 (October 30, 2024): 169–91.

Families and Work Institute. *National Study of the Changing Workforce*. 2008. https://archive.ciser.cornell.edu/studies/2849.

Farrugia, David, Julia Coffey, Steven Threadgold, Lisa Adkins, Ros Gill, Megan Sharp, and Julia Cook. "Hospitality Work and the Sociality of Affective Labour." *Sociological Review* 71, no. 1 (January 1, 2023): 47–64.

Faulkner, Robert, and Andy Anderson. "Short-Term Projects and Emergent Careers: Evidence from Hollywood." *American Journal of Sociology* 92, no. 4 (1987): 879–909.

Feagin, Joe, and Kimberley Ducey. *Elite White Men Ruling: Who, What, When, Where, and How*. Routledge, 2017.

Federici, Silvia. *Wages Against Housework*. Falling Wall Press and the Power of Women Collective, 1975.

Feltman, Charles. *The Thin Book of Trust: An Essential Primer for Building Trust at Work*. Thin Book Publishing, 2021.

Ferguson, Ann Arnett. *Bad Boys: Public Schools in the Making of Black Masculinity*. University of Michigan Press, 2000.

Fernandez, Roberto, and Roman Galperin. "The Causal Status of Social Capital in Labor Markets." In *Contemporary Perspectives on Organizational Social Networks*, vol. 40. Research in the Sociology of Organizations. Emerald Group Publishing, 2014.

Fine, Gary Alan. "Crafting Authenticity: The Validation of Identity in Self-Taught Art." *Theory and Society* 32, no. 2 (2003): 153–80.

———. "Friendships in the Work Place." In *Friendship and Social Interaction*, edited by Valerian Derlega and Barbara Winstead. Springer Series in Social Psychology. Springer, 1986.

———. "One of the Boys: Women in Male-Dominated Settings." In *Changing Men: New Directions in Research on Men and Masculinity*, edited by Michael Kimmel. Sage Publications, 1987.

Fine, Gary Alan, and Michaela de Soucey. "Joking Cultures: Humor Themes as Social Regulation in Group Life." *Journal of Humor Research* 18, no. 1 (April 20, 2005): 1–22.

Fine, Janice, Daniel Galvin, Jenn Round, and Hana Shepherd. "Strategic Enforcement and Co-Enforcement of U.S. Labor Standards Are Needed to Protect Workers Through the Coronavirus Recession." Washington Center for Equitable Growth, January 14, 2021. https://equitablegrowth.org/strategic-enforcement-and-co-enforcement-of-u-s-labor-standards-are-needed-to-protect-workers-through-the-coronavirus-recession/.

Fiske, Susan. "Interpersonal Stratification." In *Handbook of Social Psychology*, edited by Susan Fiske, Daniel Gilbert, and Gardner Lindzey. John Wiley & Sons, 2010.

Fiske, Susan, Amy Cuddy, and Peter Glick. "Universal Dimensions of Social Cognition: Warmth and Competence." *Trends in Cognitive Sciences* 11, no. 2 (February 1, 2007): 77–83.

Fitzsimmons, Emma. "New York City Moves to Require Uber to Provide a Tipping Option in Its App." *New York Times*, April 17, 2017.

Flaherty, Michael. "A Formal Approach to the Study of Amusement in Social Interaction." *Symbolic Interactionism* 5 (1982): 71–82.

Flanagan, Caitlin. "The Problem with HR." *Atlantic*, June 20, 2019.

Fleming, Peter, and Graham Sewell. "Looking for the Good Soldier, Švejk: Alternative Modalities of Resistance in the Contemporary Workplace." *Sociology* 36, no. 4 (November 1, 2002): 857–73.

Fletcher, Joyce. *Disappearing Acts: Gender, Power, and Relational Practice at Work*. MIT Press, 1999.

Flyverbom, Mikkel, Paul Leonardi, Cynthia Stohl, and Michael Stohl. "The Management of Visibilities in the Digital Age." *International Journal of Communication* 10 (January 5, 2016): 12.

Folbre, Nancy. *The Invisible Heart: Economics and Family Values*. New Press, 2001.

Foroohar, Rana. "TIME Person of the Year 2015 Runner-Up: Travis Kalanick." *Time*, December 9, 2015.

Frankenberg, Ruth. *White Women, Race Matters: The Social Construction of Whiteness*. University of Minnesota Press, 1993.

Fraser, Nancy, and Rahel Jaeggi. *Capitalism: A Conversation in Critical Theory*. John Wiley & Sons, 2018.

Freeman, James, and Richard Medoff. *What Do Unions Do?* Basic Books, 1984.

Freese, Jeremy, and David Peterson. "Replication in Social Science." *Annual Review of Sociology* 43, no. 1 (2017): 147–65.

Frenette, Alexandre, and Richard Ocejo. "Sustaining Enchantment: How Cultural Workers Manage Precariousness and Routine." In *Race, Identity and Work*, vol. 32. Research in the Sociology of Work, 2018.

Freud, Sigmund. "The Uncanny." In *The Standard Edition of the Complete Psychological Works of Sigmund Freud*, vol. 17. Bloomsbury, 1919.

Frey, Carl, and Michael Osborne. "The Future of Employment" Working paper, Oxford Martin Programme on Technology and Employment, September 1, 2013. https://www.oxfordmartin.ox.ac.uk/publications/the-future-of-employment.

Fukuyama, Francis. *Trust: The Social Virtues and the Creation of Prosperity*. Free Press, 1995.

Gallup. "Confidence in Institutions." Annual Trust Poll, 2018. https://news.gallup.com/poll/1597/confidence-institutions.aspx.

Gambetta, Diego. *The Sicilian Mafia: The Business of Private Protection*. Harvard University Press, 1996.

Gandini, Alessandro. *The Reputation Economy: Understanding Knowledge Work in Digital Society*. Springer, 2016.

Garofalo, Livia. "Doppelgangers in a Digital World." Data & Society, August 16, 2023. https://datasociety.net/points/doppelgangers-in-a-digital-world/.

Garratt, Lindsey. "Authenticity and Racism: Young Boys in Three Inner City Primary Schools in Dublin." *Journal of Ethnic and Migration Studies* 48, no. 9 (July 4, 2022): 2285–2303.

Gately, Iain. *Drink: A Cultural History of Alcohol*. Avery, 2009.

Gay, Roxane. "Jada Pinkett Smith Shouldn't Have to 'Take a Joke': Neither Should You." *New York Times*, March 29, 2022.

Gelmi, Thomas. "Leaders in the Digital Age Must Think, Act and Be Human." *Forbes*, April 25, 2023.

General Social Survey, *The Quality of WorkLife Survey Module*. 2022. https://gss.norc.org/us/en/gss/quality-of-worklife.html.

Gershon, Ilana. *Down and Out in the New Economy: How People Find (or Don't Find) Work Today*. University of Chicago Press, 2017.

Geschiere, Peter. *Witchcraft, Intimacy, and Trust: Africa in Comparison*. University of Chicago Press, 2013.

Ghaziani, Amin. *There Goes the Gayborhood?* Princeton University Press, 2014.

Ghosh, Debaleena, and Kristen Barber. "The Gender of Multiculturalism: Cultural Tokenism and the Institutional Isolation of Immigrant Women Faculty." *Sociological Perspectives* 64, no. 6 (December 1, 2021): 1063–80.

Giddens, Anthony. *The Consequences of Modernity*. Stanford University Press, 1990.

———. *Modernity and Self-Identity: Self and Society in the Late Modern Age*. Stanford University Press, 1991.

Gilligan, Carol. *In a Different Voice: Psychological Theory and Women's Development*. Harvard University Press, 1982.

Gilliom, John. *Overseers of the Poor: Surveillance, Resistance, and the Limits of Privacy*. University of Chicago Press, 2001.

Gittleman, Maury. "The 'Great Resignation' in Perspective." *Monthly Labor Review*, July 2022. US Bureau of Labor Statistics. Accessed November 27, 2024. https://www.bls.gov/opub/mlr/2022/article/the-great-resignation-in-perspective.htm.

Glenn, Evelyn Nakano. "Creating a Caring Society." *Contemporary Sociology* 29, no. 1 (January 2000): 84–94.

———. "From Servitude to Service Work: Historical Continuities in the Racial Division of Paid Reproductive Labor." *Signs* 18, no. 1 (October 1, 1992): 1–43.

———. "The Social Construction and Institutionalization of Gender and Race: An Integrative Framework." In *Revisioning Gender*, edited by Myra Ferree, Judith Lorber, and Beth Hess. Sage Publications, 1999.

Goff, Phillip Atiba, Margaret Thomas, and Matthew Christian Jackson. "'Ain't I a Woman?': Towards an Intersectional Approach to Person Perception and Group-Based Harms." *Sex Roles* 59, no. 5 (September 1, 2008): 392–403.

Goffman, Alice. "Go to More Parties? Social Occasions as Home to Unexpected Turning Points in Life Trajectories." *Social Psychology Quarterly* 82, no. 1 (March 1, 2019): 51–74.

Goldberg, Emma. "When Your Boss Is Crying, but You're the One Being Laid Off." *New York Times*, August 24, 2022.

Golden, Lonnie. "Irregular Work Scheduling and Its Consequences." Economic Policy Institute, 2015. https://www.epi.org/publication/irregular-work-scheduling-and-its-consequences/.

Goncharova, Masha. "Ride-Hailing Drivers Are Slaves to the Surge." *New York Times*, January 12, 2017.

Gordon, Dexter. "Humor in African American Discourse: Speaking of Oppression." *Journal of Black Studies* 29, no. 2 (1998): 254–76.

Gorman, Elizabeth. "Gender Stereotypes, Same-Gender Preferences, and Organizational Variation in the Hiring of Women: Evidence from Law Firms." *American Sociological Review* 70, no. 4 (August 1, 2005): 702–28.

Gorman, Elizabeth, and Sarah Mosseri. "How Organizational Characteristics Shape Gender Difference and Inequality at Work." *Sociology Compass* 13, no. 3 (2019): e12660.

Gottfried, Jeffrey, Mason Walker, and Amy Mitchell. "Americans See Skepticism of News Media as Healthy, Say Public Trust in the Institution Can Improve." Pew Research Center's Journalism Project, August 31, 2020. https://www.pewresearch.org/journalism/2020/08/31/americans-see-skepticism-of-news-media-as-healthy-say-public-trust-in-the-institution-can-improve/.

Gould, Elise, and Will Kimball. "'Right-to-Work' States Still Have Lower Wages." Economic Policy Institute, April 22, 2015. https://www.epi.org/publication/right-to-work-states-have-lower-wages/.

Gouldner, Alvin. "The Norm of Reciprocity: A Preliminary Statement." *American Sociological Review* 25, no. 2 (1960): 161–78.

———. *Patterns of Industrial Bureaucracy*. Free Press, 1964.

Graham, Laurie. *On the Line at Subaru-Isuzu: The Japanese Model and the American Worker*. Cornell University Press, 1995.

Granovetter, Mark. "Economic Action and Social Structure: The Problem of Embeddedness." *American Journal of Sociology* 91, no. 3 (November 1, 1985): 481–510.

———. *Getting a Job: A Study of Contacts and Careers*. University of Chicago Press, 1974.

———. "The Strength of Weak Ties." *American Journal of Sociology* 78 (1973): 1360–80.

Granter, Edward, Leo McCann, and Maree Boyle. "Extreme Work/Normal Work: Intensification, Storytelling and Hypermediation in the (Re)Construction of 'the New Normal.'" *Organization* 22, no. 4 (July 1, 2015): 443–56.

Gray, Mary, and Siddharth Suri. *Ghost Work: How to Stop Silicon Valley from Building a New Global Underclass*. Houghton Mifflin Harcourt, 2019.

Grazian, David. *Blue Chicago: The Search for Authenticity in Urban Blues Clubs*. University of Chicago Press, 2005.

———. "Demystifying Authenticity in the Sociology of Culture." In *Routledge Handbook of Cultural Sociology*. Routledge, 2018.

"Great Place To Work® Trust Index© Employee Survey." Accessed June 2021. https://www.greatplacetowork.com/solutions/employee-surveys.

Gregg, Melissa. *Counterproductive: Time Management in the Knowledge Economy*. Duke University Press, 2018.

———. "Hack for Good: Speculative Labour, App Development and the Burden of Austerity." *Fibreculture Journal*, no. 25 (2015): 183–201.

———. "On Friday Night Drinks: Workplace Affects in the Age of the Cubicle." In *The Affect Theory Reader*, edited by Melissa Gregg and Gegory Seigworth. Duke University Press, 2010.

———. *Work's Intimacy*. John Wiley & Sons, 2013.

Griswold, Alison. "Uber Drivers Are Using This Trick to Make Sure the Company Doesn't Underpay Them." *Quartz*, April 13, 2017. https://qz.com/956139/uber-drivers-are-comparing-fares-with-riders-to-check-their-pay-from-the-company.

Guendelsberger, Emily. *On the Clock: What Low-Wage Work Did to Me and How It Drives America Insane*. Little, Brown, 2019.

Gulesserian, Lisa, Alex Veen, and Marian Baird. "'Gig' Work and Fatherhood: A Typology of Ride-Share Fathers in Australia." In *New Technology, Work and Employment*, January 16, 2025, https://doi.org/10.1111/ntwe.12333.

Gusfield, Joseph. "Passage to Play: Rituals of Drinking Time in American Society." In *Constructive Drinking*. Routledge, 1987.

Guzman, Joseph. "Talking Shit, Egos, and Tough Skin: Humor Among Elite Black Men." *Journal of Contemporary Ethnography* 49, no. 5 (October 1, 2020): 613–37.

Hacker, Jacob. *The Great Risk Shift: The New Economic Insecurity and the Decline of the American Dream*. Oxford University Press, 2008.

Harding, Sandra. *The Science Question in Feminism*. Cornell University Press, 1986.

Hart, Paul. "Symbols, Rituals and Power: The Lost Dimensions of Crisis Management." *Journal of Contingencies and Crisis Management* 1, no. 1 (1993): 36–50.

Hartless, Jaime. "#ImWithHer or #FeelTheBern." In *The Politics of Gender*, edited by Adrienne Trier-Bieniek. Brill, 2018.

———. "Questionably Queer: Understanding Straight Presence in the Post-Gay Bar." *Journal of Homosexuality* 66, no. 8 (July 3, 2019): 1035–57.

Hatton, Erin. *Coerced: Work Under Threat of Punishment*. University of California Press, 2020.

———. "Mechanisms of Invisibility: Rethinking the Concept of Invisible Work." *Work, Employment and Society* 31, no. 2 (April 1, 2017): 336–51.

Hawkins, Andrew. "Uber Finally Caves and Adds a Tipping Option to Its App." *The Verge*, June 20, 2017.

Haylett, Jennifer. "One Woman Helping Another: Egg Donation as a Case of Relational Work." *Politics & Society* 40, no. 2 (June 1, 2012): 223–47.

Hays, Sharon. *The Cultural Contradictions of Motherhood*. Yale University Press, 1996.

———. *Flat Broke with Children: Women in the Age of Welfare Reform*. Oxford University Press, 2003.

Heaney, Jonathan. "Emotion as Power: Capital and Strategy in the Field of Politics." *Journal of Political Power* 12, no. 2 (May 4, 2019): 224–44.

Hearn, Alison. "Structuring Feeling: Web 2.0, Online Ranking and Rating, and the Digital 'reputation' Economy." *Ephemera: Theory & Politics in Organization* 10, nos. 3/4 (November 2010): 421–38.

Heidegger, Martin. *An Introduction to Metaphysics*. Yale University Press, 1953.

Heilman, Madeline. "Description and Prescription: How Gender Stereotypes Prevent Women's Ascent Up the Organizational Ladder." *Journal of Social Issues* 57, no. 4 (January 1, 2001): 657–74.

———. "Gender Stereotypes and Workplace Bias." *Research in Organizational Behavior* 32 (January 1, 2012): 113–35.

Heilman, Madeline, Suzette Caleo, and Francesca Manzi. "Women at Work: Pathways from Gender Stereotypes to Gender Bias and Discrimination." *Annual Review of Organizational Psychology and Organizational Behavior* 11 (January 22, 2024): 165–92.

Heilman, Madeline, and Julie Chen. "Same Behavior, Different Consequences: Reactions to Men's and Women's Altruistic Citizenship Behavior." *Journal of Applied Psychology* 90, no. 3 (2005): 431–41.

Heimer, Carol. "Doing Your Job and Helping Your Friends: Universalistic Norms About Obligations to Particular Others in Networks." In *Sociology of Organizations: Structures and Relationships*, edited by Mary Godwyn and Jody Hoffer Gittell. Sage Publications, 2011.

Henly, Julia., Luke Shaefer, and Elaine Waxman. "Nonstandard Work Schedules: Employer- and Employee-Driven Flexibility in Retail Jobs." *Social Service Review* 80, no. 4 (2006): 609–34.

Hersey, Tricia. *Rest Is Resistance: A Manifesto*. Little, Brown, 2022.

Hill, Jasmine Diana. "The Hustle Ethic and the Spirit of Platform Capitalism." PhD diss., Stanford University, 2020.

Hirschman, Albert. *Exit, Voice, and Loyalty: Responses to Decline in Firms, Organizations, and States*. Harvard University Press, 1970.

Hirshfield, Laura, and Tiffany Joseph. "'We Need a Woman, We Need a Black Woman': Gender and Cultural Taxation in the Academy." *Gender and Education* 24 (2012): 213–27.

Ho, Karen. "Disciplining Investment Bankers, Disciplining the Economy: Wall Street's Institutional Culture of Crisis and the Downsizing of 'Corporate America.'" *American Anthropologist* 111, no. 2 (2009): 177–89.

———. *Liquidated: An Ethnography of Wall Street*. Duke University Press, 2009.

Hoang, Kimberly Kay. *Dealing in Desire: Asian Ascendancy, Western Decline, and the Hidden Currencies of Global Sex Work*. University of California Press, 2015.

Hochschild, Arlie Russell. "The Commercial Spirit of Intimate Life and the Abduction of Feminism: Signs from Women's Advice Books." *Theory, Culture & Society* 11, no. 2 (May 1, 1994): 1–24.

———. *The Commercialization of Intimate Life: Notes from Home and Work*. University of California Press, 2003.

——. *The Managed Heart: Commercialization of Human Feeling*. University of California Press, 1983.

——. *The Second Shift*. Penguin Books, 2003.

——. *The Time Bind: When Work Becomes Home and Home Becomes Work*. Macmillan, 1997.

Hodges, Graham Russell Gao. *Taxi! A Social History of the New York City Cabdriver*. Johns Hopkins University Press, 2007.

Hodson, Randy. "Group Relations at Work: Solidarity, Conflict, and Relations with Management." *Work and Occupations* 24, no. 4 (November 1, 1997): 426–52.

——. "Worker Resistance: An Underdeveloped Concept in the Sociology of Work." *Economic and Industrial Democracy* 16, no. 1 (February 1, 1995): 79–110.

Hodson, Randy, Vincent J. Roscigno, Andrew Martin, and Steven H. Lopez. "The Ascension of Kafkaesque Bureaucracy in Private Sector Organizations." *Human Relations* 66, no. 9 (September 1, 2013): 1249–73.

Hopkins, RaQuel. "The Real Deal Around HR Confidentiality." *Forbes*, October 2, 2019.

Howard-Grenville, Jennifer, Karen Golden-Biddle, Jennifer Irwin, and Jina Mao. "Liminality as Cultural Process for Cultural Change." *Organization Science* 22, no. 2 (2011): 522–39.

Huet, Ellen. "Uber Continues to Finance Its Drivers with New Gas Credit Card." *Forbes*, June 9, 2015.

Hultin, Suzanne, Landon Jacquinot, and Anna Petrini. "Do Workers in Your State Need Portable Benefits?" National Conference of State Legislatures, 2023. https://www.ncsl.org/state-legislatures-news/details/do-workers-in-your-state-need-portable-benefits.

Husain, Fauzia. *The Stigma Matrix: Gender, Globalization, and the Agency of Pakistan's Frontline Women*. Stanford University Press, 2024.

Ibarra, Herminia, Nancy Carter, and Christine Silva. "Why Men Still Get More Promotions Than Women." *Harvard Business Review*, September 2010.

Illouz, Eva. *Oprah Winfrey and the Glamour of Misery: An Essay on Popular Culture*. Columbia University Press, 2003.

——. *Saving the Modern Soul: Therapy, Emotions, and the Culture of Self-Help*. University of California Press, 2008.

Independent Drivers Guild (IDG). "The Independent Drivers Guild Celebrates Tipping Victory over Uber." IDG, April 17, 2017. https://driversguild.org/independent-drivers-guild-celebrates-tipping-victory-uber/.

——. "On Tipping." IDG. Accessed November 25, 2024. https://driversguild.org/on-tipping/.

Infurna, Frank, and Eranda Jayawickreme, eds. *Redesigning Research on Post-Traumatic Growth: Challenges, Pitfalls, and New Directions*. Oxford University Press, 2021.

International Labour Organization (ILO). "Valid and Prohibited Grounds for Dismissal." Accessed November 3, 2023. https://eplex.ilo.org/en/valid-and-prohibited-grounds-for-dismissal.

Irani, Lilly. "Difference and Dependence Among Digital Workers: The Case of Amazon Mechanical Turk." *South Atlantic Quarterly* 114, no. 1 (January 1, 2015): 225–34.

Isaac, Mike. *Super Pumped: The Battle for Uber*. W. W. Norton, 2019.

Jackall, Robert. *Moral Mazes: The World of Corporate Managers*. Oxford University Press, 1988.

Jackman, Mary. *The Velvet Glove: Paternalism and Conflict in Gender, Class, and Race Relations*. University of California Press, 1996.

Jackson, Steven. "Rethinking Repair." In *Media Technologies: Essays on Communication, Materiality, and Society*, edited by Tarleton Gillespie, Pablo Boczkowski, and Kirsten A. Foot. MIT Press, 2014.

Jacoby, Sanford M. *Modern Manors*. Princeton University Press, 1996.

Jaffe, Sarah. *Work Won't Love You Back: How Devotion to Our Jobs Keeps Us Exploited, Exhausted, and Alone*. PublicAffairs, 2021.

James, Al. "Platform Work-Lives in the Gig Economy: Recentering Work–Family Research." *Gender, Work & Organization* 31, no. 2 (2024): 513–34.

Jerolmack, Colin, and Shamus Khan. "Talk Is Cheap: Ethnography and the Attitudinal Fallacy." *Sociological Methods & Research*, March 9, 2014.

Jerolmack, Colin, and Alexandra Murphy. "The Ethical Dilemmas and Social Scientific Trade-Offs of Masking in Ethnography." *Sociological Methods & Research* 48, no. 4 (November 1, 2019): 801–27.

Jones, Angela. "Cisgendered Workspaces: Outright and Categorical Exclusion in Cisgendered Organizations." *Social Problems*, April 25, 2023.

Jones, Rebecca, Stephen Woods, and Yves Guillaume. "The Effectiveness of Workplace Coaching: A Meta-Analysis of Learning and Performance Outcomes from Coaching." *Journal of Occupational and Organizational Psychology* 89, no. 2 (2016): 249–77.

Kalanick, Travis. "5-Year Anniversary Remarks from Uber CEO Travis Kalanick." *Uber Blog*, June 3, 2015. https://www.uber.com/newsroom/5-years-travis-kalanick.

Kalev, Alexandra. "How You Downsize Is Who You Downsize: Biased Formalization, Accountability, and Managerial Diversity." *American Sociological Review* 79, no. 1 (February 1, 2014): 109–35.

Kalev, Alexandra, and Frank Dobbin. "How Firms Turn Middle Managers into Diversity Leaders." *Seattle University Law Review* 46, no. 2 (January 1, 2023): 493.

Kalleberg, Arne. *Good Jobs, Bad Jobs: The Rise of Polarized and Precarious Employment Systems in the United States, 1970s–2000s*. Russell Sage Foundation, 2011.

Kalmoe, Nathan, and Lilliana Mason. *Radical American Partisanship: Mapping Violent Hostility, Its Causes, and the Consequences for Democracy.* University of Chicago Press, 2022.

Kaltner, Jillian. "Employment Status of Uber and Lyft Drivers: Unsettlingly Settled." *UC Law SF Journal on Gender and Justice* 29, no. 1 (January 1, 2018): 29.

Kanter, Rosabeth Moss. *Men and Women of the Corporation.* BasicBooks, 1977.

Kantor, Jodi, and David Streitfeld. "Inside Amazon." *New York Times*, August 17, 2015.

Kantor, Jod, and Arya Sundaram. "The Rise of the Worker Productivity Score." *New York Times*, August 15, 2022.

Kantor, Jodi, and Megan Twohey. *She Said: Breaking the Sexual Harassment Story That Helped Ignite a Movement.* Penguin Press, 2019.

Kay, Fiona, and Jean Wallace. "Mentors as Social Capital: Gender, Mentors, and Career Rewards in Law Practice." *Sociological Inquiry* 79, no. 4 (2009): 418–52.

Keane, Helen. "Join Us for Drinks: Intoxication, Work and Academic Conferences." In *Routledge Handbook of Intoxicants and Intoxication.* Routledge, 2022.

Keister, Lisa, and Stephanie Moller. "Wealth Inequality in the United States." *Annual Review of Sociology* 26, no. 1 (2000): 63–81.

Kellogg, Katherine. *Challenging Operations: Medical Reform and Resistance in Surgery.* University of Chicago Press, 2011.

Kelly, Erin, Samantha Ammons, Kelly Chermack, and Phyllis Moen. "Gendered Challenge, Gendered Response Confronting the Ideal Worker Norm in a White-Collar Organization." *Gender & Society* 24, no. 3 (June 1, 2010): 281–303.

Kelly, Erin, and Phyllis Moen. *Overload: How Good Jobs Went Bad and What We Can Do About It.* Princeton University Press, 2020.

Kelly, Jack. "While Google, Amazon and Others Continue to Lay Off Employees, Companies See Hybrid Work as a Cost-Saver." *Forbes*, January 12, 2024.

Khan, Shamus Rahman. *Privilege: The Making of an Adolescent Elite at St. Paul's School.* Princeton University Press, 2011.

King, Martin Luther, Jr. "A New Sense of Direction." Presented at the Southern Christian Leadership Conference, 1968.

Klein, Naomi. *Doppelganger: A Trip into the Mirror World.* Farrar, Straus and Giroux, 2023.

———. *The Shock Doctrine: The Rise of Disaster Capitalism.* Picador, 2007.

Kneese, Tamara. "Our Silicon Valley, Ourselves." *Boundary 2 Editorial Collective* (blog), August 6, 2021. https://www.boundary2.org/2021/08/tamara-kneese-our-silicon-valley-ourselves/.

Kochan, Thomas, Duanyi Yang, William Kimball, and Erin Kelly. "Worker Voice in America: Is There a Gap between What Workers Expect and What They Experience?" *ILR Review* 72, no. 1 (January 1, 2019): 3–38.

Koestler, Arthur. *The Act of Creation*. One 70 Press, 2014.
Korczynski, Marek. "Communities of Coping: Collective Emotional Labour in Service Work." *Organization* 10, no. 1 (February 1, 2003): 55–79.
Koshy, Susan. "South Asians and the Complex Interstices of Whiteness: Negotiating Public Sentiment in the United States and Britain." In *White Women in Racialized Spaces: Imaginative Transformation and Ethical Action in Literature*, edited by Rajini Srikanth and Samina Najmi. State University of New York Press, 2012.
Kramer, Roderick. "Trust and Distrust in Organizations: Emerging Perspectives, Enduring Questions." *Annual Review of Psychology* 50, no. 1 (1999): 569–98.
Krzywdzinski, Martin, and Maximilian Greb. "Teamwork: From Self-Managed to Lean and Agile Teams." In *Shifting Categories of Work*. Routledge, 2022.
Kunda, Gideon. *Engineering Culture: Control and Commitment in a High-Tech Corporation*. Temple University Press, 1992.
Lacatus, Corina, and Gustav Meibauer. "'Saying It Like It Is': Right-Wing Populism, International Politics, and the Performance of Authenticity." *British Journal of Politics and International Relations* 24, no. 3 (August 1, 2022): 437–57.
Laemmli, Taylor. "Workers and Their Foes: Customer Scapegoats in the Service Triangle." *Socius* 9 (November 9, 2023): 1–13.
Lafer, Gordon, and Lola Loustaunau. "Fear at Work." Economic Policy Institute, 2020. https://www.epi.org/publication/fear-at-work-how-employers-scare-workers-out-of-unionizing/.
Lainer-Vos, Dan. "The Practical Organization of Moral Transactions: Gift Giving, Market Exchange, Credit, and the Making of Diaspora Bonds." *Sociological Theory* 31, no. 2 (June 1, 2013): 145–67.
Lambert, Susan. "Passing the Buck: Labor Flexibility Practices That Transfer Risk onto Hourly Workers." *Human Relations* 61, no. 9 (September 1, 2008): 1203–27.
Lamont, Michèle. "Addressing Recognition Gaps: Destigmatization and the Reduction of Inequality." *American Sociological Review* 83, no. 3 (2018): 419–44.
———. *The Dignity of Working Men*. Harvard University Press, 2000.
———. *Seeing Others: How Recognition Works—and How It Can Heal a Divided World*. Simon and Schuster, 2023.
Lamont, Michèle, Stefan Beljean, and Matthew Clair. "What Is Missing? Cultural Processes and Causal Pathways to Inequality." *Socio-Economic Review* 12, no. 3 (July 1, 2014): 573–608.
Lane, Carrie. *A Company of One: Insecurity, Independence, and the New World of White-Collar Unemployment*. Cornell University Press, 2011.
Lapavitsas, Costas. "Relations of Power and Trust in Contemporary Finance." *Historical Materialism* 14, no. 1 (March 2006): 129–54.

Lasch, Christopher. *Haven in a Heartless World: The Family Besieged.* W. W. Norton, 1995.

Lawrence, Felicity. "Uber Paid Academics Six-Figure Sums for Research to Feed to the Media." *Guardian*, July 12, 2022.

Leidner, Robin. *Fast Food, Fast Talk: Service Work and the Routinization of Everyday Life.* University of California Press, 1993.

Lerma, Veronica, Laura Hamilton, and Kelly Nielsen. "Racialized Equity Labor, University Appropriation and Student Resistance." *Social Problems* 67, no. 2 (May 1, 2020): 286–303.

Levin, Sam. "Uber's Scandals, Blunders and PR Disasters: The Full List." *Guardian*, June 27, 2017.

Levine, Judith. *Ain't No Trust: How Bosses, Boyfriends, and Bureaucrats Fail Low-Income Mothers and Why It Matters.* University of California Press, 2013.

Lewicki, Roy, and Chad Brinsfield. "Trust, Distrust and Building Social Capital." In *Social Capital.* Edward Elgar Publishing, 2009.

Lewicki, Roy, and Barbara Bunker. "Developing and Maintaining Trust in Work Relationships." In *Trust in Organizations*, edited by Roderick Kramer and T. R. Tyler. Sage Publications, 1995.

Lewis, David, and Andrew Weigert. "Trust as a Social Reality." *Social Forces* 63, no. 4 (June 1, 1985): 967–85.

Lewis-Kraus, Gideon. "They Studied Dishonesty: Was Their Work a Lie?" *New Yorker*, September 30, 2023.

Lifton, Robert Jay. *Thought Reform and the Psychology of Totalism: A Study of "Brainwashing" in China.* University of North Carolina Press, 1989.

Liu, Alan. *The Laws of Cool: Knowledge Work and the Culture of Information.* University of Chicago Press, 2009.

Lizardo, Omar. "Improving Cultural Analysis: Considering Personal Culture in Its Declarative and Nondeclarative Modes." *American Sociological Review* 82, no. 1 (February 1, 2017): 88–115.

Lorde, Audre. "Uses of Anger: Women Responding to Racism." In *Sister Outsider: Essays & Speeches by Audre Lorde.* Crossing, 1984.

Lott, Eric. *Love & Theft: Blackface Minstrelsy and the American Working Class.* Oxford University Press, 2013.

Lubet, Steven. "Ethnography on Trial." *New Republic*, July 15, 2015.

Luckerson, Victor. "10 Most Lavish Job Perks in Silicon Valley." *Time*, October 14, 2014.

Luebke, Simon. "Political Authenticity: Conceptualization of a Popular Term." *International Journal of Press/Politics* 26, no. 3 (July 1, 2021): 635–53.

Luhmann, Niklas. "Familiarity, Confidence, Trust: Problems and Alternatives." In *Trust: Making and Breaking Cooperative Relations*, edited by Diego Gambetta. Basil Blackwell, 1988.

——. *Social Systems*. Stanford University Press, 1995.

——. *Trust and Power*. John Wiley & Sons, 1979.

Lyman, Peter. "The Fraternal Bond as a Joking Relationship: A Case Study of the Role of Sexist Jokes in Male Group Bonding." In *Changing Men: New Directions in Research on Men and Masculinity*. Sage Publications, 1987.

Lyng, Stephen. "Edgework: A Social Psychological Analysis of Voluntary Risk Taking." *American Journal of Sociology* 95, no. 4 (January 1990): 851–86.

——. "Sociology at the Edge: Social Theory and Voluntary Risk Taking." In *Edgework*. Routledge, 2004.

MacCannell, Dean. *The Tourist: A New Theory of the Leisure Class*. University of California Press, 1999.

MacKenzie, Donald, and Judy Wajcman, eds. *The Social Shaping of Technology*. McGraw Hill Education/Open University, 1985.

Mackenzie, Ewan, and Alan McKinlay. "Hope Labour and the Psychic Life of Cultural Work." *Human Relations* 74, no. 11 (November 1, 2021): 1841–63.

Macomber, Kristine Claire. "Men as Allies: Mobilizing Men to End Violence Against Women." PhD diss., North Carolina State University, 2012.

Madani, Doha. "Dan Patrick on Coronavirus 'More Important Things than Living.'" *NBC News*, April 21, 2020. https://www.nbcnews.com/news/us-news/texas-lt-gov-dan-patrick-reopening-economy-more-important-things-n1188911.

Madland, David, and Alex Rowell. "Combating Pay Gaps with Unions and Expanded Collective Bargaining." The Center for American Progress, June 28, 2018. https://www.americanprogress.org/article/combating-pay-gaps-unions-expanded-collective-bargaining/.

Martin, Andrew, Steven Lopez, Vincent Roscigno, and Randy Hodson. "Against the Rules: Synthesizing Types and Processes of Bureaucratic Rule-Breaking." *Academy of Management Review* 38, no. 4 (2013): 550–74.

Maruna, Shadd. *Making Good: How Ex-Convicts Reform and Rebuild Their Lives*. American Psychological Association, 2001.

Marwick, Alice. *Status Update: Celebrity, Publicity, and Branding in the Social Media Age*. Yale University Press, 2013.

Marx, Karl, and Fredrick Engels. *Economic and Philosophic Manuscripts of 1844*. Start Publishing, 2013.

Mateescu, Alexandra, and Madeline Claire Elish. *AI in Context*. Report, Data & Society, January 30, 2019. https://datasociety.net/library/ai-in-context/.

Mateescu, Alexandra, and Julia Ticona. "Invisible Work, Visible Workers: Visibility Regimes in Online Platforms for Domestic Work." In *Beyond the Algorithm: Qualitative Insights for Gig Work Regulation*, edited by Deepa Das Acevedo. Cambridge University Press, 2020.

Matthyssen, Mieke. *Ignorance Is Bliss: The Chinese Art of Not Knowing*. Springer Nature, 2021.

Mauss, Marcel. *The Gift: The Form and Reason for Exchange in Archaic Societies.* Translated by W. D. Halls. W. W. Norton, 1925.

May, Reuben Buford. *Urban Nightlife: Entertaining Race, Class, and Culture in Public Space.* Rutgers University Press, 2014.

Mayer, Roger, James Davis, and David Schoorman. "An Integrative Model Of Organizational Trust." *Academy of Management Review* 20, no. 3 (July 1, 1995): 709–34.

Mayo, Elton. *The Human Problems of an Industrial Civilization.* Routledge, 2003.

McAdams, Dan. *The Redemptive Self: Stories Americans Live By.* Oxford University Press, 2005.

McAllister, Daniel. "Affect- and Cognition-Based Trust as Foundations for Interpersonal Cooperation in Organizations." *Academy of Management Journal* 38, no. 1 (February 1, 1995): 24–59.

McCall, Leslie. "The Complexity of Intersectionality." *Signs* 30, no. 3 (March 1, 2005): 1771–1800.

McCann, Carly, Donald Tomaskovic-Devey, and M. V. Lee Badgett. "Employers' Responses to Sexual Harassment." Social Science Research Network, December 1, 2018. https://papers.ssrn.com/sol3/papers.cfm?abstract_id=3407960.

McCarthy, Justin. "U.S. Approval of Labor Unions at Highest Point Since 1965." Gallup, August 30, 2022. https://news.gallup.com/poll/398303/approval-labor-unions-highest-point-1965.aspx.

McClain, Denise, and Ryan Pendell. "Why Trust in Leaders Is Faltering and How to Gain It Back." Gallup, April 17, 2023. https://www.gallup.com/workplace/473738/why-trust-leaders-faltering-gain-back.aspx.

McCluney, Courtney, Kathrina Robotham, Serenity Lee, and Myles Durkee. "The Costs of Code-Switching." *Harvard Business Review,* November 15, 2019.

McDonald, Steve. "What's in the 'Old Boys' Network? Accessing Social Capital in Gendered and Racialized Networks." *Social Networks* 33, no. 4 (October 1, 2011): 317–30.

McDonnell, Terence, Christopher Bail, and Iddo Tavory. "A Theory of Resonance." *Sociological Theory* 35, no. 1 (March 1, 2017): 1–14.

McGoey, Linsey. *The Unknowers: How Strategic Ignorance Rules the World.* Zed Books, 2019.

McGuire, Gail. "Gender, Race, and the Shadow Structure: A Study of Informal Networks and Inequality in a Work Organization." *Gender & Society* 16, no. 3 (June 1, 2002): 303–22.

———. "Intimate Work: A Typology of the Social Support That Workers Provide to Their Network Members." *Work and Occupations* 34, no. 2 (May 1, 2007): 125–47.

McLaughlin, Heather, Christopher Uggen, and Amy Blackstone. "Sexual Harassment, Workplace Authority, and the Paradox of Power." *American Sociological Review* 77, no. 4 (August 2012): 625–47.

McLuhan, Arthur, Dorothy Pawluch, William Shaffir, and Jack Haas. "The Cloak of Incompetence: A Neglected Concept in the Sociology of Everyday Life." *American Sociologist* 45, no. 4 (2014): 361–87.

McNicholas, Celine, Margaret Poydock, Samantha Sanders, and Ben Zipperer. "Employers Spend More Than $400 Million Per Year on 'Union-Avoidance' Consultants to Bolster Their Union-Busting Efforts." Economic Policy Institute, 2023. https://www.epi.org/publication/union-avoidance/.

McNicholas, Celine, Margaret Poydock, Julia Wolfe, Ben Zipperer, Gordon Lafer, and Lola Loustaunau. "Unlawful: U.S. Employers Are Charged with Violating Federal Law in 41.5% of All Union Election Campaigns." Economic Policy Institute, 2019. https://www.epi.org/publication/unlawful-employer-opposition-to-union-election-campaigns/.

McNicholas, Celine, and Marni von Wilpert. "The Joint Employer Standard and the National Labor Relations Board." Economic Policy Institute, 2017. https://www.epi.org/publication/the-joint-employer-standard-and-the-national-labor-relations-board-what-is-at-stake-for-workers/.

McPherson, Miller, Lynn Smith-Lovin, and James Cook. "Birds of a Feather: Homophily in Social Networks." *Annual Review of Sociology* 27 (January 1, 2001): 415–44.

Mears, Ashley. *Pricing Beauty: The Making of a Fashion Model*. University of California Press, 2011.

———. "Working for Free in the VIP: Relational Work and the Production of Consent." *American Sociological Review* 80, no. 6 (December 1, 2015): 1099–1122.

Melaku, Tsedale. "Black Women in White Institutional Spaces: The Invisible Labor Clause and the Inclusion Tax." *American Behavioral Scientist* 66, no. 11 (October 1, 2022): 1512–25.

Messeri, Lisa. "Resonant Worlds: Cultivating Proximal Encounters in Planetary Science." *American Ethnologist* 44, no. 1 (2017): 131–42.

Messner, Michael, Max A. Greenberg, and Tal Peretz. *Some Men: Feminist Allies and the Movement to End Violence against Women*. Oxford University Press, 2015.

Meyer, John, and Brian Rowan. "Institutionalized Organizations: Formal Structure as Myth and Ceremony." *American Journal of Sociology* 83, no. 2 (September 1, 1977): 340–63.

Meyers, Joan. *Working Democracies: Managing Inequality in Worker Cooperatives*. Cornell University Press, 2022.

Mickey, Ethel. "The Organization of Networking and Gender Inequality in the New Economy: Evidence from the Tech Industry." *Work and Occupations* 49, no. 4 (November 1, 2022): 383–420.

Miller, Candace, and Josipa Roksa. "Balancing Research and Service in Academia: Gender, Race, and Laboratory Tasks." *Gender & Society* 34, no. 1 (February 1, 2020): 131–52.

Miller, Claire Cain. "The World 'Has Found a Way to Do This': The U.S. Lags on Paid Leave." *New York Times*, October 25, 2021.

Miller, Laura. "Not Just Weapons of the Weak: Gender Harassment as a Form of Protest for Army Men." *Social Psychology Quarterly* 60, no. 1 (1997): 32–51.

Mills, Charles. *The Racial Contract*. Cornell University Press, 2022.

Mishel, Lawrence, and Celine McNicholas. "Uber Drivers Are Not Entrepreneurs." Economic Policy Institute, 2019. https://www.epi.org/publication/uber-drivers-are-not-entrepreneurs-nlrb-general-counsel-ignores-the-realities-of-driving-for-uber/#:~:text=In%20reality%2C%20Uber%20drivers%20do,do%20is%20drive%20more%20hours.

Misztal, Barbara. *Trust in Modern Societies: The Search for the Bases of Social Order*. Polity Press, 1996.

Mitra, Diditi. "Driving Taxis in New York City." *WorkingUSA* 7, no. 2 (2003): 76–99.

Mizrachi, Nissim, Israel Drori, and Renee Anspach. "Repertoires of Trust: The Practice of Trust in a Multinational Organization amid Political Conflict." *American Sociological Review* 72, no. 1 (February 1, 2007): 143–65.

Möllering, Guido. *Trust: Reason, Routine, Reflexivity*. Emerald Group Publishing, 2006.

Molm, Linda, Nobuyuki Takahashi, and Gretchen Peterson. "Risk and Trust in Social Exchange: An Experimental Test of a Classical Proposition." *American Journal of Sociology* 105, no. 5 (March 1, 2000): 1396–1427.

Montell, Amanda. *Cultish: The Language of Fanaticism*. Harper, 2021.

Morduch, Jonathan, and Rachel Schneider. *The Financial Diaries: How American Families Cope in a World of Uncertainty*. Princeton University Press, 2019.

Moreno, Edward. "Business Groups Sue to Stop F.T.C. from Banning Noncompete Clauses." *New York Times*, April 24, 2024.

Morrison, Toni. "Grendel and His Mother." In *The Source of Self-Regard: Selected Essays, Speeches, and Meditations*. Knopf Doubleday Publishing Group, 2019.

Mosseri, Sarah. "Being Watched and Being Seen: Negotiating Visibility in the NYC Ride-Hail Circuit." *New Media & Society* 24, no. 3 (March 1, 2022): 600–620.

———. "Finding Middle Ground: The Relationship Between Cultural Schemas and Working Mothers' Work-Family Strategies." *Community, Work & Family* 24, no. 3 (May 27, 2021): 331–56.

———. "Managed Absence: Unequal Time in Elite Occupations." Presented at Section on Organizations, Occupations and Work Paper Session: Gender

Inequality in Organizations of the American Sociological Association's Annual Meeting, Chicago, IL, August 12, 2025.

Mosseri, Sarah, Ariadne Vromen, Rae Cooper, and Elizabeth Hill. "Between Frustration and Invigoration: Women Talking about Digital Technology at Work." *Work, Employment and Society*, 37, no. 6 (December 2023): 1681–98.

Mueller, Charles, Stacy De Coster, and Sarah Beth Estes. "Sexual Harassment in the Workplace: Unanticipated Consequences of Modern Social Control in Organizations." *Work and Occupations* 28, no. 4 (2001): 411–46.

Munsch, Christin. "Strength, Stamina, and Structural Violence in the Social Sciences." *Journal of Men's Studies* 30, no. 3 (October 1, 2022): 402–24.

Murphy, Alexandra, Colin Jerolmack, and DeAnna Smith. "Ethnography, Data Transparency, and the Information Age." *Annual Review of Sociology* 47, no. 1 (2021): 41–61.

Murphy, Scott Patrick. "Humor Orgies as Ritual Insult: Putdowns and Solidarity Maintenance in a Corner Donut Shop." *Journal of Contemporary Ethnography* 46, no. 1 (February 1, 2017): 108–32.

Musto, Michela. "Brilliant or Bad: The Gendered Social Construction of Exceptionalism in Early Adolescence." *American Sociological Review* 84, no. 3 (June 2019): 369–93.

Naidu, Suresh, and Michael Carr. "'If You Don't like Your Job, Can You Always Quit?': Pervasive Monopsony Power and Freedom in the Labor Market.'" Economic Policy Institute, 2022. https://www.epi.org/unequalpower/publications/pervasive-monopsony-power-and-freedom-in-the-labor-market/.

Nance-Nash, Sheryl. "How Corporate Diversity Initiatives Trap Workers of Colour." *BBC*, September 13, 2020.

Natanson, Hannah. "Trust in Teachers Is Plunging amid a Culture War in Education." *Washington Post*, September 8, 2022.

National Conference of State Legislatures. "At-Will Employment—Overview," 2008. https://www.ncsl.org/labor-and-employment/at-will-employment-overview.

———. "Right-to-Work Resources." 2023. https://www.ncsl.org/labor-and-employment/right-to-work-resources.

Neely, Megan Tobias. "Fit to Be King: How Patrimonialism on Wall Street Leads to Inequality." *Socio-Economic Review* 16, no. 2 (April 1, 2018): 365–85.

———. *Hedged Out: Inequality and Insecurity on Wall Street*. University of California Press, 2022.

———. "The Portfolio Ideal Worker: Insecurity and Inequality in the New Economy." *Qualitative Sociology* 43, no. 2 (June 1, 2020): 271–96.

Neff, Gina. "The Changing Place of Cultural Production: The Location of Social Networks in a Digital Media Industry." *ANNALS of the American Academy of Political and Social Science* 597, no. 1 (January 1, 2005): 134–52.

———. *Venture Labor: Work and the Burden of Risk in Innovative Industries*. MIT Press, 2012.

Nelson, Alondra. *Body and Soul: The Black Panther Party and the Fight Against Medical Discrimination*. University of Minnesota Press, 2013.

New York City Health Department. *Paid Family Leave: A Strategy for Promoting Health and Economic Equity for New York City's Families*. 2016. https://www.nyc.gov/assets/doh/downloads/pdf/hca/paid-family-leave-report1.pdf.

New York State Attorney General. "Attorney General James Joins New York City Uber and Lyft Drivers to Celebrate Historic $328 Million Settlement." Press Release, January 18, 2024.

New York State Senate. *Hearing, Examination of the Gig Economy*. Standing Committee on Internet and Technology, October 16, 2019. https://www.nysenate.gov/calendar/public_hearings/october-16-2019/public-hearing-examination-gig-economy-hear-stakeholders.

New York Taxi Workers Alliance. "$328 Million Uber/Lyft Wage Theft Settlement." Press Release, July 25, 2024.

Newcomer, Eric. "In Video, Uber's CEO Argues with a Driver Over Falling Fares." *Bloomberg*, February 28, 2017. https://www.bloomberg.com/news/articles/2017-02-28/in-video-uber-ceo-argues-with-driver-over-falling-fares.

Newton, Casey. "Facebook Says It Will Permanently Shift Tens of Thousands of Jobs to Remote Work." *The Verge*, May 21, 2020. https://www.theverge.com/facebook/2020/5/21/21265699/facebook-remote-work-shift-workforce-permanent-covid-19-mark-zuckerberg-interview.

Nietzsche, Friedrich. *On the Genealogy of Morality*. Edited by Keith Ansell-Pearson. Translated by Carol Diethe. Cambridge University Press, 1887.

Nixon, Sean, and Ben Crewe. "Pleasure at Work? Gender, Consumption and Work-Based Identities in the Creative Industries." *Consumption Markets & Culture* 7, no. 2 (June 1, 2004): 129–47.

Noble, Safiya. *Algorithms of Oppression: How Search Engines Reinforce Racism*. New York University Press, 2018.

North, Henry Ringling, and Alden Hatch. *The Circus Kings: Our Ringling Family Story*. University Press of Florida, 2008.

Nuwer, Hank. *Hazing: Destroying Young Lives*. Indiana University Press, 2018.

O'Brien, Rourke. "Depleting Capital? Race, Wealth and Informal Financial Assistance." *Social Forces* 91, no. 2 (2012): 375–95.

O'Brien, Tim. *The Things They Carried: A Work of Fiction*. Broadway Books, 1990.

Ocejo, Richard. *Masters of Craft: Old Jobs in the New Urban Economy*. Princeton University Press, 2017.

Offer, Shira. "Negative Social Ties: Prevalence and Consequences." *Annual Review of Sociology* 47 (July 31, 2021): 177–96.

O'Flynn, Micheal, Lee Monaghan, and Martin Power. "Scapegoating During a Time of Crisis: A Critique of Post-Celtic Tiger Ireland." *Sociology* 48, no. 5 (October 1, 2014): 921–37.

Oldenburg, Ray. *Great Good Place*. Marlowe & Company, 1999.

Oliver, Melvin, and Thomas Shapiro. *Black Wealth/White Wealth: A New Perspective on Racial Inequality*. Routledge, 2013.

Olson, Carly. "There's No Labor Shortage—Just Not Enough Good Jobs." *Los Angeles Times*, July 2, 2021.

Open Science Collaboration. "Estimating the Reproducibility of Psychological Science." *Science* 349, no. 6251 (August 28, 2015).

Organisation for Economic Co-operation and Development (OECD). Statistics, "Trade Union Density." 2019. https://data-explorer.oecd.org.

Ortlieb, Renate, and Barbara Sieben. "Balls, Barbecues and Boxing: Contesting Gender Regimes at Organizational Social Events." *Organization Studies* 40, no. 1 (2019): 115–34.

Orwell, George. *1984*. Harcourt, Brace, 1949.

Osterman, Paul. *Employment Futures: Reorganization, Dislocation, and Public Policy*. Oxford University Press, 1988.

Paap, Kris. *Working Construction: Why White Working-Class Men Put Themselves—and the Labor Movement—in Harm's Way*. Cornell University Press, 2006.

Pachucki, Mark, Sabrina Pendergrass, and Michèle Lamont. "Boundary Processes: Recent Theoretical Developments and New Contributions." *Poetics*, 35, no. 6 (December 1, 2007): 331–51.

Pager, Devah, and Diana Karafin. "Bayesian Bigot? Statistical Discrimination, Stereotypes, and Employer Decision Making." *ANNALS of the American Academy of Political and Social Science* 621, no. 1 (January 1, 2009): 70–93.

Pager, Devah, Bruce Western, and Bart Bonikowski. "Discrimination in a Low-Wage Labor Market: A Field Experiment." *American Sociological Review* 74, no. 5 (October 1, 2009): 777–99.

Palmer, Annie. "Amazon Workers Walk Out over 'Lack of Trust' in Leadership." *CNBC*, May 31, 2023. https://www.cnbc.com/2023/05/31/amazon-workers-plan-to-walk-out-over-lack-of-trust-in-leadership.html.

Parker, Kim, and Juliana Menasce Horowitz. "Majority of Workers Who Quit a Job in 2021 Cite Low Pay, No Opportunities for Advancement, Feeling Disrespected." Pew Research Center, March 9, 2022. https://www.pewresearch.org/short-reads/2022/03/09/majority-of-workers-who-quit-a-job-in-2021-cite-low-pay-no-opportunities-for-advancement-feeling-disrespected/.

Parreñas, Rhacel Salazar. *Illicit Flirtations: Labor, Migration, and Sex Trafficking in Tokyo*. Stanford University Press, 2011.

Parrott, James, and Michael Reich. *An Earnings Standard for New York City's App-Based Drivers: Economic Analysis and Policy Assessment*. A Report for

the New York City and Limousine Commission. Center for New York City Affairs and Center on Wage and Employment Dynamics, July 2018.
Pascoe, C. J. *Nice Is Not Enough: Inequality and the Limits of Kindness at American High*. University of California Press, 2023.
Paules, Greta. *Dishing It Out: Power and Resistance Among Waitresses in a New Jersey Restaurant*. Temple University Press, 1991.
Payton, L'Oeral Thompson. "Black Women and the Glass Cliff: 'I Was Supposed to Bring Some Kind of Black Girl Magic.'" *Fortune*, November 6, 2022.
Pearce, Jone. "Employability as Trustworthiness." In *Relational Wealth: The Advantages of Stability in a Changing Economy*, edited by Carrie Leana and Denise Rousseau. Oxford University Press, 2000.
Pedersen, Vivi Bach, and Suzan Lewis. "Flexible Friends? Flexible Working Time Arrangements, Blurred Work-Life Boundaries and Friendship." *Work, Employment and Society* 26, no. 3 (June 1, 2012): 464–80.
Pedulla, David, and Devah Pager. "Race and Networks in the Job Search Process." *American Sociological Review* 84, no. 6 (December 1, 2019): 983–1012.
Pérez, Raúl. "Learning to Make Racism Funny in the 'Color-Blind' Era: Stand-up Comedy Students, Performance Strategies, and the (Re)Production of Racist Jokes in Public." *Discourse & Society* 24, no. 4 (July 1, 2013): 478–503.
———. *The Souls of White Jokes: How Racist Humor Fuels White Supremacy*. Stanford University Press, 2022.
Perrow, Charles. *Normal Accidents: Living with High Risk Technologies*. Princeton University Press, 1984.
Petersen, Anne Helen. "What Is Anne Hathaway Trying to Tell Us?" *Culture Study*, May 22, 2024.
Petersen, Morten. "How Leaders Can Build a Culture of Trust—and Why They Should." *Fast Company*, December 21, 2020.
Peterson, Richard A. *Creating Country Music: Fabricating Authenticity*. University of Chicago Press, 2013.
———. "In Search of Authenticity." *Journal of Management Studies* 42, no. 5 (2005): 1083–98.
Pew Research Center. "American Trends Panel Wave 40." July 2019. https://www.pewresearch.org/dataset/american-trends-panel-wave-40/.
Pew Research Center. *Public Trust in Government: 1958–2017*. December 14, 2017. https://www.pewresearch.org/politics/2017/05/03/public-trust-in-government-remains-near-historic-lows-as-partisan-attitudes-shift/#3066c1c1ffe016698ae30ceb67d107b5.
Pfeffer, Fabian, and Alexandra Killewald. "Generations of Advantage: Multigenerational Correlations in Family Wealth." *Social Forces*, 96, no. 4 (June 2018): 1411–42.
Pierce, Jennifer. *Gender Trials: Emotional Lives in Contemporary Law Firms*. University of California Press, 1995.

Piketty, Thomas. *Capital in the Twenty-First Century.* Harvard University Press, 2014.

Pillemer, Karl. *Fault Lines: Fractured Families and How to Mend Them.* Penguin, 2022.

Piore, Michael, and Andrew Schrank. *Root-Cause Regulation.* Harvard University Press, 2018.

Plater, Allister Pilar. "Symbolic Aesthetic Labor." Presented at Section on Sociology of Sex and Gender Paper Session: Embodied Labor and Intersectional Inequalities of the American Sociological Association's Annual Meeting, Seattle, WA, August 21, 2016.

Pollman, Elizabeth. "The Supreme Court and the Pro-Business Paradox." *All Faculty Scholarship*, November 10, 2021.

Porter, Theodore. *Trust in Numbers.* Princeton University Press, 1996.

Portes, Alejandro. "Social Capital: Its Origins and Applications in Modern Sociology." *Annual Review of Sociology* 24, no. 1 (1998): 1–24.

Portes, Alejandro, and Julia Sensenbrenner. "Embeddedness and Immigration: Notes on the Social Determinants of Economic Action." *American Journal of Sociology* 98, no. 6 (1993): 1320–50.

Price, Ryan. "NYCC Transportation Committee Public Comment." Independent Divers Guild, 2017. https://driversguild.org/nycc-transportation-committee-public-comment/.

Project for Public Spaces. "Ray Oldenburg." Accessed November 23, 2024. https://www.pps.org/article/roldenburg.

Pugh, Allison. "Connective Labor as Emotional Vocabulary: Inequality, Mutuality, and the Politics of Feelings in Care-Work." *Signs: Journal of Women in Culture and Society* 49, no. 1 (September 2023): 141–64.

———. *The Last Human Job: The Work of Connecting in a Disconnected World.* Princeton University Press, 2024.

———. *The Tumbleweed Society: Working and Caring in an Age of Insecurity.* Oxford University Press, 2015.

———. "What Good Are Interviews for Thinking About Culture? Demystifying Interpretive Analysis." *American Journal of Cultural Sociology* 1, no. 1 (February 2013): 42–68.

Pugh, Allison, and Sarah Mosseri. "Trust-Building vs. 'Just Trust Me': Reflexivity and Resonance in Ethnography." In Special issue, "Ethnography in the Open Science and Digital Age: New Debates, Dilemmas, and Issues," *Frontiers in Sociology* 8 (2023).

Pultz, Sabina, and Ofer Sharone. "The Intimate Dance of Networking: A Comparative Study of the Emotional Labor of Young American and Danish Jobseekers." In *Professional Work*, edited by Elizabeth Gorman and Steven Vallas, vol. 34. Research on the Sociology of Work, 2020.

Putnam, Robert. *Bowling Alone.* Simon and Schuster, 2000.

Puwar, Nirmal. *Space Invaders: Race, Gender and Bodies Out of Place.* Berg Publishers, 2004.

Quadagno, Jill. "Welfare Capitalism and the Social Security Act of 1935." *American Sociological Review* 49, no. 5 (1984): 632–47.

Quinn, Beth. "The Paradox of Complaining: Law, Humor, and Harassment in the Everyday Work World." *Law & Social Inquiry* 25, no. 4 (October 2000): 1151–85.

Racabi, Gali. "Effects of City–State Relations on Labor Relations: The Case of Uber." *ILR Review* 74, no. 5 (October 1, 2021): 1155–78.

Raman, Aneesh, and Maria Flynn. "When Your Technical Skills Are Eclipsed, Your Humanity Will Matter More Than Ever." *New York Times*, February 14, 2024.

Rao, Aliya Hamid, and Megan Tobias Neely. "What's Love Got to Do with It? Passion and Inequality in White-Collar Work." *Sociology Compass* 13, no. 12 (2019).

Rath, Tom. *Vital Friends: The People You Can't Afford to Live Without.* Simon and Schuster, 2006.

Ravenelle, Alexandrea. *Hustle and Gig: Struggling and Surviving in the Sharing Economy.* University of California Press, 2019.

Ray, Victor. "A Theory of Racialized Organizations." *American Sociological Review* 84, no. 1 (February 1, 2019): 26–53.

Reed, Isaac Ariail. "Charismatic Performance: A Study of Bacon's Rebellion." *American Journal of Cultural Sociology* 1, no. 2 (June 1, 2013): 254–87.

Reid, Erin, Olivia Amanda O'Neill, and Mary Blair-Loy. "Masculinity in Male-Dominated Occupations: How Teams, Time, and Tasks Shape Masculinity Contests." *Journal of Social Issues* 74, no. 3 (2018): 579–606.

Reid, Erin, and Lakshmi Ramarajan. "Seeking Purity, Avoiding Pollution: Strategies for Moral Career Building." *Organization Science* 33, no. 5 (September 2022): 1909–37.

Reilly, Katie. "Culture Wars Could Be Coming to a School Board Near You." *Time*, March 23, 2022.

Reskin, Barbara, and Patricia Roos. *Job Queues, Gender Queues: Explaining Women's Inroads Into Male Occupations.* Temple University Press, 1990.

Ribas, Vanesa. *On the Line: Slaughterhouse Lives and the Making of the New South.* University of California Press, 2015.

Richardson, Amanda. "You Want Your Employees to Return to the Office, But Why?" *Forbes*, May 19, 2023.

Ridgeway, Cecilia. *Framed by Gender: How Gender Inequality Persists in the Modern World.* Oxford University Press, 2011.

Ridgeway, Cecilia, and Shelley Correll. "Unpacking the Gender System: A Theoretical Perspective on Gender Beliefs and Social Relations." *Gender & Society* 18, no. 4 (August 1, 2004): 510–31.

Ridgeway, Cecilia, Rachel Korn, and Joan Williams. "Documenting the Routine Burden of Devalued Difference in the Professional Workplace." *Gender & Society* 36, no. 5 (October 1, 2022): 627–51.

Rinaldo, Rachel, and Jeffrey Guhin. "How and Why Interviews Work: Ethnographic Interviews and Meso-Level Public Culture." *Sociological Methods & Research* 51, no. 1 (February 1, 2022): 34–67.

Rivera, Lauren. *Pedigree: How Elite Students Get Elite Jobs*. Princeton University Press, 2016.

Robbins, Mike. *We're All in This Together: Creating a Team Culture of High Performance, Trust, and Belonging*. Hay House, 2022.

Roberts, Dorothy. *Fatal Invention: How Science, Politics, and Big Business Re-Create Race in the Twenty-First Century*. The New Press, 2012.

Robinson, Laura, and Jeremy Schulz. "Eliciting Frontstage and Backstage Talk with the Iterated Questioning Approach." *Sociological Methodology* 46, no. 1 (August 1, 2016): 53–83.

Romero, Eric, and Kevin Cruthirds. "The Use of Humor in the Workplace." *Academy of Management Perspectives* 20, no. 2 (May 2006): 58–69.

Romero, Mary. "Crossing the Immigration and Race Border: A Critical Race Theory Approach to Immigration Studies." *Contemporary Justice Review* 11, no. 1 (March 1, 2008): 23–37.

Rosalsky, Greg. "You May Have Heard of the 'Union Boom': The Numbers Tell a Different Story." *NPR*, February 28, 2023. https://www.npr.org/sections/money/2023/02/28/1159663461/you-may-have-heard-of-the-union-boom-the-numbers-tell-a-different-story.

Rosenblat, Alex. *Uberland: How Algorithms Are Rewriting the Rules of Work*. University of California Press, 2018.

Rosenblat, Alex, Karen Levy, Solon Barocas, and Tim Hwang. "Discriminating Tastes: Uber's Customer Ratings as Vehicles for Workplace Discrimination." *Policy & Internet* 9, no. 3 (2017): 256–79.

Rosenblat, Alex, and Luke Stark. "Algorithmic Labor and Information Asymmetries: A Case Study of Uber's Drivers." *International Journal of Communication* 10 (July 27, 2016): 27.

Rosenfeld, Jake. *What Unions No Longer Do*. Harvard University Press, 2014.

Rosenthal, Brian. "As Thousands of Taxi Drivers Were Trapped in Loans, Top Officials Counted the Money." *New York Times*, May 19, 2019.

Roscigno, Vincent J., and Randy Hodson. "The Organizational and Social Foundations of Worker Resistance." *American Sociological Review* 69, no. 1 (2004): 14–39.

Rossman, Gabriel. "Obfuscatory Relational Work and Disreputable Exchange." *Sociological Theory* 32, no. 1 (March 1, 2014): 43–63.

Roth, Louise Marie. "The Right to Privacy Is Political: Power, the Boundary Between Public and Private, and Sexual Harassment." *Law & Social Inquiry* 24, no. 1 (1999): 45–71.

———. "The Social Psychology of Tokenism: Status and Homophily Processes on Wall Street." *Sociological Perspectives* 47, no. 2 (June 1, 2004): 189–214.

Rousseau, Denise, Sim Sitkin, Ronald Burt, and Colin Camerer. "Not So Different After All: A Cross-Discipline View of Trust." *Academy of Management Review* 23, no. 3 (July 1, 1998): 393–404.

Roy, Donald. "'Banana Time' Job Satisfaction and Informal Interaction." *Human Organization* 18, no. 4 (1959): 158–68.

Royster, Deirdre. *Race and the Invisible Hand: How White Networks Exclude Black Men from Blue-Collar Jobs.* University of California Press, 2003.

Rumens, Nick. "Firm Friends: Exploring the Supportive Components in Gay Men's Workplace Friendships." *Sociological Review* 58, no. 1 (February 1, 2010): 135–55.

Rumens, Nick. "Researching Workplace Friendships: Drawing Insights from the Sociology of Friendship." *Journal of Social and Personal Relationships* 34, no. 8 (2017): 1149–67.

Rushbrook, Dereka. "Cities, Queer Space, and the Cosmopolitan Tourist." *GLQ: A Journal of Lesbian and Gay Studies* 8, no. 1 (2002): 183–206.

Rushin, Kate. "The Bridge Poem." In *This Bridge Called My Back: Writings by Radical Women of Color*, State University of New York Press, 2015.

Ryan, Michelle, and Alexander Haslam. "The Glass Cliff: Evidence That Women Are Over-Represented in Precarious Leadership Positions." *British Journal of Management* 16, no. 2 (June 1, 2005): 81–90.

Saguy, Abigail C., and Mallory E. Rees. "Gender, Power, and Harassment: Sociology in the #MeToo Era." *Annual Review of Sociology* 47 (2021): 417–35.

Said, Edward. *After the Last Sky: Palestinian Lives.* Columbia University Press, 1999.

Salisbury, Meredith, and Jefferson Pooley. "The #nofilter Self: The Contest for Authenticity Among Social Networking Sites, 2002–2016." *Social Sciences* 6, no. 1 (March 2017): 10.

Sallaz, Jeffrey. "The House Rules: Autonomy and Interests among Service Workers in the Contemporary Casino Industry." *Work and Occupations* 29, no. 4 (November 2002): 394–427.

———. *The Labor of Luck: Casino Capitalism in the United States and South Africa.* University of California Press, 2009.

Sandberg, Sheryl, and Adam Grant. *Option B: Facing Adversity, Building Resilience, and Finding Joy.* Knopf, 2017.

Santora, Marc, and John Surico. "Uber Drivers in New York City Protest Fare Cuts." *New York Times*, February 2, 2016.

Sasson-Levy, Orna, and Avi Shoshana. "'Passing' as (Non)Ethnic: The Israeli Version of Acting White." *Sociological Inquiry* 83, no. 3 (2013): 448–72.

Satran, Joe. "An Intimate Look at 'Family Meal,' the Staff-Only Food Customers Will Never Get to Eat at a Restaurant." *Huffington Post*, June 23, 2015.

Schawbel, Dan. "Why Work Friendships Are Critical for Long-Term Happiness." *CNBC*, November 13, 2018. https://www.cnbc.com/2018/11/13/why-work

-friendships-are-critical-for-long-term-happiness.html#:~:text=Our%20work%20friendships%20impact%20our,becomes%20blurrier%20by%20the%20day.

Scheiber, Noam. "Uber Drivers Are Contractors, Not Employees, Labor Board Says." *New York Times*, May 14, 2019.

———. "Uber Has a Union of Sorts, but Faces Doubts on Its Autonomy." *New York Times*, January 20, 2018.

———. "Uber to Repay Millions to Drivers, Who Could Be Owed Far More." *New York Times*, May 23, 2017.

Schilke, Oliver, Martin Reimann, and Karen S. Cook. "Trust in Social Relations." *Annual Review of Sociology* 47, no. 1 (2021): 239–59.

Schneider, Daniel, and Kristen Harknett. "Hard Times: Routine Schedule Unpredictability and Material Hardship Among Service Sector Workers." *Social Forces* 99, no. 4 (June 1, 2021): 1682–1709.

Schwab, Stewart, and Randall Thomas. "An Empirical Analysis of CEO Employment Contracts: What Do Top Executives Bargain For." *Washington and Lee Law Review* 63, no. 1 (2006): 231–70.

Schwarz, Ori. "The Symbolic Economy of Authenticity as a Form of Symbolic Violence: The Case of Middle-Class Ethnic Minorities." *Distinktion: Journal of Social Theory* 17, no. 1 (January 2, 2016): 2–19.

Seligman, Adam. *The Problem of Trust*. Princeton University Press, 2021.

Sennett, Richard. *The Corrosion of Character: The Personal Consequences of Work in the New Capitalism*. W. W. Norton, 1997.

———. *The Culture of the New Capitalism*. Yale University Press, 2006.

Serazio, Michael. *The Authenticity Industries: Keeping It "Real" in Media, Culture, and Politics*. Stanford University Press, 2023.

Shane, Tommy. "The Semiotics of Authenticity: Indexicality in Donald Trump's Tweets." *Social Media + Society* 4, no. 3 (July 1, 2018): 1–14.

Sharma, Sarah. *In the Meantime: Temporality and Cultural Politics*. Duke University Press, 2014.

Sharone, Ofer. *Flawed System/Flawed Self: Job Searching and Unemployment Experiences*. University of Chicago Press, 2014.

———. "LinkedIn or LinkedOut? How Social Networking Sites Are Reshaping the Labor Market." In *Emerging Conceptions of Work, Management and the Labor Market*, vol. 30. Emerald, 2017.

———. "Social Capital Activation and Job Searching: Embedding the Use of Weak Ties in the American Institutional Context." *Work and Occupations* 41, no. 4 (November 1, 2014): 409–39.

Sheppard, Blair, and Dana Sherman. "The Grammars of Trust: A Model and General Implications." *Academy of Management Review* 23, no. 3 (1998): 422–37.

Sherman, Jennifer. *Those Who Work, Those Who Don't: Poverty, Morality, and Family in Rural America*. University of Minnesota Press, 2009.

Sherman, Rachel. *Class Acts: Service and Inequality in Luxury Hotels*. University of California Press, 2007.

———. *Uneasy Street: The Anxieties of Affluence*. Princeton University Press, 2019.

Shiao, Jiannbin Lee. "The Meaning of Honorary Whiteness for Asian Americans: Boundary Expansion or Something Else?" *Comparative Sociology* 16, no. 6 (November 23, 2017): 788–813.

Shierholz, Heidi, Margaret Poydock, and Celine McNicholas. "Unionization Increased by 200,000 in 2022: Tens of Millions More Wanted to Join a Union, but Couldn't." Economic Policy Institute, 2023. https://www.epi.org/publication/unionization-2022/.

Shierholz, Heidi, and John Schmitt. "The Court Decision Invalidating the 2016 Overtime Rule Was Based on Fundamentally Flawed Economic Logic." Economic Policy Institute, 2022. https://www.epi.org/publication/the-court-decision-invalidating-the-2016-overtime-rule-was-based-on-fundamentally-flawed-economic-logic/.

Showers, Fumilayo. "Moving Onward and Upward in a 'Dead-End' Job: Extrinsic Motivations and Rewards in Health Care Work." *Sociological Forum* 37, no. 2 (2022): 443–64.

SHRM. "Why HR Confidentiality Is Essential for Protecting Employee Info." Accessed November 24, 2024. https://www.shrm.org/topics-tools/tools/hr-answers/confidentiality-critical-to-human-resources.

Silva, Jennifer. *Coming Up Short: Working-Class Adulthood in an Age of Uncertainty*. Oxford University Press, 2015.

Simko, Christina. "Oprah and the Politics of Consolation." *Culture and Society* 56, no. 3 (June 1, 2019): 273–81.

Simmel, Georg. *The Philosophy of Money*. Edited by David Frisby and Charles Lemert. Routledge, 1978.

———. *The Sociology of Georg Simmel*. Translated by K. H. Wolf. Free Press, 1950.

Sinek, Simon. "Why Good Leaders Make You Feel Safe." *Ted Talk*, May 19, 2014. https://www.youtube.com/watch?v=lmyZMtPVodo.

Singer, Natasha. "Twisting Words to Make 'Sharing' Apps Seem Selfless." *New York Times*, August 8, 2015.

Sismondo, Christine. *America Walks into a Bar: A Spirited History of Taverns and Saloons, Speakeasies and Grog Shops*. Oxford University Press, 2011.

Slingerland, Edward. *Drunk: How We Sipped, Danced, and Stumbled Our Way to Civilization*. Little, Brown, 2021.

Smelser, Neil. "The Rational and the Ambivalent in the Social Sciences: 1997 Presidential Address." *American Sociological Review* 63, no. 1 (1998): 1–15.

Smith, Adam. *Wealth of Nations*. Hayes Barton Press, 1994.

Smith, Gabriella. "Woke: Performing Progressive Whiteness in a Racially Liminal Time." PhD diss., University of Virginia, 2019.

Smith, Pamela, and Jennifer Overbeck. "The Leaders' Rosy Halo: Why Do We Give Power Holders the Benefit of the Doubt." In *Power, Politics, and*

Paranoia: Why People Are Suspicious of Their Leaders, edited by Jan-Willem van Prooijen and Paul van Lange. Cambridge University Press, 2014.

Smith, Sandra Susan. "'Don't Put My Name on It': Social Capital Activation and Job-Finding Assistance Among the Black Urban Poor." *American Journal of Sociology* 111, no. 1 (2005): 1–57.

——. *Lone Pursuit: Distrust and Defensive Individualism Among the Black Poor*. Russell Sage Foundation, 2007.

——. "Race and Trust." *Annual Review of Sociology* 36, no. 1 (2010): 453–75.

Smith, Vicki. *Crossing the Great Divide: Worker Risk and Opportunity in the New Economy*. Cornell University Press, 2001.

——. "New Forms of Work Organization." *Annual Review of Sociology* 23, no. 1 (1997): 315–39.

Snyder, Benjamin. *The Disrupted Workplace: Time and the Moral Order of Flexible Capitalism.*: Oxford University Press, 2016.

Sobering, Katherine. *The People's Hotel: Working for Justice in Argentina*. Duke University Press, 2022.

——. "The Relational Production of Workplace Equality: The Case of Worker-Recuperated Businesses in Argentina." *Qualitative Sociology* 42, no. 4 (December 1, 2019): 543–65.

——. "Watercooler Democracy: Rumors and Transparency in a Cooperative Workplace." *Work and Occupations* 46, no. 4 (November 1, 2019): 411–40.

Stack, Carol. *All Our Kin: Strategies for Survival in a Black Community*. Basic Books, 1974.

Standing, Guy. *The Precariat: The New Dangerous Class*. Bloomsbury Publishing, 2016.

Stark, Evan. *Coercive Control: How Men Entrap Women in Personal Life*. Oxford University Press, 2023.

Starr, Evan, J. J. Prescott, and Norman Bishara. "Noncompete Agreements in the U.S. Labor Force." *Journal of Law and Economics* 64, no. 1 (February 2021): 53–84.

Stehle, Maria, and Beverly Weber. *Precarious Intimacies: The Politics of Touch in Contemporary Western European Cinema*. Northwestern University Press, 2020.

Stickel, Darryl. *Building Trust: Exceptional Leadership in an Uncertain World*. Simon and Schuster, 2022.

Stiglitz, Joseph. *The Price of Inequality: How Today's Divided Society Endangers Our Future*. W. W. Norton, 2012.

Stone, Katherine, and Alexander Colvin. "The Arbitration Epidemic: Mandatory Arbitration Deprives Workers and Consumers of Their Rights." Briefing Paper. Economic Policy Institute, December 7, 2015. https://www.epi.org/publication/the-arbitration-epidemic/.

Strauss, Anselm. "Work and the Division of Labor." *Sociological Quarterly* 26, no. 1 (1985): 1–19.

Strong, W. F. “The Texan Origins of the Word ‘Maverick.’” *Texas Standard* (blog). Accessed November 24, 2024. https://www.texasstandard.org/stories/the-texan-origins-of-the-word-maverick/.

Suchman, Lucy. *Human-Machine Reconfigurations: Plans and Situated Actions.* Cambridge University Press, 2007.

Summers-Effler, Erika. “The Micro Potential for Social Change: Emotion, Consciousness, and Social Movement Formation.” *Sociological Theory* 20, no. 1 (2002): 41–60.

Sweet, Paige. *The Politics of Surviving: How Women Navigate Domestic Violence and Its Aftermath.* University of California Press, 2021.

———. “The Sociology of Gaslighting.” *American Sociological Review* 84, no. 5 (October 1, 2019): 851–75.

Swidler, Ann. “Culture in Action: Symbols and Strategies.” *American Sociological Review* 51, no. 2 (April 1986): 273.

Szerszynski, B. “Risk and Trust: The Performative Dimension.” *Environmental Values* 8, no. 2 (May 1, 1999): 239–52.

Tapper, James. “Quiet Quitting: Why Doing the Bare Minimum at Work Has Gone Global.” *Observer*, August 6, 2022.

Tarasov, Katie. “Unions Are Forming at Starbucks, Apple and Google: Here’s Why Workers Are Organizing Now.” *CNBC*, August 5, 2022. https://www.cnbc.com/2022/08/05/why-starbucks-apple-and-google-are-unionizing-now-for-the-first-time.html#:~:text=CNBC%20talked%20to%20workers%20inside,voted%20to%20unionize%20in%20April.

Tate, Greg. *Everything But the Burden: What White People Are Taking from Black Culture.* Crown, 2003.

Tavory, Iddo. “The Situations of Culture: Humor and the Limits of Measurability.” *Theory and Society* 43, no. 3 (July 1, 2014): 275–89.

Tavory, Iddo, and Gary Alan Fine. “Disruption and the Theory of the Interaction Order.” *Theory and Society* 49, no. 3 (April 1, 2020): 365–85.

Taxi & Limousine Commission (TLC). “2018 Factbook.” 2018. https://www.nyc.gov/assets/tlc/downloads/pdf/2018_tlc_factbook.pdf.

———. “Notice of Promulgation of Rules on Tipping,” 2017. https://www.nyc.gov/assets/tlc/downloads/pdf/proposed_tipping_rule_promulgated.pdf.

Tedeschi, Richard, and Lawrence Calhoun. “Posttraumatic Growth: Conceptual Foundations and Empirical Evidence.” *Psychological Inquiry* 15, no. 1 (2004): 1–18.

Thakore, Bhoomi. “Must-See TV: South Asian Characterizations in American Popular Media.” *Sociology Compass* 8, no. 2 (2014): 149–56.

Thomas, William Isaac, and Dorothy Swaine Thomas. *The Child in America: Behavior Problems and Programs.* A. A. Knopf, 1928.

Thompson, Derek. “Three Myths of the Great Resignation.” *Atlantic*, December 8, 2021.

Thorp-Moscon, Jennifer, Alixandra Pollack, and Olufemi Olu-lafe. *Empowering Workplaces Combat Emotional Tax for People of Colour in Canada.* Catalyst, n.d.

Ticona, Julia. *Left to Our Own Devices: Care & Control in a Connected Age.* Oxford University Press, 2022.

Ticona, Julia, and Alexandra Mateescu. "Trusted Strangers: Carework Platforms' Cultural Entrepreneurship in the on-Demand Economy." *New Media & Society* 20, no. 11 (November 1, 2018): 4384–4404.

Tikhomirov, Alexey. "The Regime of Forced Trust: Making and Breaking Emotional Bonds between People and State in Soviet Russia, 1917–1941." *Slavonic and East European Review* 91, no. 1 (2013): 78–118.

Tilly, Charles. *Durable Inequality.* University of California Press, 1998.

———. *Why?* Princeton University Press, 1998.

Tinkler, Justine, Sarah Becker, and Kristen Clayton. "'Kind of Natural, Kind of Wrong': Young People's Beliefs About the Morality, Legality, and Normalcy of Sexual Aggression in Public Drinking Settings." *Law & Social Inquiry* 43, no. 1 (2018): 28–57.

Tolentino, Jia. "The Gig Economy Celebrates Working Yourself to Death." *New Yorker*, March 22, 2017.

Tomaskovic-Devey, Donald, and Dustin Avent-Holt. *Relational Inequalities: An Organizational Approach.* Oxford University Press, 2019.

Tomassetti, Julia. "Does Uber Redefine the Firm: The Postindustrial Corporation and Advanced Information Technology." *Hofstra Labor & Employment Law Journal* 34, no. 1 (2017 2016): 1–78.

Tone, Andrea. *The Business of Benevolence: Industrial Paternalism in Progressive America.* Cornell University Press, 1997.

Travis, Dnika, Jennifer Thorpe-Moscon, and Courtney McCluney. *Emotional Tax: How Black Women and Men Pay More at Work and How Leaders Can Take Action.* Catalyst, 2016.

Trimble, Lindsey, and Julie Kmec. "The Role of Social Networks in Getting a Job." *Sociology Compass* 5, no. 2 (February 1, 2011): 165–78.

Tripodi, Francesca Bolla. *The Propagandists' Playbook: How Conservative Elites Manipulate Search and Threaten Democracy.* Yale University Press, 2022.

Tung, Irene, Jared Odessky, and Paul Sonn. "Just Cause Job Protections: Building Racial Equity and Shifting the Power Balance Between Workers and Employers." National Employment Law Project, April 29, 2021. https://www.nelp.org/insights-research/just-cause-job-protections-building-racial-equity-and-shifting-the-power-balance-between-workers-and-employers/.

Turco, Catherine. *The Conversational Firm: Rethinking Bureaucracy in the Age of Social Media.* Columbia University Press, 2016.

———. "Cultural Foundations of Tokenism Evidence from the Leveraged Buyout Industry." *American Sociological Review* 75, no. 6 (December 1, 2010): 894–913.

Turner, Victor. *Dramas, Fields, and Metaphors: Symbolic Action in Human Society*. Cornell University Press, 2018.

———. "Liminality and Communitas." In *Ritual*. Routledge, 2010.

———. *The Ritual Process: Structure and Anti-Structure*. Transaction Publishers, 2011.

Tweedy, Amy. "Laboring Lesbians: Queering Emotional Labor." *Journal of Lesbian Studies* 23, no. 2 (2019): 169–95.

Uber. "Drive When You Want, Make What You Need." Accessed November 5, 2023. https://www.uber.com/.

US Bureau of Labor Statistics. "Contingent and Alternative Employment Arrangements—May 2017." 2018. https://www.bls.gov/cps/labor-force /contingent-alternative-arrangements-may-2017.htm.

———. "Multiple Jobholders by Selected Characteristics." Labor Force Statistics from the Current Population Survey, 2024. https://www.bls.gov/cps/cpsaat 36.htm.

———. "Number of Jobs, Labor Market Experience, Marital Status, and Health for Those Born 1957-1964." Economic News Release, 2023. https://www.bls .gov/news.release/nlsoy.nro.htm.

———. "Union Members—2022." News release, 2023. https://www.bls.gov/news .release/archives/union2_01192023.pdf.

US Congress. National Labor Relations Act/National Labor Relations Board. 29 U.S.C. §§ 151–66 (Suppl. 2 1934). Accessed November 2, 2023. https://tile .loc.gov/storage-services/service/ll/uscode/uscode1934-00302/uscode1934 -003029007/uscode1934-003029007.pdf.

US Department of Labor. "Comparison of State Unemployment Laws 2022." 2022. https://oui.doleta.gov/unemploy/comparison/2020-2029/comparison 2022.asp.

———. "Department of Labor Announces Proposal to Restore, Extend Overtime Protections for 3.6 Million Low-Paid Salaried Workers." 2023. https://www .dol.gov/newsroom/releases/whd/whd20230830#:~:text=WASHINGTON %20%E2%80%93%20The%20U.S.%20Department%20of,week%2C %20about%20%2455%2C000%20per%20year.

———. "FY 2020 Congressional Budget Justification." 2019. https://www.dol.gov /sites/dolgov/files/general/budget/2020/CBJ-2020-V3-04.pd.

US Department of the Treasury. "Labor Unions and the Middle Class." 2023. https://home.treasury.gov/system/files/136/Labor-Unions-And-The-Middle -Class.pdf.

———. "The State of Labor Market Competition." 2022. https://home.treasury .gov/system/files/136/State-of-Labor-Market-Competition-2022.pdf.

US Equal Employment Opportunity Commission. "Charge Statistics (Charges Filed with EEOC) FY 1997 through FY 2019." 2020. https://www.eeoc.gov /data/charge-statistics-charges-filed-eeoc-fy-1997-through-fy-2022.

———. "Diversity in High Tech." 2024. https://www.eeoc.gov/sites/default/files/migrated_files/eeoc/statistics/reports/hightech/diversity-in-high-tech-report.pdf.

———. "Job Patterns for Minorities and Women in Private Industry (EEO-1)." 2020. https://www.eeoc.gov/data/2018-job-patterns-minorities-and-women-private-industry-eeo-1-raw-datasets.

US House of Representatives. *Hearing, "Examining the Future of Transportation Network Companies"*. Subcommittee on Highways and Transit, Committee on Transportation and Infrastructure, October 16, 2019. https://www.congress.gov/event/116th-congress/house-event/LC65343/text.

Uzzi, Brian. "Embeddedness in the Making of Financial Capital: How Social Relations and Networks Benefit Firms Seeking Financing." *American Sociological Review* 64, no. 4 (August 1, 1999): 481–505.

Vallas, Steven. "The Adventures of Managerial Hegemony: Teamwork, Ideology and Worker Resistance." *Social Problems* 50, no. 2 (2003): 204–25.

———. "Empowerment Redux: Structure, Agency, and the Remaking of Managerial Authority." *American Journal of Sociology* 111, no. 6 (May 1, 2006): 1677–1717.

Vallas, Steven, and Angèle Christin. "Work and Identity in an Era of Precarious Employment: How Workers Respond to 'Personal Branding' Discourse." *Work and Occupations* 45, no. 1 (February 1, 2018): 3–37.

Vallas, Steven, and Emily Cummins. "Personal Branding and Identity Norms in the Popular Business Press: Enterprise Culture in an Age of Precarity." *Organization Studies* 36, no. 3 (March 1, 2015): 293–319.

Vallas, Steven, and Andrea Hill. "Conceptualizing Power in Organizations." In *Rethinking Power in Organizations, Institutions, and Markets*. Emerald, 2012.

Van Gennep, Arnold. *The Rites of Passage*. Translated by David I. Kertzer, Monika B. Vizedom, and Gabrielle L. Caffee. University of Chicago Press, 2019.

Van Green, Ted. "Few Americans Are Confident in Tech Companies to Prevent Misuse of Their Platforms in the 2020 Election." Pew Research Center, September 9, 2020. https://www.pewresearch.org/short-reads/2020/09/09/few-americans-are-confident-in-tech-companies-to-prevent-misuse-of-their-platforms-in-the-2020-election/.

Van Oort, Madison. *Worn Out: How Retailers Surveil and Exploit Workers in the Digital Age and How Workers Are Fighting Back*. MIT Press, 2023.

Vasel, Kathryn. "The Pandemic Forced a Massive Remote-Work Experiment: Now Comes the Hard Part." *CNN Business*, March 9, 2021. https://edition.cnn.com/2021/03/09/success/remote-work-covid-pandemic-one-year-later.

Vaughan, Diane. *The* Challenger *Launch Decision: Risky Technology, Culture, and Deviance at NASA*. University of Chicago Press, 1997.

Volpe, Allie. "Holiday Dread: At Gatherings This Year, 'Someone Is Going to Be Offended.'" *Guardian*, November 25, 2021.

Wade, Peter. "Michelle Obama Talks Morality, Pressure of Being First with Colbert." *Rolling Stone*, December 1, 2018.

Wagner-Pacifici, Robin, and Iddo Tavory. "Politics as a Vacation." *American Journal of Cultural Sociology* 5, no. 3 (October 1, 2017): 307–21.

Walker, Bernard, and Robert T. Hamilton. "Employee–Employer Grievances: A Review." *International Journal of Management Reviews* 13, no. 1 (2011): 40–58.

Walker, Margaret Urban. *Moral Repair: Reconstructing Moral Relations After Wrongdoing*. Cambridge University Press, 2006.

Wallerstein, Joseph. "Risky Ties and Taxing Ties: The Multiple Dimensions of Negativity." *Qualitative Sociology* 46, no. 3 (September 1, 2023): 349–73.

Waring, Amanda, and Justin Waring. "Looking the Part: Embodying the Discourse of Organizational Professionalism in the City." *Current Sociology* 57, no. 3 (May 1, 2009): 344–64.

Waters, Mary. *Ethnic Options: Choosing Identities in America*. University of California Press, 1990.

Weaver, Simon. *The Rhetoric of Racist Humour: US, UK and Global Race Joking*. Ashgate Publishing, 2011.

Weber, Linda, and Allison Carter. *The Social Construction of Trust*. Springer Science & Business Media, 2003.

Weber, Max. *Economy and Society: An Outline of Interpretive Sociology*. University of California Press, 1922.

———. *The Protestant Ethic and the Spirit of Capitalism*. Routledge, 1904.

———. "The Social Psychology of World Religions." In *From Max Weber: Essays in Sociology*. Routledge, 1970.

Weeden, Kim. "Occupational Segregation." State of the Union. Stanford Center on Poverty and Inequality, 2019. https://inequality.stanford.edu/sites/default/files/Pathways_SOTU_2019_OccupSegregation.pdf.

Weeks, Kathi. "Down with Love: Feminist Critique and the New Ideologies of Work." *WSQ: Women's Studies Quarterly* 45, no. 3–4 (2017): 37–58.

———. *The Problem with Work: Feminism, Marxism, Antiwork Politics, and Postwork Imaginaries*. Duke University Press, 2011.

Weil, David. *The Fissured Workplace*. Harvard University Press, 2014.

Wells, Katie, Kafui Attoh, and Declan Cullen. *Disrupting D.C.: The Rise of Uber and the Fall of the City*. Princeton University Press, 2023.

———. "'Just-in-Place' Labor: Driver Organizing in the Uber Workplace." *Environment and Planning A: Economy and Space* 53, no. 2 (March 1, 2021): 315–31.

Wherry, Frederick. "The Social Sources of Authenticity in Global Handicraft Markets: Evidence from Northern Thailand." *Journal of Consumer Culture* 6, no. 1 (March 1, 2006): 5–32.

Wherry, Frederick, Kristin Seefeldt, and Anthony S. Alvarez. "To Lend or Not to Lend to Friends and Kin: Awkwardness, Obfuscation, and Negative Reciprocity." *Social Forces* 98, no. 2 (December 1, 2019): 753–93.

Wilcox, Annika, and Amanda Koontz. "Workplace Well-Being: Shifting from an Individual to an Organizational Framework." *Sociology Compass* 16, no. 10 (2022): e13035.

Wilkinson, Adrian, and Michael Barry. "Voices from Across the Divide: An Industrial Relations Perspective on Employee Voice." *German Journal of Human Resource Management* 30, nos. 3–4 (2016): 338–44.

Williams, Christine. *Gaslighted: How the Oil and Gas Industry Shortchanges Women Scientists.* University of California Press, 2021.

———. "The Glass Escalator: Hidden Advantages for Men in the 'Female' Professions." *Social Problems* 39, no. 3 (August 1, 1992): 253–67.

———. "Life Support: The Problems of Working for a Living." *American Sociological Review* 86, no. 2 (April 1, 2021): 191–200.

Williams, Christine, and Catherine Connell. "'Looking Good and Sounding Right': Aesthetic Labor and Social Inequality in the Retail Industry." *Work and Occupations* 37, no. 3 (August 1, 2010): 349–77.

Williams, Christine, Chandra Muller, and Kristine Kilanski. "Gendered Organizations in the New Economy." *Gender & Society: Official Publication of Sociologists for Women in Society* 26, no. 4 (August 2012): 549–73.

Williams, Jhacova. "Laid Off More, Hired Less: Black Workers in the COVID-19 Recession." RAND, September 29, 2020. https://www.rand.org/pubs/commentary/2020/09/laid-off-more-hired-less-black-workers-in-the-covid.html.

Williams, Joan. *Unbending Gender: Why Family and Work Conflict and What to Do About It.* Oxford University Press, 1999.

Williams, Joan, Mary Blair-Loy, and Jennifer Berdahl. "Cultural Schemas, Social Class, and the Flexibility Stigma." *Journal of Social Issues* 69, no. 2 (2013): 209–34.

Williams, Joan C., and Nancy Segal. "Beyond the Maternal Wall: Relief for Family Caregivers Who Are Discriminated Against on the Job." *Harvard Women's Law Journal* 26 (2003): 77–162.

Wilson, Eli. *Front of the House, Back of the House: Race and Inequality in the Lives of Restaurant Workers.* New York University Press, 2020.

Wingfield, Adia Harvey. "Are Some Emotions Marked 'Whites Only'? Racialized Feeling Rules in Professional Workplaces." *Social Problems* 57, no. 2 (May 1, 2010): 251–68.

———. *Flatlining: Race, Work, and Health Care in the New Economy.* University of California Press, 2019.

———. *Gray Areas: How the Way We Work Perpetuates Racism and What We Can Do to Fix It.* HarperCollins, 2023.

———. "The Modern Mammy and the Angry Black Man: African American Professionals' Experiences with Gendered Racism in the Workplace." *Race, Gender & Class* 14, nos. 1/2 (2007): 196–212.

———. *No More Invisible Man: Race and Gender in Men's Work*. Temple University Press, 2013.

———. "Racializing the Glass Escalator: Reconsidering Men's Experiences with Women's Work." *Gender & Society* 23, no. 1 (February 1, 2009): 5–26.

———. "Where Work Has Been, Where It Is Going: Considering Race, Gender, and Class in the Neoliberal Economy." *Sociology of Race and Ethnicity* 6, no. 2 (April 1, 2020): 137–45.

Wingfield, Adia Harvey, and Renée Skeete Alston. "Maintaining Hierarchies in Predominantly White Organizations: A Theory of Racial Tasks." *American Behavioral Scientist* 58, no. 2 (February 2014): 274–87.

Wingfield, Adia Harvey, and Koji Chavez. "Getting In, Getting Hired, Getting Sideways Looks: Organizational Hierarchy and Perceptions of Racial Discrimination." *American Sociological Review* 85, no. 1 (February 1, 2020): 31–57.

Wingfield, Adia Harvey, and John Harvey Wingfield. "When Visibility Hurts and Helps: How Intersections of Race and Gender Shape Black Professional Men's Experiences with Tokenization." *Cultural Diversity & Ethnic Minority Psychology* 20, no. 4 (2014): 483–90.

Wong, Julia Carrie. "Uber Admits Underpaying New York City Drivers by Millions of Dollars." *Guardian*, May 23, 2017.

Wood, Alex. *Despotism on Demand: How Power Operates in the Flexible Workplace*. Cornell University Press, 2020.

———. "Powerful Times: Flexible Discipline and Schedule Gifts at Work." *Work, Employment and Society* 32, no. 6 (December 1, 2018): 1061–77.

Wooten, Melissa, and Lucius Couloute. "The Production of Racial Inequality Within and Among Organizations." *Sociology Compass* 11, no. 1 (2017): e12446.

Wright, Ronald. *A Short History of Progress*. Carroll & Graf, 2004.

Wynn, Alison. "Misery Has Company: The Shared Emotional Consequences of Everwork Among Women and Men." *Sociological Forum* 33, no. 3 (2018): 712–34.

Wynn, Alison, and Aliya Hamid Rao. "Failures of Flexibility: How Perceived Control Motivates the Individualization of Work–Life Conflict." *ILR Review* 73, no. 1 (January 1, 2020): 61–90.

Xygalatas, Dimitris. *Ritual: How Seemingly Senseless Acts Make Life Worth Living*. Little, Brown, 2022.

Yamagishi, Toshio. "Trust as a Form of Social Intelligence." In *Trust in Society*, edited by Karen Cook. Russell Sage Foundation, 2001.

Yavorsky, Jill. "Cisgendered Organizations: Trans Women and Inequality in the Workplace." *Sociological Forum* 31, no. 4 (2016): 948–69.

Yglesias, Matthew. "Uber's Toxic Culture of Rule Breaking, Explained." *Vox*, March 21, 2017. https://www.vox.com/new-money/2017/3/21/14980502/uber-toxic-culture-rule-breaking-explained.

Young, James. "Against Redemption: The Arts of Countermemory in Germany Today." In *Symbolic Loss: The Ambiguity of Mourning and Memory at Century's End*, edited by P Homans. University of Virginia Press, 2000.

Zaleski, Annie. "We Are All 'Amabots' Now: Jeff Bezos Just Perfected the 'Burn and Churn' Philosophy That's Sucking American Workers Dry." *Salon*, August 18, 2015. https://www.salon.com/2015/08/18/we_are_all_ambots_now_jeff_bezos_just_perfected_the_burn_and_churn_philosophy_thats_sucking_american_workers_dry/.

Zelizer, Viviana. "How I Became a Relational Economic Sociologist and What Does That Mean?" *Politics & Society* 40, no. 2 (June 1, 2012): 145–74.

———. *The Purchase of Intimacy*. Princeton University Press, 2007.

———. *The Social Meaning of Money*. Princeton University Press, 2004.

Zerubavel, Eviatar. *Don't Take It Personally: Personalness and Impersonality in Social Life*. Oxford University Press, 2024.

Zimmer, John. "The Third Transportation Revolution." *Medium* (blog), September 20, 2016. https://medium.com/@johnzimmer/the-third-transportation-revolution-27860f05fa91.

Zucker, Lynne. "Production of Trust: Institutional Sources of Economic Structure, 1840–1920." *Research in Organizational Behavior* 8 (1986): 53–111.

Zuckerberg, Mark. "Update on Meta's Year of Efficiency." *Meta* (blog), March 14, 2023. https://about.fb.com/news/2023/03/mark-zuckerberg-meta-year-of-efficiency/.

Zuckerman, Ethan. *Mistrust: Why Losing Faith in Institutions Provides the Tools to Transform Them*. W. W. Norton, 2021.

Index

Founded in 1893,
UNIVERSITY OF CALIFORNIA PRESS
publishes bold, progressive books and journals on topics in the arts, humanities, social sciences, and natural sciences—with a focus on social justice issues—that inspire thought and action among readers worldwide.

The UC PRESS FOUNDATION
raises funds to uphold the press's vital role as an independent, nonprofit publisher, and receives philanthropic support from a wide range of individuals and institutions—and from committed readers like you. To learn more, visit ucpress.edu/supportus.

www.ingramcontent.com/pod-product-compliance
Lightning Source LLC
Chambersburg PA
CBHW020840270326
41928CB00006B/490
9780520387379